THE
HOOD
TO HELL & BACK

QUIETSTRENGTH

authorHOUSE®

AuthorHouse™
1663 Liberty Drive
Bloomington, IN 47403
www.authorhouse.com
Phone: 1 (800) 839-8640

Published by AuthorHouse 11/20/2019

ISBN: 978-1-7283-0929-3 (sc)
ISBN: 978-1-7283-0930-9 (hc)
ISBN: 978-1-7283-0928-6 (e)

CONTENTS

THIS BOOK IS DEDICATED TO:

1. *God*, for always being there in my darkest hours of real need and teaching me the rules of life in his Ten Commandments.
2. *Cheyenne*, my beautiful, loyal and adorable lassie collie, who was the only friend I had in my deepest despair and has been loyally at my side for well over a decade, through the good, the bad and the ugly in my roller-coaster life. She is much more than a pet to me; she is and always will be my best friend.
3. *Michelle and Iona*, my two gorgeous daughters, who taught this old dog what hope, friendship and love really mean. They showed me for once that the only person I need to prove myself to is myself.
4. *my parents and family*, whose genuine yet tough love gave me strength to get through the worst times.
5. *Sharon Bard*, my guardian angel, who never deserted me and truly saved my life.
6. *my ex-wife, Carol, and all my girlfriends,* who were all true friends and lovers and helped me overcome my shyness.
7. *the Yukon and North Shore homeless shelter staff,* who for well over a year kept me off the streets.
8. *the Richmond Hospital psych ward staff,* who cured not only my psychosis but also its very real cause, my prescription drug addiction.
9. *all the friends I lost on my way,* including my Scottish rippers, Ally and Martin; the best athlete I have ever met, Rob; my Canadian bodybuilding champion, Ray; my beloved feline friends, Cayman,

Arran and Rori; and last but certainly not least, my gorgeous childhood golden retriever, Vharie.

10. *all my really good friends* (way too many to mention here, but know who they are) who did the impossible: get past my walls, earn my trust and motivate me to push the envelope in everything I do.

11. *Michael Jackson and the Jackson 5*: Michael's music is the soundtrack to my life and still is my voice when I'm at my lowest and can't find the light or the words.

12. *every songwriter, musician and dancer* who has touched my life. For as far back as I can remember, music and its human expression through dance has always been my port from all the storms I have faced.

13. *all my sports coaches and sponsors*, who made it possible for me to follow and even realize some of my athletic dreams.

14. *all the great doctors and medical professionals*, who brought me back from the brink so many times.

15. *the cities and towns* of Aberdeen and Stonehaven in Scotland and Vancouver and Whistler in Canad*a*

16. *AuthorHouse and all their staff*, who accepted *The Hood* manuscript and gave me the avenue and inspiration to share my true story with the world.

17. *every unsung hero* who has touched and/or helped me throughout my life.

From my mother:

You have made it through the rain and now the sun is coming out tomorrow. We are *proud of you*. You are an *Austin*, and you are about to begin a new life and finally put the past behind you.

From Iona and Michelle

The important thing about my dad is he is loving! My dad is the best *dad* in the whole universe.

I love how he is always confident and persuades us to get into more sports.

My dad loves to talk so much, I bet he could get on the world record book for it.

My dad loves to bike, ski, snowboard and do his martial arts.

He is crazy about music and is a great dancer.

But the most important thing about my dad is he is loving!

CHAPTER 1

HEAL THE WORLD

As I lie by the side of a beautiful pool in gorgeous Tenerife, part of the Spanish Canary Islands just off Morocco in Africa, I reflect on what would be best described as my chaotic past decade, and indeed my seriously messed-up life story. At this very moment, what I would guess to be a 10-year-boy goes dancing past me, rocking out to his dad's MP3 player with not a care in the world. I find myself totally immersed in the innocence of childhood and pray he never loses that wonder of youth.

As if by magic, the voice of Michael Jackson, my lifelong idol, comes on my own player with one of my all-time favourite songs of his: "Will You Be There." It immediately transports me back three months to when I was doubled over in writhing agony in a hospital bed in Vancouver General Hospital. It was the middle of the night on my 45th birthday, and I was all alone and listening to exactly the same song.

The very next day, as I recall, brought the guilty verdict in the Dr. Conrad Murray case. I intentionally cranked up the TV volume in my hospital room so that everyone could hear, especially those heartless physicians who write prescriptions just to support their lavish lifestyles. It was a doctor like that who ultimately killed my hero, Michael, as well as way too many others like him.

Was it a coincidence that I was discharged the following day, even though every one of them knew I was still in terrible pain and was going to be living on the streets again? Or was it, as I genuinely believe, the revenge of these modern-day drug dealers who call themselves physicians? Were they just trying to silence another protestor by writing out a death sentence to protect their social status and criminally negligent behaviour?

My only comfort was that maybe Michael's death would not be in vain but would spark a revolution. In all honesty, though, I doubt it. The prescription drug cartels—or as the diplomatically correct media calls them, the pharmaceutical lobbies—are stronger than those willing to stand up and be counted. Like it or not, money talks in this modern world we live in.

This reminds me of a program about Cesar the dog whisperer. It explained so intimately that unlike the animal kingdom—which is all about love, affection and family—humanity has mapped its own course seeking greed, power, hate and vengeance. It's almost akin to the amazing *Star Wars* saga, with the small but growing army of environmentalists like the Jedi against the now too-strong dark side of the Empire. I know I am not the only one who thinks this way. Everyone on this planet should see *An Inconvenient Truth*, featuring Al Gore, and Michael Moore's priceless *Capitalism: A Love Story*.

You'll find that I frequently refer to films and especially music. My mother introduced me to music at a very early age, and I have used it as a way to not only explain my seriously messed-up thoughts and emotions but as my favourite happy place. Much more than just another medium for entertainment, it's like a religion or spiritual escape.

Hip hop's "the hood," Elvis's and Kayne West's "the ghetto," or the dance world's "step up" and Streetdance's "the streets"—all depict a very dark place that most of us will never see. But we think we know all about such places as we walk down our local sidewalks of life and see these ever-increasing, very weird, almost inhuman street people who look like characters from *Mad Max* with their stolen grocery carts full of all of their earthly belongings. We see them panhandling, begging for their next meal, which really means to most of them their next fix.

When I had my millions and almost every toy known to man, my descriptions for such people ranged from the obvious—*weirdos*, *druggies*, *hookers*, *psychos*, *dumpster-jumpers*—to the even more judgmental, like *losers*, *suckers*, *leeches* and *outcasts*. I threw my pittance of a helping hand into their caps, and that somehow eased any guilt trip I might have taken. I took salvation in the fact that I was indeed a good Samaritan.

It wasn't until I actually visited their world in the hardest possible way that I realized these people are not the scum of the earth but rather the ultimate survivors—the forgotten clan, if you like. I am truly amazed how so many of the people I have now met live outside under the stars, sometimes for well over a decade, and don't die. How do they get up every day and find a "Reason to Believe," to quote Springsteen? I never thought I would experience that kind of life firsthand, but trust me, I have. I've also faced the temptation of suicide, the easy way out.

There's an age-old saying that, to be honest, I never understood until recently: "It's not the destination, it's the journey." This is a critical piece of the puzzle we call life, as we live, learn and hopefully grow as people. Like Eminem's hard-hitting lyrics that helped me make it through the worst times, I never ever thought "I would ever pick up a pen and vent" and write my story, as reliving it is almost as hard as doing it all over again. Still, as messed-up as my past has been, maybe writing about it will bring me some solace and even closure.

More importantly, the very few people I have opened up and told my story to have advised me to write about it to inspire others not to ever travel down the rough side of the road—and to help those still stuck there to realize that escape is possible, though incredibly hard. Even now, I desperately struggle every second of every minute of every hour of every day to come back from that experience.

As I lie here in what feels like heaven compared to the hell-and-back I've been through, I am reeling from yet another celebrity death. The angelic singing legend Whitney Houston is gone, another fantastic talent sucked in and spit out by our all-consuming disposable society. It was a mere two years ago that I tried to do exactly the same thing: commit suicide in a bathtub in my penthouse yuppie pad in Yaletown with a lethal cocktail of painkillers, antidepressants and sleeping pills—enough to kill a bull, according to the paramedics. Just how my lungs didn't stop pumping oxygen to my bloodstream is a mystery to me. Maybe God wasn't ready for me yet.

Unfortunately for what many of us believe was the best female voice since Ella Fitzgerald, Whitney succeeded in her attempt to end her life. To me, it's yet another testament to just how precious life really is. We must go out and live it to the fullest—or as another one of my fallen icons, Lance Armstrong, states in one of his thrilling autobiographies: "Every second counts." Two of my favourite songs that helped me through my remaining days in the Yukon shelter, by the incomparable Hedley, are "One Life" and "Invincible." The videos and lyrics encapsulate my every emotion and help me keep my head up despite being more than rundown.

It really pains me to see a star like Whitney rise so high, contribute so much, and then fall so fast into oblivion. All the warning signs were there: the vicious cycle of stress, distress and crisis; drug abuse; financial ruin and impending bankruptcy; and failing health. She had to brush all that off and deal with the incredible pressure of an upcoming Grammy performance and immortalization in a movie role.

Was I the only one who saw a similarity to Michael Jackson and his 50 sold-out O2 concerts and riveting but oh-so-sad movie *This Is It*? Somehow, no one was able to save her. Like Amy Winehouse the year before, she succumbed to a combination of legal drugs like alcohol and prescriptions and so-called illegal street drugs. Her light that shone so bright only a few decades earlier with timeless classics like "I Will Always Love You and "Greatest Love of All" was extinguished.

Of course, these Hollywood and *Billboard* stars are only the tip of the iceberg. For every one of them who dies, how many more no-names perish in the ghettos of this planet? Most of them receive no proper funeral, tombstone or memorial through biographies or multimillion-dollar movies like *Walk the Line* or *Ray*. No one will know about their daily fight to stay alive.

What is so unbelievable to me after meeting these unknown soldiers, as I like to call them, is that their stories are even more worthy of a film than these international superstars. Rather than praising and rewarding those who have the most money, awards, fame, power, corruption and greed, shouldn't we recognize today's truest celebrities—the ones living with practically nothing but still willing to help other human beings? They are the heroes in my book.

I have met so many men and women who deserve to have a movie made of their crazy life on this earth, as they have survived through the darkest times. Most of them are still on the streets, addicted to their drug of choice. Most have major mental-health issues.

I ask you, what has happened to our world when the car you drive, your fancy personalized licence plate, the size of your suburban house, the fashion brands you wear, how cool your phone is or how many toys you have in your garage determines how great a human being you are? I too spent the majority of my life accepting the philosophy that "whoever has the most toys wins." Can we not all slow down and see how frankly insane our materialistic and utterly ridiculous success criteria are? Dear God, when are we going to realize that these status and power fantasies are not only killing us but killing our planet?

You gain a whole new perspective on life when your roof is the clouds crying all over you. Rain seeps into your very soul and keeps you awake all night. And even on clear cold nights, the intense gut pain inflicted by hunger pangs, drug withdrawal and pure fear of being attacked by fellow desperados trying to survive life on the streets is indescribable. Please spare a thought for these orphans, drug addicts, sex-trade workers, sexual-abuse victims and the critically mentally ill of this world—the truly forgotten warriors—the next time you bitch about how bad a day you had and how much you hate your job, your marriage or, worse still, your life. Maybe then the lyrics of Michael Jackson's anthem "Heal the World" will resound with a new meaning for this thing we so ironically call the human "race."

CHAPTER 2

CHILDHOOD

No matter where I go, I can't escape my past. I go to this paradise called Tenerife, one of the most idyllic places on earth, and I'm back in the very where I was at my absolute worst. I can't even remember when it was I was last there. My only real memory is of funneling pills down my throat every chance I could, as my Crohn's disease or IBS pain dictated. I think I either slept most of that trip or was in the kind of drug-infested daze so brilliantly described in Pink Floyd's timeless classic "Comfortably Numb." That song nails what it's like when you get your hit, whether IV, oral liquid or pill.

The best way I can describe my youth is that I was an out-of-control, crazy, troubled kid whose only mission in life was to have fun. According to my mum, not too much has changed. Her nickname for me was and still is Peter Pan (coincidently, the same as was levelled at my idol MJ). Even now, I relate better to kids and animals than I ever will to adults. Every time I meet up with my own children—which is way too infrequently for my liking—they always ask for another stupid "Dad as a kid" story. I have so many to choose from.

I'm still just a big kid at heart, and I make no apology for that. I genuinely believe the answers we seek will come from the brilliance of youth, as kids are closer to what God intended us to be. We all become twisted by our new existence into unrecognizable selfish monsters who are only concerned about one thing: ourselves! I also believe that we are only as old as we feel—a concept perfectly depicted in songs like "Young at Heart" by the Bluebells and "Forever Young" by Jay-Z.

If I was born today, I am sure I would be popping ADHD pills. Actually, I think I should be taking them now, as attention is definitely not my strong suit. I get so easily distracted by everything and anything. All my life, if I wasn't risking my health and wellness in some way or another, getting my buzz of adrenalin and challenging myself beyond belief, I was bored silly.

When I was growing up, we lived in a small city in Scotland called Aberdeen, home of Annie Lennox and Emily Sande; North Sea oil; and more than its fair share of inventors. I was the second of three boys. This had advantages and disadvantages. My older brother took most of the parental discipline, as I flew under the radar. I found this to be a great strategy very early on in life, and it probably helped save my life later on.

On the other hand, I always felt like the forgotten red-headed stepchild who got all my brother's hand-me-downs. They never really fit me, as we are totally different builds. Looking back at photos from then, I think I invented the baggy skate, surf and boarder look by total accident. It sure wasn't trendy then. If you look at old pictures of Larry Bird or Jimmy Connors, you'll remember those exceptionally bad tight shorts that were in style. Most of mine were down to my knees.

The crucial exception was my most hated and most used pair: my grey school uniform shorts, which were always bought new and simply sucked to wear, especially when you are around 13 and on the cusp of morphing into manhood. Thanks to those horrendous uniforms, you still looked the same as you did when you were 5.

My rock, both then and now, was always my four-legged furry angels— my beautiful dogs. They truly were God's biggest and best blessing. When I was around 2 years old, my dad agreed to look after a golden retriever for a friend who had just moved into an apartment that did not allow dogs. No surprise, the supposed two weeks of dog-sitting turned into a lifetime, as we all fell head over heels for this gorgeous golden, especially me. I couldn't understand how this magical bond we have with dogs worked, but who cares?

She really was my and Dad's dog, as we were the ones who walked her every day. I never complained; it was my private time alone with her.

There are no words for the genuinely deep, warming, unconditional love we had for each other. Every time I was down from another rough day, she was my go-to friend. I guess it was similar to kids who use a pacifier, blanket or imaginary friend to access their happy place and deal with life's burdens. For many adults, drugs fill that purpose.

I hated being away from my pal for family holidays. Almost every summer, we took a trip to stay with my old man's mum in the tiny yet picturesque town of West Kilbride, quite simply the most boring place on earth when you're a kid. When we returned and our dog was released from the kennels, she would always make a beeline for me and knock me over with her affectionate joy. I will take to my grave walking up Law Hill and looking over to the lovely Isle of Arran and on clear days, over to the Eilsa Andrew, and just sitting with my best friend in complete peace and freedom. I remember training her in the massive local parks, getting her to stay until she was almost a dot on the horizon, and then whistling to her and watching her come at full gallop. I dearly miss that dog. She was my very first experience of total and complete unconditional love.

Sometimes I wish I could get along with people (especially girls) as well as I do with pretty much any dog. I think we have yet to truly tap into dogs' potential. Dogs are now proving to be able to find things the electronic gadgets we boast about can't—like diseases, drugs, explosives and ammunition. Even more importantly, they give us the unconditional love we all seek, and their friendship is a powerful remedy for all types of human diseases and weaknesses. To me, it is absolutely no coincidence that *DOG* spelt backwards is *GOD*.

My love for my childhood dog was so strong, I still to this day have a picture of my adorable Vharie by my bedside, and I say goodnight to her each and every night. Despite all the crazy highs and lows of my silly life, the day I lost my best friend is still my hardest, roughest and saddest day. I was 15 years old, and I have never felt such an immense loss and been so lost. I swore that I would never have another dog, as I could never bear the deep pain of losing something so near and dear to my heart and soul ever again. But of course, never say never.

I was introduced to music at a very early age, mainly by my mother, and I immediately connected with it as a way to express and deal with my emotions. One of my anthems was "Billy Don't Be a Hero" by Black Lace

THE HOOD

(I actually saw them perform that very song here in Tenerife decades later). I always wanted to be that hero, and I did some stupid things to impress my friends and prove my courage. I think that's why I pursued sports and became the biggest jock of all time. "Win or die trying" was my way to prove my manhood—to myself more than anyone else.

My older brother, Ian, and I had been sent to a private all-boys school called Gordon's College, which all the kids my age referred to as Gay Gordon's. Ian did everything to hide from the world that he was more than very in touch with his feminine side. It all came to a head when a vicious rumour surfaced that he was caught having sex with an older man up on the Hazelhead golf course. I tried to rationalize that this was simply impossible; as a teenager, Ian didn't fit the usual limp-wristed homosexual mold but was rather more the Hell's Angel/Freddy Mercury hard-man type. He tried to own every conversation and had this insanely annoying habit of answering every fucking question for me.

As a result, I ended up getting an unbelievably embarrassing lisp, which wasn't much fun when you lived at 66 Queens Road and were born on 6 November 1966. I was an insecure teenager, so the lisp was further exacerbated when I spoke to girls. With the benefit of hindsight—and with no disrespect to speech-impeded people, as I know firsthand how it affects one's self confidence—it probably sounded like I was the gay one. It took me well over four years of intense after-school speech therapy to finally conquer my speech defect, but even today, I have to really concentrate on some words that have *S* in them, like *sleep* and *sheep*.

All of this had a profound effect on me. I honestly never questioned my own sexuality, as I knew I had never been attracted to any male. I was infatuated with the female body, in sexy lingerie even more than totally naked. I liked a little mystery. Lingerie left the all-important pink bits to your imagination; in truth, they were usually better in the imagination anyway.

Going through adolescence, I had a massive crush on my nana Irene, to the extent that I would actually steal her underwear and get off on it as my fantasy focal point. I have never admitted this to anyone, but before starting this book, I decided that honesty is not just the best but the *only* policy. I'm not going to sugar-coat anything either. I know I'm not the only guy out there who had a secret stash of Victoria's Secret fashion-show videos on their hard drives and got a golden boner just by being in their shops.

To be painted by the same brush as my brother was hurtful and truly made me hate most of my school years and, unfortunately, all gay men. This was further compounded when, in grade 10 (third year in Scottish secondary terminology), my form and physics teacher, "Belly" Simmons, took me aside one day in class and physically abused me by putting his hand down my pants. I was so young and so ashamed that I hid it from everyone, doing my old-school macho-man shit, storing it up inside where it eats at you. As Britney puts it, "the tears come at night" rather in front of anyone, as real men don't cry.

Thankfully, someone *did* deal with it properly. He was caught the following year doing the same to another kid, and that kid told all. After the inevitable firing from his position and before he was summoned to trial, Belly took his own life. That was my first contact with suicide, and it was like seeing *Jaws* and *The Exorcist* when I was way too young. I was devastated, and I considered suicide as a very real option to having to go through the inevitable failing of my high school exams.

Sport was everything to me. I was on pretty much every team I wanted to be on in school, but my folks always maintained that "sports will not pay your mortgage." I always felt like that dumb black sheep of the family. My school operated on a hierarchical system based on academic achievement and potential, with the clever ones (like my both my brothers) being in A or B and the dense ones being in D or E. I was in *"D for dunce."* To this day, I hate that letter, almost slipping to *"E for epi"*—epileptic retardation, as we used to somewhat harshly call it.

The whole structure of Gordon's was based around mental rather than physical excellence, so I simply rebelled in the biggest way possible—actually earning the record for the amount of belting received in a calendar year at well over 200, an increase of more than 50 from the previous record. A song that seemed to sum up my predicament and suicide plot was "Seasons in the Sun" by Terry Jacks, with the line "Goodbye papa, please pray for me, I was the black sheep of the family, you tried to teach me right from wrong." I sang it over and over again when I was enduring the pain of the scud (the strap) or my most dreaded punishment, detention and lines.

THE HOOD

My parents, to my extreme frustration, could never decide which was better: the glitz of city life in Aberdeen (which Mum preferred because of her Belfast past and social butterfly traits) or the rural commuter satellite village that was Stonehaven 15 miles to the south (which Dad preferred from his small-town only-child upbringing). I have to give a shout-out to my many exploits in Stonehaven with females like Vivian and Joanne. I think my brothers and I gained from being the new kids on the block, and many saw us as millionaires because of our private schooling and the fact that we owned the most prestigious hotel in town, which was like a miniature Balmoral castle. It couldn't be further from the truth, as I recall my folks scrimping and saving wherever they could, with my old dear calling on her mum for help.

I think that this is where I got my work ethic. To earn pocket money, I had to help in the hotel doing a variety of duties. My worst chore came every Christmas Day after the presents were opened, when I did the dishes in the hotel's restaurant. We were obviously fully booked, and that was our chance to max out our revenue before the slacker winter months kicked in. I got into this weird festive ritual that dictated we weren't allowed to open our presents until after the work was done, which was when we got our own turkey feast, late in the afternoon.

It never fails to amaze me just how much influence your upbringing has on you and how much you either resist or resent some of your parents' ethics but deliver the agreeable ones onto your own offspring. Every Christmas day when Carol and I and the girls were together, we would only open the down-the-chimney stocking-filler presents and then go skiing or riding, as it was the quietest morning of any on the mountain. We opened our own personal gifts in the evening after our feast.

To overcome the sheer boredom of our rural surroundings in Stoney, one of my few friends, Dean Kerr (or Kermit, as he was affectionately nicknamed), introduced me to my first-ever addiction: smoking tobacco. By the time I eventually managed to quit this highly addictive social habit at age 27, I had actually smoked for longer than I hadn't, and it was because the doctor warned me about my very annoying predisposition to asthma. That blew my career fantasy of growing up to be a firefighter or, best of all, a fighter pilot like Maverick and Goose on their epic eighties *Top Gun* adventure. It was made clear to me that if I did any of that, I would end up in an asthma ward by the time I was 40.

My brother and I decided to pony up for some second-hand DJ equipment, which also satisfied our mutual love of music and my love of dance. It was easily the best job (if you can even call it a job) that I have personally ever had. It came so totally naturally to me that to this day, I am my own personal DJ, every spare second I get.

We managed to secure our first gig at the local community centre youth club, which was pure magic. It was the ideal place to pick up local talent from our "target-rich environment." I have never really understood why being a pretty decent DJ and dancer was so desirable to the opposite sex, but there was something there, and I was at the perfect coming-of-age moment to take full advantage. I simply have never scored so many birds (or chicks, as they say in North America) in my life. It was amazing to me, but it made my popularity plummet with the local guy crew, a feeling I have experienced throughout my life.

My intense and tenacious competitiveness made us better. We put on progressively more professional gigs every Saturday night. Word got out about our DJ unit, and we were invited to play the adult discos, which were a whole different beast to slay.

I remember my first one so well: I was nervous, as we were in the town's largest hotel, the Commodore, and in front of adults who probably had very different taste in music than we did. We thought it might be hard to garner their respect as two adolescent kids, but in actual fact, it was dead easy. The simple formula was to play fair-to-middling records up to about 11 p.m., when the locals started to get their alcohol courage, and then play your best tracks up until around 1 a.m., after which you could quite honestly play any old shit and they would still dance. The guys would pull out their best lines, armed with beer-goggled bravery, and it was absolutely hilarious to watch.

It was an early introduction to adult life and the difference between dating when you're a kid and when you're adult. It was so simple then: boy meets girl, cute innocent chase for a few days, then boom, she's yours. There was none of the attitude, ego and battle of the sexes you get involved in when you grow up. I blame it squarely on sex, marriage, babies and death. As you get older, you soon find out that from some men's perspective, this isn't too far from the truth. I know that's not male chauvinist crap, as I know for a fact that I ain't the only man, or woman for that matter, who feels this way. Anyway, how could I ever be a male chauvinist after 23 years of faithful romance and marriage and two adorable daughters?

Only now do I have an understanding of what my mum had to deal with for so long as the only female in our family. Instead of my kids growing up with Action Men, Hot Wheels, train sets and Transformers like me, I was surrounded by Barbies and Kens, dress-up, tea parties and unicorns. All I can say is, listen closely to the advice your best man and friends try to give you on what has to be the best night of your life, the stag party, before the completely different reality of married life descends.

Back in our DJ days, it was fucking easy: you liked her; found a way to tell her to her face; impressed her in some way, like at sports or on the dance floor; and it was a done deal. I ask you, who has the better method, kids or adults? The kids win with a decisive knockout every time.

My love life always had this very weird relationship with the number three when it came to girls, just like those three little words that are said too much and not enough. My romances lasted as follows:

1. three days with girls I thought I liked but were pretty much like driving that lemon of a new car off the lot; as soon as I kissed them, I realized the fantasy was better than the reality.
2. three weeks with the ones who were the light of my life, but something better always came along as the radar pointed out the latest bombshell, must-have girl.
3. three years on, coincidentally, three occasions.

My first three-year relationship was with a cute chick called Wendy, who I truly loved. I think that's the reason I got so into Bruce Springsteen— the Boss—who owns more space in my iTunes library than any other artist, including even Michael. I can't quite explain it, but I almost always religiously buy Springsteen's records as soon as they come out, and I don't give a shit if punters view it as old-school or boring.

His music mystifies me to this day. He is a pure genius at putting words to my every emotion, life experience, love, everything, the full nine yards. I remember going to his sensational concert in Vancouver just after he dropped *The Rising* in response to the chaos that followed the Twin Towers attack. Amazingly, he sang every note and played every instrument, every song, with no band, no backing singers or dancers, no pyro, nothing. It was a unique musical achievement that is a bucket-list highlight for sure. I think my ex hated every minute of it, but that was payback for having to endure the way-too-girlie Celine Dion in the Chrysler Theatre at Caesar's Palace in Vegas years later.

To this day, every time I hear Springsteen's rock-and-roll rebel anthem "Born to Run," with lyrics like "Wendy let me in, I want to be your friend, I want to guard your dreams and visions, just wrap your legs around these velvet straps ... your hands around my engines," it brings me back to laying Wendy so hard on my favourite ninth-hole tee of our local golf course, where I really had my best-ever "power drive" as the sun set on the scenic Aberdeen landscape. The other great line, "I want to die with you on the streets in an everlasting kiss," has more significance now than then. But yes, that was our song, and what a truly killer power ballad to fall in love to.

Only one problem: her family knew what we were up to. As in so many cases, they decided that if you were fucking their daughter, you had to man up and give her a ring. They knew full well that there would be something wrong with you if sex wasn't involved by that time. Truth is, we had been screwing each other's brains out for ages with some of the best sex I have ever had. To this day, I still don't even know how to use a rubber, and I can't believe I haven't had any unwanted babies or STDs. Maybe the expert timing and reactions I was blessed with from my sports was the key.

That marriage pressure was, sadly, what drove us apart. Her family desperately wanted it, but I knew I was too young and there was many more fish in the sea I needed to trawl for. My folks never approved of Wendy, as she came from the other side of the tracks, living in a council housing estate. I tried to visit it on my bike last time I was in Aberdeen, but it has been transformed into yet another million-dollar suburb for oil-wealthy Aberdeen tycoons.

Her brother was the army's lightweight boxing champion, as her parents proudly kept boasting to me. I later learned it was more of a threat that "if you screw our sweetheart over, you die, punk." Those were her father's very words when he got the feeling I was going to end it. Funny thing is, I honestly wasn't scared. I'd had so many fights back then, I knew I could at the very least hurt him back, if not counter his one-dimensional attack. Though my boxing skills were limited, I was passionate about martial arts, and thanks to my training in that area, I had turned the tables on the many bullies I had to face in the early years because of my diminutive size.

I had kickboxed and done some Shotokan karate to make up for the inherent weaknesses of tae kwon do, but it was the Korean foot-fist discipline that I particularly loved, gaining my brown belt in almost record time. I also gained respect in competitions, often beating larger and higher-belted opponents.

The best fight I ever had was against a black-belt second-degree karate expert who, right off the bell, did this crouching tiger pose resembling something out of the great old-school *Karate Kid* movies (another one of my favorite flicks and my main catalyst for studying karate, because I was sick of getting bullied). As with bent and splayed knees he went into this very cool low position I had never seen before, with his arms over his head pointed directly at me, I was in awe, pure and simple. What he intended for me was totally unknown.

With nothing to lose, I just thought, *Fuck it: if he wants to put his head there, I'm going to kick the living hell out of it.* I unleashed and connected perfectly with the sweetest, fastest, most powerful kick I have ever thrown.

Most coaches will tell you fear is no motivator, but trust me, it works, and it has gotten me out of some very scary spots, as my opponent soon found out to his detriment. He lay unconscious on the mat, and my club erupted behind me. I was a mere green belt at that time.

Another fight I'll never forget happened when I was working behind the bar at Kenny's Fish and Chips. This drunk came in around 1 a.m. and ordered a regular fish supper. Just another punter, I assumed as I gave him his chippie—at which point he grabbed my shirt and gave me a Glasgow kiss. That is, he head-butted me, one of the sorest, hardest-to-defend-against blows known to man. My nose was broken, I was gushing everywhere, and I lost it. I ran out from behind the counter, got the guy on the ground, and laid into him until the doormen pulled me off, threatening police involvement if I didn't stop.

A horrible and horrific temper that I inherited from my dad had reared its ugly head from as far back as I remember. On my first day of primary/elementary school, as we were all lined up outside our classroom, the guy behind me pushed me. I grabbed him by the neck and wouldn't stop banging his head against the wall. I inadvertently hit his head off the clothes hook and hurt him way more than I actually meant to.

Years later, on my first day of senior or high school, after a school assembly that was basically singing hymns and getting bored stupid listening to teachers sound off about dull news, I was caught talking. The goodie-two-shoes prefects, who I had learned to hate, pulled me up to the front after the teachers were gone and hit me hard over the head with their hymn books. Despite the huge size discrepancy, I retaliated with every ounce of my strength. I picked out the head boy and brought him to his knees, to the vast approval of every student in the crowd. Obviously, after that, he was out for me.

In a strange twist of fate, that morning assembly was the only place I ever got any kind of recognition for my athletic endeavours, as it was there that they announced the successes and failures of the various sporting teams. It brings me back to a time when I actually got on the swim team. I thought I was quite good (especially at the breaststroke) until this guy Colin joined and beat me by a whole length in a 4 ´ 25-meter backstroke race. I was so gutted that I decided that maybe I would be better at diving. In fairness to me, this Colin bloke eventually ended up winning a bronze for the Great Britain team at the Los Angeles Olympics.

So off to the springboard this budding Greg Louganis or Alex Despatie went. I decided I would throw in a spin, as I got bored with straight diving, swallows or pikes. I got dialed fairly easily off the higher boards, but unfortunately, my foot slipped off the springboard at the time of my jump and totally ruined my trajectory. Instead of ending up in the water, I flew toward the side of the pool, bashing my head off the concrete corner, which not only split my head open like a can of sardines but knocked me clean out. I endured my first of many concussions, winding up unconscious and bleeding on the bottom of the pool until my teacher/coach dove in along with some pupils to save my sorry ass.

There was just something about diving boards that engrossed me ever since I was a very young kid. As a family, we always seemed to holiday in and around Spain and its southern tourism magnet—the Costa del Sol and islands like Majorca. With my dad being the stereotypical tight-ass Scot, we always were booked into the cheapest and best-value-for-money hotels.

THE HOOD

We would be told to just pretend we were staying there as we snuck into the higher-end hotels with the cool pools.

This one vacation I was sitting in the kids' pool with my rubber ring and just became obsessed watching people jumping of the springboard. That was it: like so many times in my life, I just had to experience it for myself. There I was, this 4-year-old boy, walking up the steps, petrified yet determined to make this leap of faith. I stood there for approaching half an hour, walking up to the end but then getting too scared and retreating.

I looked around, and to my amazement, everyone around the pool area had stopped what they were doing to watch me. How could I give in to my many fears with such an audience? I dug deep and somehow found the courage to jump. Holding my nose, I flung myself off that perceived life-ending cliff-drop into the pool.

Unfortunately, when I entered the water, I went straight through my rubber ring, and before I knew what was going on, I was at the bottom of the pool, completely helpless, as I hadn't learned to swim by then. With one of my nine lives gone, my dad and this other saint dived in to save me, the latter ruining his very expensive watch in the process.

A few years later, I was doing exactly the same in our local Aberdeen Bon Accord baths. My bravery had me walking up the steps to the top Olympic-sized board, jumping, then diving off, with my heart in my mouth—again, the higher the risk, the higher the glory. As Lance Armstrong stated, "Pain is temporary, but glory is forever." Believe me, you don't want to know how many times I have silently said that to myself over the years I have spent on this planet.

I could go on and on with my complete dumb-ass childhood stories, but I will finish with what I think is the pièce de résistance and the crème de la crème. It still amazes me to this day. I always knew before my report card came out what my teachers were going to say: *Andrew would do so much better if he only applied himself blah blah blah*. Although I knew they were right, I just hated being in an all-boys super-strict school and really wanted to go to the local public school, so I rebelled. In an attempt to finally get a good report card, I concocted a scam.

When they gave me my report card, I decided I was going to doctor it by using liquid eraser over the comments and adding my own, and then cutting out squares to cover up the marks and inputting my make-believe ones. Then I took it to the nearest Prontaprint (a printing place) and photocopied it. I just told my folks the school lost the original, and they actually believed it. For the first time in ages, I could enjoy Christmas holiday.

Then the next term, we made these coffee tables in woodworking—but when my folks gave the money to buy it, I spent the cash instead on these top-of-the-range darts, as I was starting to get damn good at it in my folks' hotel, and I wanted a new pimping set. Instead of buying my table, I wandered into the woodworking shop and took the best one as mine. It was done by the class nerd, Darren, who I hated more than life itself. He was the teacher's pet, and I remember chasing him around the physics lab with a stroboscope trying to induce his epilepsy. Nasty or what?

I walked out of the school quadrangle with another person's table. Why I never thought I would get caught, God knows. I bunked off for over two weeks before the phone call came down the line. It coincided with the end-of-year concert. As I was in the choir, I had to attend—and deal with all the dirty looks from teachers and parents alike.

The next day was my judgment day, with the vice headmaster Goofy Gordon. After a real ribbing and belting, he let me off with a suspension. But that was just so much me back then—the original wild child, with more than a cat's nine lives.

CHAPTER 3

THE WAY YOU MAKE ME FEEL

So, out of school … now what? I didn't have a clue what I wanted to be, and with next to no qualifications, my choices were limited to all those minimum-wage jobs that my private-school upbringing made fun of. That was something I never fully understood: if we were all born equal and someone had to do those jobs, why judge anyone for their chosen profession, right?

At that point in my life, my old man had just accepted a position with much higher wages in Hemel Hempsted, just north of London. I had no idea how I would love or hate the move, but it was major, as all I had ever known was the northeast of Scotland. I was actually kind of excited to expand my horizons and check out the rest of this big badass world.

It was like we didn't just move to another place in the UK but had just landed on Mars. Everything seemed alien to me. My folks had checked out the local technical colleges because I didn't have enough grades to even get close to any university. But what course to do? I decided that these cool new computer machines (imperfect as they were in their early days) were going to become way bigger than anyone could predict back then. I enrolled in computer studies with math, as I was always good at arithmetic and algebra at school. Little did I know that these choices were going to be way beyond anything I had ever done before, partly because the Scottish and English education systems didn't mesh well, and I was way behind the eight ball on all my courses.

Computer programming, starting with binary code, was a fucking mystery, like those crazy Roald Dahl creepy stories or *The Twilight Zone* that I loved but could never really understand. How the fuck could 1 + 1 = 0? God knows; it went against everything I had ever been taught. I desperately tried to get a handle on it, but after about a month, I realized I was a round peg in a square hole. My old man's super-logical flow-diagram brain would have excelled at it, but I had my mum's emotional/coach type of brain, which meant I was simply dumfounded by every class I took.

On top of that, the culture was completely foreign to me. I just wanted to pack up my shit and hitchhike back to Aberdeen. When this was not possible, I did what I always do in that situation: rebel. I started bunking classes, and even when I was there, I spent most of my time in the common room playing pool and chatting up the oh-so-fine English girls.

After a few more mind-numbingly boring months looking for an elusive job, I'd had enough of this place. I took a few cool trips to the big smoke that was London, checking out the bright lights of the extensive club scene, and then I was ready to go home. My lasting memory of London is that when you jumped on the Underground rail system, no matter what time, there was no conversation. You were greeted with a wall of newspapers that everyone hid behind. The *Times*, *Guardian*, *Daily Express* or whatever paper would go up if you tried to engage in eye contact with any of your fellow travellers. Pretty strange!

After yet another bad day in class, I'd had enough. I went home and told my folks that I was going to catch the train to Aberdeen, as I honestly hated the pretentious place. My only good friend I had down there, Dave—a six-foot-five-inch gentle giant of a guy—followed me back to Aberdeen. We found the cheapest of cheap B & Bs, filled with unemployed stoners. This was pretty much my first taste of the non-working dole class, with the massive temptation just to get baked from as soon as they woke up. My folks and my sports had drilled the anti-drug message into me, so I just replied "Not my scene man" to their offers to turn me into one of them.

I knew I needed a way out, and the key was a job. I eventually took one in the retail superstore where we'd always bought our weekly groceries— Fine Fare at the Bridge of Dee. I didn't have enough qualifications or motivation to go on and do any more education. I always viewed university as a place for silver-spoon kids and ivory-tower geeks with no grasp of the real world. Sure, I knew back then it was the ticket to a well-paid, high-powered career, but I didn't care. I had more wedge in my pocket than I'd ever had, and it was time to chase women.

Fine Fare was a great pick-up environment. It was a large supermarket, and I was the king of the car accessories aisle. I'd always drooled over cars, and I knew that one day, I would have a set of hot wheels. To me, cars are like usable works of art, and I have loved them since I was a kid. I could name any car just by the light of the headlights at night. I found it really ironic that my main responsibility was to look after that portion of the store, but I soon got totally bored and frustrated talking about car swag when I didn't even own one myself. So I was moved to cashier, which was mint, as there were more girls in that team to chat up and impress with how quickly you could "input the data." This was before the barcode era.

You usually got a conversation from the customers, too, but as with everything I do, once I get to a certain proficiency at anything, I want to move on to the next challenge. This is a trait I genuinely hate and wish I would lose. My mother used to talk about "contented cow syndrome"— you know, those people who are more than content in doing whatever God chose for them, something I could never understand but truly wished I could be, rather than the control freak I admittedly am.

I decided that working in a warehouse would be a good experience and bulk me up, as I was never the biggest kid muscle-wise; rather, I relied on my very high strength-to-weight ratio. Somewhere along the way, you get conned into thinking that women like muscles and you can intimidate other males with them. It worked, and I started gaining mass; the downside was I often had to work night shifts, which seriously impeded my social life. But in a strange way, I grew to love working at night. It was somehow more peaceful. Inner peace is something I have been striving for in vain all my life, hence my love for the stupendously hilarious *Kung Fu Panda* movies. Quite honestly, I am a real-life version of him.

In the warehouse, I had my very first glimpse into the God Squad. A relationship with the Almighty is something I truly cherish, but in my own time and space. I vowed with my Irish side that I would never have an argument about religion but rather accept and respect others' opinions on the subject. Instead, I was inflicted with Sunday School, which was almost mandatory back in those days in middle-class Scotland. I told myself *I will never ever force my kids to endure the boredom of these sermons* as we counted down the minutes before we would disappear through the back to our kids' time.

I could never figure out how our Scottish Presbyterian Church could make religion so dull and boring—kind of like how the various Ski and Snowboard Instructor Associations I have been actively involved in made some of the most enjoyable winter pursuits so dull and grey. I had by then watched all these uplifting black-gospel-music-driven ceremonies on TV and thought I would actually enjoy getting kitted out for a Sunday service like that. Just google "Scots and Rye New Year's special" and you won't stop laughing; it sums up perfectly how dour our religion is in the auld country.

I had to work with this guy Kelvin, a born-again Christian who, within two minutes, brought every conversation back to the Almighty. After a couple of weeks of late nights, I thought I was going crazy. Every night, he urged me to go home and pray, meaning I had to close my eyes with absolutely no distractions (not ever my greatest strength with my ADHD) and ask God to come into every part of my heart and soul.

I really did try, but He didn't join me like He did with Kelvin. I opted for the more karma yin and yang deal and/or *Star Wars* force theory and the genuine belief that there is something magical and bigger than we will ever be running this universe. Even if you don't believe, you can try to follow the Ten Commandments. That's easier said than done in this cutthroat society, especially when you have no money.

I managed to get moved over to the much smaller non-foods warehouse side, where I met Des, one of those guys who everyone loves. That's something I had always dreamed of being, but I am too brutally honest. I wear my heart on my sleeve and can't hide my non-verbal communication when I don't like someone. Some call it rude and crude; I call it being real, genuine and honest. Why the fuck should you be two-faced, saying hello to people you can't stand, and you know the feeling is mutual? I have always called a spade a spade. I will always give people my utmost respect as long as they deserve it. But it stops there. You won't find any brown on my nose.

To begin with, Des and I got on like a house on fire, as we seemed to be very similar, really upbeat and unable to sit still, like human versions of the Energizer bunny. I never could figure out what it was about him, but you know when you just get this hunch that there is something not right about someone? My misgivings about him soon proved right. I was up one of the many ladders getting some of my old aisle's car accessories stock and passing it down to Des, who was below me, when completely out of left field I felt this hand on my groin. Talk about revisiting a ghost from the past, with horrific memories of my now-deceased form teacher's "indiscretion."

After I regained my composure, I almost lost more than just my grip on the ladder. Thankfully, rather than following my initial urge to unleash the fiercest back kick on him, I shuffled down the ladder, pinned him against the wall and told him point-blank that I would fucking kill him if he ever pulled a stunt like that on me ever again. I was left wondering if this was a strategy of gay men: suck you in with charisma, jokes and fun, then make their move. Kind of similar to how guys court girls, I guess. In hindsight, that horrible experience, amongst others, only heightened my distrust of other guys and my discomfort around gay guys.

Compounding this, I met this guy Greg in Fine Fare, and we immediately hit it off. Again, this was a super-bubbly guy who was really popular with the girls. It was bizarre; he seemed to know exactly what made them tick and how to make them laugh. He almost blended into them to the point where they would tell him anything. How I never translated this trait to him being gay, I will never know. It was on a holiday with Greg to Ibiza that I found out the hardest way possible that my initial "he is very in touch with his feminine side" assessment was a complete understatement, and he decided to come out at my expense.

I had scored pretty well that holiday with a few English birds, mainly because of him. He helped me overcome my nervousness at making the initial hit on girls, as I hated rejection more than anything, and I seemingly have nothing in common with them if they don't like sports. He seemed to be able to go up to any female on the planet, start up a conversation and have her laughing within minutes—which made me green with envy.

On the second to last night, I found out why: he was one of them! I have never been so close to murdering a fellow human being. Greg made his move on me by climbing into my bed naked and starting to spoon and touch me. There aren't words for the trauma and sheer disgust I felt in my very being. *Not again!* Pure anger filled my thoughts. It brought me full circle to my past, when I was rumoured to be a homo because of my brother's exploits and the school I attended (neither of which were my choice).

I recalled my form teacher putting his hands down my pants and Des groping me on the ladder in Fine Fare, and I started asking myself, was I indeed a closet gay? Why the fuck were they always hitting on me? I still to this day cannot figure out what a man can see in another man (and for that matter, quite what girls see in a guy's body). It will always be a mystery I know I will never find an answer to. But a question more important to me even now is, why on earth do gay guys continue to hit on me? Do I subconsciously emit some signal? Am I game prey for them? I don't understand what's going on, but leave me the fuck alone.

Despite what you might think, I actually respect their choice. I genuinely support gay marriage and have had some amazing gay friends. Why can't they respect my choice to be straight? Because of my past, as much as I hate that part of me, I think I will always harbour some deep homophobic paranoia.

After some time at Fine Fare, I realized this was not my calling in life, although the green was really nice. Just like anything, there was a honeymoon period before I said to myself, *Do I want to do this for the rest of my life?* I asked my folks what to do, as I knew as much as I really didn't want to do any more education—it just wasn't me—the only escape from a close-to-minimum-wage job for the rest of my life was going back to college. They came up with business studies, reasoning that there will always be companies, so there will always be jobs for business-school graduates.

Suffice to say, I had nowhere near the qualifications to get into university, so I enrolled in the local Aberdeen College of Commerce. It wasn't ideal, as my old dear worked there and I knew she'd have easy access to my progression, but I really had no choice. The only other college in town was the technical college, and my next-to-useless hands counted me out of any kind of trade.

The summer that followed was quite simply my best. My parents had followed me back to Aberdeen, but when they left for a three-week excursion around the states, it was like an invitation to party. I still had the rich pickings of the Fine Fare crew, which definitely favoured female employment. The Los Angeles Olympics came on at the same time every night—around 11, just in time for us to be fairly well liquored up—and went through the early morning. I had fallen off a ladder at work and hurt my back, so I was on sick leave and drowned any pain I had by drinking it away. I remember all of our money went for beer; we stole our neighbour's milk and used up everything in the food cupboards until the only thing left was my old man's All Bran.

I had just passed my driver's license test in my usual crazy Andrew style. My folks gave me the money for 10 driving lessons for my birthday, but I spent almost all of it getting hammered and picking up chicks. I had enough left for two lessons and couldn't even afford to get a car for the actual exam. I borrowed the old man's Rover 3.5 and used it to take my test. Fuck if I didn't nail everything except the last test, the parallel park deal, when I smoked the damn curb. It was an automatic fail. The examiner gave me the bad news, and to his shock, I pulled away on my own. I will never forget that face as long as I live.

After finding my parents' car keys, we went *Cannonball Run*–style street racing—so much so that when my father returned, the car would hardly start, as it had been accustomed to a short trip to go shopping and the very occasional 16-mile trip to Banchory—nothing like the 130-miles-per-hour races we'd had with cars way out of its league. The car literally billowed black smoke out of it and couldn't get above 40 miles per hour, so my dad filled it full of oil and traded it in as soon as he figured out what had happened. Saying he wasn't too pleased is a gigantic understatement.

Actually, my parents returned a week early; they had been booked for four weeks. I will never forget lying in their bed, with a girl either side of me and what Rihanna describes as "a little (no a lot) of last night on the sheets," and hearing my mum's familiar Irish accent shouting hello as the front door opened. I don't think I have ever panicked as bad in my life. Shock doesn't even come close to describing the look on my parents' faces when they saw easily 20 girls with next to nothing on darting about frantically trying to find the rest of their clothes and get the fuck out of there ASAP. They knew that what was going to go down wouldn't be pretty, and they didn't want to have any part in it.

The final straw was that I had decided to test my dad's favourite toy— his top-of-the-line audio-visual equipment—to the absolute max. This was right in line with my love for music and DJing. (It wasn't until I left home that our suburban neighbours ratted me out, telling them just how loud we cranked the music, sometimes until 6 a.m. Better neighbours no man could ever ask for.) It was no surprise that I had blown up his Goodman's sub, and in hindsight, I would be pissed too if anyone did that to mine, as one of the few things Dad and I share is devotion to the reproduction of top-quality sight and sound. That's what he did for a living as the chief engineer for the region's TV station. It was kind of a cool gig. From a very young age, I got to meet celebrities and realize that, apart from their infinite wealth and fame, they were just normal human beings with all the demons and insecurities that face us all.

Even though I thought it was way overboard at the time, they quite rightly threw me out, and I got my first insight into being homeless. It was also, apart from cigarettes, my first real adventure in the world of addiction. We had drunk so much every day and night over those epic three-and-a-half weeks that the night I was thrown out onto the street, I went over to my girlfriend's place in Tory looking for booze—but to my surprise, her folks had no booze in their house. In absolute desperation, I scoured every off-license in her hood (Tory is a pretty rough part of Aberdeen at night), but not one was open. Weird sweats, awake all night shaking uncontrollably—this was all very, very scary when you're only 19 years old. Afterward, I vowed I would never let that happen to me ever again. It never did ... well, not with alcohol.

This incident, combined with the usual Christmas and Hogmany festivities, made me very cautious and careful about consuming alcohol in copious amounts. It was what we referred to then as "the season to get bleezing." After the mandatory three-week lead-up to the big day, Christmas came and went with no problem. New Year's Eve night was the jewel in the crown of the festivities that seemed to last for almost a week. Trust me, celebrating is something the Gaels do better than anyone.

The night started out as always: a few beers with friends and then on to our local pub, Henry J Beans, then to Queen's Cross Church, as we always did on Christmas Eve. We left the Kirk and sang and danced around the Queens Cross roundabout for longer than we usually did, as if you couldn't score with the chicks on that night, you'd better consider switching teams.

THE HOOD

Unlike our usual one a.m. time of going back to the folks' place to celebrate with the usual Runrig's Bonnie Banks of Loch Lomond and Queen's greatest anthems in the background, we didn't stumble in until almost 2:30 a.m. We were met by a rather pissed old man (both on a drunk and anger basis) going off about *where the fuck you have you been, it just shows what we mean to you* rant. It all came to a head, as it always seems to do at parties, in the kitchen. My old man decided to give in to his temper and start pounding me with punches.

Something just snapped in me after all the years of bottled-up anger, brutal tough love and corporal punishment. I just lost it on him, delivering a beating I didn't even know I was capable of—especially with my own father. I was in such a rage, I literally can't remember any of the details. Suffice to say it was payback, motherfucker, for all the years of *wait till your father gets home* shit I'd had to deal with from as far back as I can remember. All I can remember is leaving him fucked up and gushing on the floor. I told him, "Don't ever fuck with me again," and he never did.

I suddenly realized that all the restraint I had when I was sober went out the window when I had a few beers inside me. If provoked, I could turn into the meanest, dirtiest, angriest asshole ever. It wasn't until he came around to apologize a few days later that I saw firsthand what my fists and kicks can do to someone when the beast is unleashed. I honestly could hardly recognize my father with his two black eyes, broken nose and broken jaw. I was so distraught about my actions, I have treated alcohol very carefully ever since—not because, as my haters like to claim, I am gay or a big girl in disguise, but because it turns me into an uncontrollable animal that I really don't like or trust.

My internal control mechanism now throws up red flags after four or five beers, and I very rarely ignore it. Honestly, I'm scared that my inbred temper could not only hurt but kill someone and get me locked up for a very long time because all of my martial arts training and street-fighting skills. Add in my older brother's army training, which he passed onto me, and I was armed and dangerous.

Why do we still use these archaic macho male symbols—like beer and *boys have to be joined at the hip* and *to be a real man's man you have to drink real beer—no light is acceptable as that's pussy beer* will never fail to amaze me. Whatever happened to the idea that a real man must be strong, work hard, and protect and love his family before anything else? I'm sick of hearing women say it is so hard to be a woman in this day and age of stereotypes. Believe me, it is equally hard on the other side of the fence, when we have to be all this plus loving, affectionate, romantic and passionate.

I just say be yourself. We might all be created equal, but we are also born different and unique. If the world doesn't want to accept you because you're different, so be it. Be proud of your distinctiveness and uniqueness. I know about this all too well, as I have never really fit in anywhere.

It was around this time that my older brother managed to outdo himself on the stupid idiotic stakes. He had gone to Aberdeen University to study law—not really for himself but to fulfill my parents' dream of having a lawyer, doctor and who knows what else in the family. Only problem was, he hated it and wanted to emulate one of his heroes, Steve McQueen in *The Great Escape*. Of course, he had to do it in the most dramatic fashion possible.

One day, we woke up and found that Ian was gone—to where, no one knew. After about a week, my mum started stressing bad and phoned the university directly to get to the bottom of his disappearance. A guy who Ian had befriended came forward with the almost unbelievable news that both he and Ian had discussed running away to join the French Foreign Legion, What the fuck! No one in my family even knew there was such a thing, but after a frantic dash for information about this highly secretive organization—much harder back then without the Internet—it became clear that if indeed you wanted to find a real-life invisibility cloak like in Harry Potter, this is where you want to be.

To our amazement, this elite fighting force required no ID. When you were enveloped by this mercenary unit, you did indeed disappear. As such, it was made up of the world's most hardened criminals, as even serial killers can't be found by anyone once they enter the legion. It was quite simply the hardest place for my folks to find Ian, never mind get him home.

I could give you a blow-by-blow account of this crazy drama, which lasted for almost two months. It eventually came to a scary conclusion, with Ian running away from their headquarters in Southern France. If you believe Ian's story, he escaped under shots fired, as they really made their own rules. I could never get on the same wavelength as my brother;

we really were the epitome of chalk and cheese. I just shook my head and looked up to the heavens in disbelief over another unlikely chapter of our family history.

Back to college: despite all my self-talk about needing college to escape the Fine Fare minimum-wage trap, I took my usual academic approach of just doing enough to get by. Unfortunately, it was only enough in my eyes. Just before Christmas, the vice principal pulled me into his office and gave the biggest wake-up call I'd ever had up to that point. He told me, in the most basic terms, that if I didn't turn things around in a hurry, I would fail and end up stocking shelves in some retail store for the rest of my life. To this day, I credit old Rory for giving me a new chance at life with the inspirational pep talk to really try at academics for the first time ever.

My logic was: *Fuck it, I don't want to ever see Fine Fare's or any other superstore's car accessories aisle or warehouse ever again. What the hell. Let's see what I can do if I try with everything I've got, like I always did with sports.*

To say that I surprised myself isn't strong enough. I remember walking the five miles every morning, usually in the pouring rain, listening to my Walkman, getting amped up to work as hard as I possibly could that day. I think that's where I first decided to take life one day at a time. Though my U-turn didn't happen overnight, slowly but surely, my grades started improving.

After two full terms of hell, I found a strength inside me I didn't know existed. I proved that if I outworked my peers, I could prove that nothing was impossible. All I needed to do was transplant how I succeeded at sports to all of life's arenas. Harking back to when I was a kid in the hotel and doing my family chores, I quickly realized that it is not always the most gifted who win; it is often the one who works the hardest and has the mental toughness. Of course, if the gifted person also does this, then you get a phenom like Michael Phelps, Usian Bolt or Shawn White. But in my experience, it rarely happens, as naturals usually rest on their God-given talent.

After what seemed an eternity, I came out as the top student, which blew me away. I had never excelled at the academic stuff. My mentor, Rory, went to bat for me and recommended that I go on to a business studies degree even though my new-found qualification, an HNC in business studies, was not officially recognized as an entry certificate to the honours degree course at Robert Gordon's University, the university of the private school I went to. All of a sudden, someone who had seemed like a real hater turned into one of my biggest fans, and I will forever be in his debt.

To my absolute amazement, I got the word: I was accepted to the degree course. To be honest, I was scared stupid. I knew I was going against all the school keen beans, as I called them: the four-eyed nerd crew who, I was convinced, had some kind of brain that was just so much better than mine.

On the very first day, this tall guy came up to me after getting our assignment asking me how many highers (high school graduation in different subjects) I had. To my embarrassment, I had none. It was just another naysayer taking a shot at me, but it was the best medicine I could have hoped for, as reverse psychology is where I shine. I went to bed that night going, *Screw all you silver-spoon kids who just got out of school and have no life trials to build from to gain the motivation I have to not ever go back to a dead-end supermarket job ever again.* It was on.

I remember spending every minute outside of class doing this *War and Peace* project to prove to the world I was no dunce. Talk about psyched: when I got the marks back, I had a 10 percent higher mark than anyone else. But it also put a target on my back to all the keeners to shoot at. I couldn't believe it. I had turned into one of them with this *fuck it, I am just going to outwork every one of my competitors* strategy. Like another one of my old dear's one-liners: you will never get fired for working too hard.

I also figured out that it was going to be tough to beat the brainers on my own, so I started my own crew. I recruited a really hard worker in this Dutch guy called Karl and a supercomputer brain called Del. God, it was almost impossible to have a normal conversation with Del, as everything he said seemed to be the biggest word possible. It felt like the guy wasn't from another country but another planet. But I knew he was easily the brainiest guy on the roster, and I needed help. There was serious competition to be top student.

This was the biggest challenge I had ever had to face. I could compete with anyone in sports, but despite the confidence boost of proving I had a brain, I felt like I was competing in the Academic Olympics. Street smarts and an exceptionally high work ethic were my secret weapons, and I wasn't going to tell anyone. My rivals weren't stupid, but even when they picked up their game, I just took mine to another level.

Suffice to say, I wasn't Mr. Popular, but I didn't care, as I wasn't there to make friends. I was there to get a new career, and as such, I was determined to beat the hell out of my peers. I suddenly realized that getting a degree wasn't really about how many brain cells you had or how good you were at your chosen subject; it was all about who worked the hardest and who had the best memory. Working hard is for sure part of it, and so it should be, but memory tests? Really? What year are we in, people? That's for all the ivory-tower professors to figure out, I guess, but please, there must be a better method of teaching.

As always, my internal SWOT analysis kicked in, and I found a way to beat the system. I developed this foolproof plan for beating the silver-spoon kids at their own game. After every term, I would go through all my notes and rewrite them into my form of shorthand, condensing them into as small a folder as possible, which tricked my brain into believing it was less info to retain. I was simply crap at scanning. I am more than sure I am dyslexic, and therefore, I never read books. This is the main reason that to this day, I still can't spell to save myself. Thank God for spell-check is all I can say.

Well, I passed everything they threw at me with flying colors. I was the most hated student ever, but every time I doubted myself, I just engaged my memory banks and reminded myself how much more I hated being Mr. Car Accessories Aisle in Fine Fare earning minimum wage. I knew I could never ever go back there. It wasn't really the low pay I hated; it was how mind-numbingly boring the job was. Although I knew I was never gifted with school smarts, what I lacked there I more than made up for in street smarts. The song "Us Against the World" was my anthem and motivation.

I had to pay my way through uni, so I found a sweet job in an off-license called the Wine Lodge. It was another minimum-wage deal, but it had its perks, because like every student, I liked to party. I scored big-time on cheap booze and made a whole bunch of connections for when I finally graduated. Of course, trust my luck, Davie the manager was as gay as they come—but you know, he was one of the best guys I ever met. He helped me see that my homophobia was totally misguided, as you couldn't meet a nicer guy, and he 110 percent respected my straight choice, never coming close to crossing that line. The only thing I resent Davie for is not giving me the Saturday off from work to go see the original Live Aid when I had an in to get tickets.

I will never forget this lovely old woman, Megan, who used to come in every day of the week for her bottle of Harvey's Bristol Cream sherry. I thought she was obviously a sad old girl numbing her sorrows and loneliness in alcohol. But then, after a few weeks of not seeing her, this younger version of her came in who turned out to be her daughter. The old woman had passed away but had told her daughter how much she enjoyed my company and that I was the only reason she had to leave the house every day. It was never about the booze.

This gave me an indelible insight into the challenges faced by too many members of our aging population and how sad they really can be. It's another injustice we as a society need to correct with proper facilities and community centres, especially tailored to the people who really deserve our respect and attention. To my amazement, Megan's daughter told me that they found more than 300 bottles of Harvey's in her house when they were cleaning it out.

I can't remember which year it was, but one night, we decided to do the brotherly love gig by going out to a club and getting messed up. We went to the latest and greatest club in Aberdeen, and after more than a few beers, my brother and I ended up in this super-stylish club. We were just chilling, watching the chicks doing their thing on the dance floor, and bingo—Ian decided to pinch the ass of the girl next to him. So off they headed to the floor, leaving me in an awkward position with her best friend.

The song "La Bamba" came on. Why I ever picked that song to have my first dance with this hottie, I will never know, as it is one of the hardest songs ever to dance to. Little did I know this was my future wife! Her name was Carol, as I later found out. She hated that name, so you had to call her Carol.

I have never understood my taste in women. Forget the sleazy Keisha, Nicki Minaj, Kim Kardashian, Miley Cyrus types. To this day, they don't do it for me. I go for Reese Witherspoon, Britney Spears, Halle Berry, and yes, Carol was in that vein. "A cute yet adorable beauty" was the best way I could describe her.

THE HOOD

One trait I know for sure I got from my mum: every time I get nervous—which is always when I'm chatting up a girl, as much as I try everything to hide it—I do the fake-it-to-make-it method and talk too much. My favorite one-liner back then, which I still use it to this day because it works better than any other I have heard and tried, is "I am actually really shy, but I have to say you're very pretty." I think the line worked so well because I wasn't making up bull like most of the guys. I was genuinely telling the truth.

By the end of the night, we managed to get the girls back to our pad. Ian disappeared into his bedroom with Fiona, and I hit the games room with Carol. At that point, we had moved just around the corner from where I worked in a very prestigious neighborhood in Aberdeen called Carlton Place. It was always a bonus to take them back to the West End, because they thought we were loaded. In actual fact, we were loaded, but not with coin—with alcohol.

In fact, our parents *were* rich, but we had been brought up with the tough love theory, which like any discipline, we hated. Now, in later life, I can how it's possible to be rich in assets but cash-flow poor. Investing in real estate can significantly improve your net worth, but because they were paying large school fees for my younger brother and a huge mortgage, they really didn't have a ton of leftover disposal income.

In our house, we had this real chill converted attic space where we could do practically anything we wanted. Music and dance were always my passion. I hooked up my decent sound system in the games room where I mixed tunes, watched music videos and danced my heart out—more often than not to MJ's incredible music videos, trying in vain to copy his moves.

Back to Carol: after four hours of me blabbing endlessly, her friend came out of my brother's bedroom, which was also located up there, with all the telltale signs of having had some passionate sex. She suggested to Carol it was time to leave. At that, I nearly died. My shyness was about to get the better of me again. I had talked nonstop for hours; was I really going to take the easy way out and let her go? Hell no! Not this time!

There was nothing left to do but grab her and kiss her. I had a real hunch she was at least as shy if not more so than me. To say it was love at first sight is an overstatement, but there was something about this girl that did something to me I had never felt before. Despite all my crazy busy life between my studies, part-time job and sports, I simply couldn't think about anything else. She took up my every thought 24/7, and I just knew she was not only different from the other girls, she was as close to perfection as I had ever found: smart, classy, humble and a hell of a cute face. I ask you: what else do you need? For me, nothing.

Even better, she was a nurse. With their reputations and my short-skirt-nurse's-uniform fantasy, I tried my best to hide every time I entered her nurse's complex. To her credit, she was actually completely the opposite from their nymph rap—and talk about earning every inch of my home-base hunt. As my mum would say countless times, marrying a nurse was the best thing I ever did. With all my sports injuries, my numerous physiotherapists agreed that I should have been born with a helmet on my head to protect me from all my crazy dangerous stunts.

Three months with Carol flew past, and none of my usual three curses came to fruition: day, week, month. They never even entered my head. Quite simply, I had finally found a girl I truly loved—that oh-so-rare mixture of friendship and love. She was like my best friend as well as my lover. It was a love that we all dream of, even if very few of us admit to it these days, as we are all too busy doing our play-it-cool image crap.

Then just like my life always seems to do when things are going my way, I got a curveball to the face when she hit me with, "I'm moving to Dunfermline to train as a midwife." I hid it well, but I was shattered. In a very emotional *Bachelor*-style farewell at the rose gardens at Duthie Park, I plucked the most gorgeous red rose for her and revealed a necklace in an attempt not to lose her. As it happens, she felt the same and wanted to try a long-distance relationship.

Thankfully, her move happened when I was entered my third work-experience gap year. I had managed to score a marketing assistant role with Stewart Milne Construction, a pioneer of timber-framed buildings which were starting to catch on in Scotland because of cost, warmth and speed of building. My role was to collect as much information as possible about their competitors in the rapidly growing segment of the industry.

In a weird twist of fate, I had to visit all of the competing companies' head offices to get quotes on this particular type of house. I felt really torn about this, as even back then I hated lying, but hey, it paid the bills and was way better than Fine Fare or my Wine Lodge roles. More importantly, it gave me the freedom to travel all over the country—and the perfect excuse to go down and see my sweetheart in Stirling and Dunfermline. Carol's best school friend Elaine, who had also moved to Aberdeen to become a nurse, nicknamed our sexual pursuits "market research."

Truth be told, although we were definitely ramping up the sensual stuff, I take my hat off to her: it was almost four months before she put out, which, looking back on it, was probably the reason I was so into her. Like it or not, our internal caveman loves the challenge of the chase, and my respect for her was immeasurable.

I would work my ass off Monday through Friday and then jump into my beloved first car my folks bought for me, a lime green Ford Cortina, and drive the 100-plus miles to kick it with my boo over the weekend. Looking back on it, I have no clue how I didn't crash when driving back to Aberdeen in the small hours of Monday morning after next to no sleep, as there were better things to pass our time with like alcohol, checking out the hood and tons of sex. The big film of the day was *Dirty Dancing*, and it was the soundtrack I would invariably listen to when I was on the road.

All good things have to come to an end, and after a very successful year out, I had to return to university to complete my last year and a half. I had elected to do honours, which was basically an extra term with a huge thesis to compile. I decided to dedicate everything I had to getting a first-class honours and/or be the best student. The best way of achieving this, it seemed to me, was to spend as little time on the thesis, which, to be honest, I straight-out copied. I compiled a whole crop of newspaper articles on the subject and manufactured them into a very impressive thesis— nearly a full-scale book—which I wish I could actually understand. Thankfully, my lecturers did and loved it, even though they remarked it was very journalistic. Oh, if they only knew!

Instead of wasting my time on that project, I spent days in the college library studying the previous semesters' exam papers on every subject we had studied for the past almost five years. I had decided that as long as I could answer the recurring core questions, I would have more than enough to pass with flying colors, and I could just BS the ones I didn't see coming. Then I would go through my summarized term notes and highlight the appropriate sections for the answer to each of the high-percent-chance subjects.

I went over my notes and memorized every single line by taking two at a time to remember. After about a paragraph, which in actual fact usually related to weeks of lecture notes, I turned over the page and tried to rewrite each line as closely as possible. After completing my memory sessions, I would get Karl over to test me randomly on each page until I literally had committed to memory ever single word, line and page.

Because I was so comprehensive in my exam research, the unforeseen tricky questions only amounted to one or at most two per paper. These I always left to last, as I have always had a turbocharged subconscious that would figure out the best possible answer from my memory test information. I just tried to throw in everything and the proverbial kitchen sink to form a suitable answer and wrote as much as possible to hopefully gain some points for effort.

Far and away, the subject area that worried me the most was accountancy. I have learnt the hardest way possible that although we are born equal, we all have our unique strengths and weaknesses. For me, accountancy was most definitely the latter. It was a topic that was reverse logic to me, as when I worked out where a figure belonged, however hard I tried, I always figured it to be on the opposite side of the cash flow, profit and loss, balance sheet, etc. The only option was to forget about using my brain and just remember where the fuck it went on each document in the books. I could never comprehend how the hell you calculate things like depreciation. Just like trig before it, and later electricity, it was a subject that I could never and even to this day still cannot comprehend.

So then came the big day: finals. It seems like an eternity when you are waiting for them. It was the first time I couldn't sleep—serious insomnia—and I found chamomile tea. We worked so hard over the months beforehand, especially Karl, who, if I remember correctly, was actually in danger of failing going into finals week. We just went for it. I taught Karl my technique in return for nothing, as he was my best friend and had helped me out with so much over the previous three years. I felt it was appropriate payback. His friendship was more than I had expected—so much so that the bastard called on me after uni was done to be his best man.

If you have ever done a best man's speech, you will sympathize, as it is easily the hardest speech I have ever had to write. We got up to some real stupid shit over our time at school—not quite appropriate material for such a speech. After meeting his parents, I thought I'd have to do a total rewrite, as they were real conservative old-school Dutch, and I had some very edgy things in there. Finally, I just said, *Fuck it; if they don't approve, tough shit.* Everyone else in the place loved it, including the bride and groom.

Maybe one day, my little brother, Stuart, will get hitched—but I told him not to ask me to make a speech, as public speaking has always terrified me ever since I was a kid. Although I've never been diagnosed, I know I'm dyslexic. That, combined with my inherent shyness, make me a nervous wreck every time I'm asked to hold the floor or the microphone.

Back to finals: I had most of the questions covered in my cramming, but there were always a few that I was clueless about, so again, I did the bullshit baffles brains deal. Then I waited with bated breath for my results. I had never been so tired. I was Mr. Stress Cadet; I was determined to get a first-class honours, so I hardly slept. It was the conclusion of almost seven years of study, if you include my tech college days.

Was it a strange twist of fate that I, the red-headed stepchild, might become the first and only Hunter ever to graduate? The black sheep of the family, especially academically, was on the cusp of proving all the naysayers wrong that I was too thick to get anywhere in this life apart from stocking shelves. I will always remember my school report cards, every term/year saying the same thing: *If Andrew applied himself, he has potential.* Finally, I did. I have always loved proving the haters wrong. The best thing you can say to me is that I can't do something, because I will prove you wrong or die trying.

It was easily the most bittersweet moment of my life to date when I saw my name right at the top of the list, a percentile of 69 percent, a mere 1 percent away from a first class. It was cool to be the best student, but it hurt not to achieve my first-class honours because of the ludicrously low mark in business policy thanks to this fucking tool of a lecturer, Tim Maston, who always despised me. The feeling was mutual. Only he will know whether personal bias crept into his mark that was way below any of my other marks and was the reason I fell short of my dream. Bastard! Suffice to say, I was chuffed and chocked, all in the same breath.

As a bonus, I was one of the very few students who also passed the Chartered Institute of Marketing diploma—quite how, I will never know, as we had next to no study time for it. The amazing thing was that Karl also passed. We chipped in for a bottle of the finest Dom Perignon champagne we could afford, and did we ever get oiled that night! No idea what the fuck we did, but I had a killer hangover for a few days.

The stress I'd piled on myself with my win-at-all-costs ideology was for the first time starting to play havoc on my body. I was diagnosed with two duodenal ulcers that killed under stress or after a night out. Dear Lord, what I would give to have the hindsight to know what I know now: as much as my mind loves and truly thrives on competition, my body has an inherent weakness in dealing with stress.

The real bitter pill to swallow came later that month when we had our graduation ceremony. Carol and I had decided a few months prior that we should move in together, which shocked my conservative (in politics and outlook on life) parents. My old dear hated me during that period, as "living in sin" in her world was worse than non-virgins walking down the aisle in white or me getting a stud in my ear way back when. Totally unbeknownst to me, she decided that was reason enough for her and my old man not to attend my graduation.

Disbelief is not strong enough to describe my reaction. The family dumb child had finally come good and proved that it was not all about ivory-tower smarts; you can succeed with street smarts or, as we call it, good old common sense. Combine that with the highest work ethic possible, and you get my recipe for success in any of life's arenas. Here was the perennial D-grader doing something my far more academically gifted brothers could not do: wear those weird grad clothes. Trust me, if you could be in my shoes that day, you might understand how hurt I was. Even to this day, when I see grads celebrating, it brings a tear to my eye, because I never got to properly rejoice with my family.

Thankfully, Carol was there. Although we really couldn't afford it, we booked a night at the Andrewendarroch up Royal Deeside (just around the corner from Balmoral Castle and beyond five-star). I still think, to this day, it was the best sex we ever had. We stripped the wallpaper off the walls. In later years, I would look back and wonder why we could never recapture the passion and sensuality of that rampant unadulterated sex ever again.

Despite my folks' no-show, I felt an inner peace, contentment and pride I had never felt before. I had come through in something that I really sucked at and bested all my peers at their own game, More importantly, I knew that it was something no one could ever take away from me as long as I live. I still, to this day, maintain that a university education at any level does not, as most people think, prove a higher standard of excellence in our chosen field or a measure of IQ/brain power. Rather, it proves you can apply yourself and work your ass off for years to get something you really want.

CHAPTER 4

OFF THE WALL

I sn't it weird that you spend most of your life gaining qualifications that will supposedly make you a very marketable product in the job market, but it takes an eternity to actually find a job? What exactly do people want from you? You spend your life trying to be something you think society wants you to be or do, but you still can't catch a break. It's the story of my life, then and now.

Thankfully, just when I was afraid I'd have to go back to my job at Fine Fare, I was invited to a ceremony to acknowledge my prize for winning the best marketing student two years in a row, setting a precedent. There, I met this guy Alistair who worked for a local business and marketing consultancy. He asked me if I was interested in coming along for an interview. I agreed; if someone offers an opportunity, I will grab it with gusto every chance I get.

Before I knew what was going on, I was in a business suit and tie every weekday, visiting with mainly construction-based companies to tell them how to improve their business but focusing mainly on their sales and marketing efforts. The irony never left me that I was telling successful business people how to run their enterprises more efficiently and effectively when I had never even had a real job before, never mind attempted to run my own business.

Suffice to say, I did what I always do: partly fake it to make it and also bullshit baffles brains. The latter was particularly true, as these businesses were founded by tradesmen with absolutely no idea how to sell themselves. It wasn't very hard to find the suggestions they needed to justify our exorbitant prices for the production of a business and marketing plan.

The only downside to my first business career was that my new boss was so old-school, meaning career success wasn't based on how good your concepts were but rather who stayed in the office the latest. Why, in this day and age, we are still are predominately a nine-to-five Monday-to-Friday society when most of us could be realistically working whenever we work best is beyond me. Even if we don't adhere to the madness of this antiquated regime, why aren't stores, banks and doctor's offices open when the rest of the world is off?

I believe the Internet will revolutionize the way we buy things and drastically change our antiquated shops on the high street. You should be able to order anything on the Web and get it customized to your own preference, like color and artwork, completely customizing any product from everyday stuff like clothing and kicks to bigger purchases like cars. These will be delivered to our door along with everything else, including groceries. If you're like me, you too absolutely hate the weekly grocery shopping.

With everything seemingly going my way, something came over me that I still don't really understand. I always said I would never get married, partly because of my folks' relationship. *Argument* is not a strong enough word to describe their disagreements; try full-blown battles in a seemingly never-ending war between the sexes.

One of the best fights I can remember came one night when my old man hooked up with his best bad-boy buddy, Fred the Bed. He stumbled in totally hammered and did what he always did: started to pound the walls with his stereo cranked up. After about an hour of eardrum-busting bass, my old dear had had enough. She came charging down the stairs like a raging bull and let them both have it. My old man wasn't dumb, though, so after switching the music off for a few minutes, he put it back on, playing his heaviest rock album; I think it was Queen's greatest hits. It blared for at least a couple of hours until my old dear, whose bedroom was right over the living room where the music was coming from, again stormed downstairs. My old man was nowhere to be found; he had retired to the third-floor converted loft and was fast asleep.

Talk about pissed! The next day was like a clip out of *Mr. and Mrs. Smith* or a Lily Allen LDN music video. My mum decided to get her own back. She opened his bedroom window out to the main street and threw every single piece of clothing from his closet onto the main drag, with all our nosy rich suburban neighbours looking on. Pretty mad or what?

I started to believe every marriage was like my folks', or certainly most of them, so why the hell settle down with someone? However, I somehow believed that mine and Carol's relationship was different. It was based on true and pure love. We truly did love each other on every level. Don't get me wrong—we also fought like cats and dogs, especially after she returned to Aberdeen from Stirling. When you move in together, you get to see each other naked, literally and metaphorically. All the annoying habits became abundantly clear when you lose your independence, but you also lose the loneliness. It's a balancing act that is still one of life's hardest to figure out.

All things considered, Carol was indeed my soulmate. I was sure I could live very happily with this girl for the rest of my life. One Saturday night, pissed out of my head, I decided to propose. Quite rightly, I got shot down in flames, with probably the hardest *no* I have ever experienced. My response was to go out of the pub and kick the back door of my beloved Ford Cortina.

After a big argument that night, I decided to ask her again in the morning, but this time properly. It was a beautiful summer day, and we drove out to my childhood home in Stonehaven and onto a stunningly spectacular and picturesque spot: Dunnottar Castle. Nothing in my head and heart had changed since the night before, so I went down on one knee overlooking the picture-perfect scenery and asked her for her hand in marriage. This time got the answer I wanted: *yes!* Because I had not prepared for the ultimate day, I had no ring, so I used a Pepsi can opener. Before too long, she picked an earth-ring-colour blue topaz as her engagement ring.

All too quickly, wedding arrangements took over our lives. My mum was determined to host a full-scale church wedding with all the bells and whistles. Any prospective groom I think would concur that the plans get so intensely girlie you started wondering if you are actually required to show up. The wedding day is not about the guy but the girl's lifelong dream coming true. Eventually, I got so hacked off with all the dumb female fights about who to invite, what band, where people are seated and so on that I just threw up a white flag up and did the usual guy's deal: "You know what, honey, do what the fuck you want. Quite frankly, I don't give a damn anymore. I just want you to be my wife."

If I ever go down that road again, which seems unlikely, a beautiful exotic island wedding with only the very closest family and friends is where it's at for sure, rather than almost 200 guests (who, in truth, I mostly didn't know) in the granite city's typical summer day of pouring rain. That wasn't exactly my original vision of our blessed wedded bliss, but I grinned and bore it with a constant thought of *just get through today*. The best was still to come: the exotic and erotic harmony of our honeymoon.

The worst thing about our wedding day was not the pouring rain, which screwed up any chance of getting special photos, or all the old people coming up to me saying how cute a baby I was in my nappies. No, it was something way beyond any of those minor irritants. My brothers and close friends decided to throw me a wild stag, which I was kind of anxious about, because the last stag I went to was that of a fellow rugby team member who ended up naked, locked in the bathroom of a British Rail train with no money, no phone—nothing but his birthday suit— heading for Kings Cross station in London. He returned the favour with interest on a road trip with the team; when I fell asleep, he shaved one of my eyebrows and put toothpaste on my man bag, which burnt worse than you can ever imagine. So cold!

To be honest, I would have preferred that fate. Instead, they took me to my local pub, Henry J Beans, and organized some real ugly strippers. Only God knows how many shots of tequila I had. I even ate the worm for the first and only time, I was so messed. Then, on our way to a club, my youngest brother did his usual passive-aggressive shit, calling out some random guys on the street. Before I knew what the fuck was going on, a massive fight between my mates and these guys ensued. The police arrived in earnest, and when they cuffed my little brother very aggressively, my older army brother Ian decked the cop, so we all spent time in the slammer that night. It was my first and only time in a police cell.

My dad somehow heard about what had gone down and came to our aid around 5 a.m., but I was still so drunk they couldn't wake me up from my drunken stupor, so I wound up walking home around three hours later. It was like something out of the hilarious *Hangover* trilogy. My face and entire body felt sore from bailing out my little brother's ass for the umpteenth time because of his big mouth. I was still drunk as a skunk.

This was far from the first time Stuart had done stupid shit. He was always the golden child. My old man had had enough kids, but my mum desperately wanted a baby girl. My dad eventually capitulated with a "Fine, but as long as you look after it." Then Stuart was born—yes, another boy. I must admit I grew to hate him growing up because all I can remember was my entire family falling in love with this pretty boy with his blond curly locks and dashing blue eyes. Just like most late ones, he was spoiled rotten, with a whole new wardrobe instead of the hand-me-downs I had been graced with. I don't know if it was that upbringing that moulded him into the person he was, but like my older brother, he was always a hit with the ladies, which I envied beyond belief.

As Stuart grew up, he grew to love partying more than life itself. All of a sudden, this cute Goody-Two-shoes turned into the most arrogant, in-your-face-attitude kid who rubbed most people the wrong way. I can't count how many times I had to bail his loose mouth out of potentially dangerous situations, both on the playground at school and, more ominously, on the mean streets of Aberdeen.

It all came to a head on a summer snowboard trip to Austria's Stubia Glacier. After my first day on this one-plank variety, my foolish insistence that I can do anything by myself, I don't need lessons, drove me to head down slopes far above my ability level. By the end of my first day, I had more bruises than from any of my many fights. I was so damn sore— especially my bum—I even had to take a pillow to sit down on in the local restaurant.

Skiing is an amazing sport, but it's very similar to learning to ride a bike: you need to find the sweet spot of balance. It's almost like life itself, I guess. Eventually, I got to a pretty advanced skill level for both skiing and snowboarding, and I've had some of my best-ever life experiences on a snowboard.

Back to Stuart: After a drunken orgy at a local night club, he managed to slam his head really bad, so much so that if it wasn't for Carol being a qualified ER nurse, he probably wouldn't be with us anymore. If I remember right, it was the usual idiotic male peer pressure bet/dare to attempt a front flip over a metal railing. Instead of doing any kind of flight or flip, Stuart basically slammed his head full on into this railing. It was incredibly funny until we realized that this was no joke. He was not only gushing blood but completely unconscious.

Carol immediately diagnosed his head injury, and before we knew what the fuck was going on, he was in the intensive care unit of Innsbruck Hospital. When my mum found out, she dropped everything and was on the first flight to be by his bedside.

If that wasn't enough, if I remember right, within a year, we were returning home after another wild party night when we hit our usual gas station to buy beer, munchies and some smokes. As soon as Stuart lit up, this other drunk got in his face with something along the lines of, "You prick, what the fuck are you lighting up in a petrol station?"

The answer from Stuart's lips, not surprisingly, was "Fuck you."

Before I knew it, we were entangled in a street gang fight. After I managed to deck my opposition, I looked over to see if Stu was okay, just to be treated to one of the most traumatic and horrific images I had ever seen. Stu's assailant had him on his back on the ground—and then, after a few kicks, he jumped on my brother's already fragile head, rendering him completely unconscious with very nasty bleeding wound. There followed another trip to the ICU, this time at Aberdeen Royal Infirmary, and a lengthy surgery to repair the damage and ensure no infection would get into his brain.

Street fights are a whole different beast from the playground stuff, or even any of my martial arts sparring, as there is no referee, judge, prefect or teacher to save your sorry ass from serious injury. In fairness to Stuart, he learned his lesson the hardest way possible. Although he still drinks like we're going to go back to prohibition, he has mellowed beyond belief—but he still possesses that really annoying passive-aggressiveness, so much that you just want to slap him when he is drunk. Unfortunately for most of us who have experienced trauma, it changes you to your very core, but not always as the rebirth depicted on reality-TV programs.

I digress again. Back to my stag night. As soon as I got home, I was met by my frantic fiancée, who quite rightly lost it as soon as she saw the state I was in. Forget the extensive body bruises; it was the two black eyes because of yet another broken nose that she couldn't believe. For an entire week prior to our wedding, I had to lie flat on my back with a mixture of frozen peas and cucumbers on my eyes whilst trying to watch the football World Cup. I even had to miss the dress rehearsal the night before and got married with my mother-in-law's eye makeup on. To this day, I have no idea how no one noticed, as its use is so clear in my wedding photos.

Only I knew where we were going on our honeymoon. I had planned a lavish fortnight in paradise, split between Florida's Disney, Universal, Sea World, etc. and the Cayman Islands. To this day, it stands as the best holiday I have ever had. Carol was completely clueless so kept asking me why the hell we were killing ourselves the first week, hitting every theme park, as she knew nothing of our second week somewhere else.

Because it was my first trip to the states, I was amazed at the stupidest things. One day, we were so hungry, but in typical Scottish style, Carol was concerned by the inflated prices at the parks, so we went hungry and waited until we got back to the hotel and ordered a pizza. Only thing was, I was so ravenous by then, I ordered the biggest extra-cheese-and-pepperoni pizza they had. I had no idea you could make a pizza that grandiose. I have never ever seen food that big. The delivery boy had to put it vertical for it to fit through the door. Suffice to say it lasted us almost the whole week, but really, how the hell anyone could want that much food was beyond me.

Same thing happened when we went to this rodeo night, where we were greeted with the largest steak ever. We were struggling to finish just my plateful, never mind Carol's. All I could think of was, *Did you really get cows that big, and how the fuck could anyone eat that much food themselves? No wonder some parts of the world are starving.* As the famous UK comedian Jasper Carrot put it so eloquently, "Have fat people not figured out your mouth hole is much bigger than your asshole?"

The other amusing thing was that our holiday timing coincided with the North American paintball championship, and I'm sure most of the competitors were staying at our accommodations. I had never seen redneck nation like that ever before: beer-belly bald guys with their Stetsons and country music pumping out of their monster trucks and their partners looking like a cross between nasty female strippers and UFC fighters. Listening to their obviously exaggerated BS stories while doing our laundry at the site's communal machines truly was more than enlightening. I exercised the greatest restraint to keep from cracking up.

THE HOOD

After a packed week of some of the coolest roller coasters, rides, attractions and animals, it was time to pack up and head for the Cayman Islands. Actually, the best thrill ride on our US trip was not a theme park ride but a connecting flight to the next airport. In the pitch black of the night, we hit one of the worst electrical storm I had ever witnessed. We were in this tiny twin-propeller Cessna-type plane. It is at times like this that you really see how small and insignificant we are when compared to the wrath Mother Nature can deliver anytime, anywhere in the world if we keep messing with her. We all know deep down inside there is only one outcome, and it won't be a victory for us.

Carol was like, "Where on earth are we going?" We nearly never made it, as I left all our vital travel documents on our first connecting flight. Thankfully, I noticed just in time and darted back to the plane, where the cleaners handed me everything they'd found. We just caught the Cayman Airways flight. Quite unbelievably, but as to plan, Carol still didn't have a clue what was going on until just before landing, when the pilot announced we were such-and-such away from the Cayman Islands so please put our seatbelts on.

Carol looked at me and said so cutely, "Where are the Cayman Islands?"

To say it's paradise doesn't do it justice. My big overdraft loan came through large, as it was the most romantic, scintillatingly beautiful place either of us had ever seen or been, and boy, did we make the most of it. Sure, there were trips to hell with this dope turtle farm and Stingray Bay on a motocross bike in a monsoon that Carol wasn't so into, but yes, the best sex ever. The whole meal deal blew our minds, but that was exactly the plan. It was all that and then some.

Back home, it was time to put my nose to the grindstone to pay off the loan. The best thing about Roy Stewart Consultancy was that not only did I gain invaluable practical commercial experience that complemented my academic theoretical knowledge but also I was like a fish in water for the first time. Lateral thought, problem-solving and idea generation have always been some of my greatest strengths—or as the marketers amongst us would say, unique selling points—so it wasn't long before I passed the probationary period and got a very nice pay raise. Things couldn't be better: I had a great job with an excellent salary, and Carol was a fully qualified midwife working in the ER at Royal Aberdeen Infirmary. We had bought our first apartment, 546 Great Western Road, and were rapidly paying off our mortgage with our salaries and a little help from Carol's dad.

But as usual for me, when I've made it, I want more—a fresh challenge. Quite why, I'll never know. I had tried snowboarding a few winters prior and was convinced that this new snow craze was going to take over the world. I wanted a piece of the action. I came up with my own business plan for a start-up of my own. My parents had passed on their risk-taking entrepreneurial traits to me, and so Freedom Sports was born: a combination of snowboarding, skateboarding and surf shop. In fairness, I couldn't have done it without a loan of 5,000 pounds—which, to this day, I wish Dad had never given me, as without it, I would have probably have never gone down the stupid roller coaster that has been my life.

I had always vowed that I would never have children, and I had even made Carol agree to the no-babies clause before I proposed. As much as I loved kids, I could see how they changed the relationship in not only my folks' marriage but so many other couples', including some of my friends'. I wanted no part of it. Yeah, right. Catch yourself on if you think like I did; after a few years, all of a sudden, the only topic people (well, women) will talk about is when they are going to hear the patter of little feet. This is especially the case for the prospective grandmothers, whose pleas all of a sudden put a sparkle in a new wife's eyes, and you know it's only a matter of time.

I tried the cat trick, where we picked up this rescue pussycat from the SPCA who was the cutest yet shyest black-and-white. We named her Cayman after our honeymoon destination. This gave me breathing room of about a year before the wee one conversation began in earnest.

In all honesty, at this point, I didn't really care. Something had changed in me, and the thought of leaving this planet without something that was part me became a very credible argument against my fear of making a commitment to a child. One of our favorite movies was *The Lion King*, and just as Simba carried on Mufasa's legacy, having a baby that would be the first for either set of kids on both my Hunter bloodline and my new Fyfe family became appealing to me. And hey, who knows, it might mean killer sex for both of us in the short term.

After growing up with two brothers and going to an all-boys elementary and high school, I thought it would be cool to have a little daughter and see how different it was growing up as a girl rather than a boy in this world. I was so curious that the need for knowledge outweighed everything else. All I had ever known was the testosterone-fed male way rather than the estrogen-heavy female way.

Unfortunately, the hope for rampant sex was quashed by the fact that my swimmers were far too good. Before I knew what was going on, Carol surprised me over a dinner in our favourite Chinese restaurant by telling me she had missed her period and, according to a few of those clear-blue-type tests, she was indeed pregnant. Although I was genuinely chuffed beyond belief, I did worry about the financial side of things, as Freedom Sports was only paying me a pittance. *Fuck it*, I thought. *I'll deal with it. Time to man up, Andrew, and be the very best father you can possibly be.*

I will never forget Carol getting bigger. I don't get the "women positively glow" crap when they are pregnant. No: they are fat, moody and clingy, period! The only bright side was her boobs, which grew to enormous proportions. Hey, maybe I would get to fulfill the breast milk fantasy! Trust me, guys, that one definitely doesn't live up to the hype. Go with the threesome every time.

The prenatal classes were a mixture of total boredom combined with TMI. The only thing that made it manageable was that after the first one, I joked to Carol that the midwife leader of the group not only looked a bit like but honestly sounded like Yoda from *Star Wars*. Carol and I would have a good giggle when she mirrored our portrait of her. I still to this day have no idea why we ever went to see her, as she would put the fear of God into us by going through every possible pregnancy-and-childbirth-gone-wrong scenario. Carol was a midwife herself, so she knew all this stuff intimately.

Well, just like a birthday, Christmas, vacation or whatever special occasion, the time flew by. Before I could pinch myself with what the hell was going on, it was almost D-Day. All the crap Yoda had instilled in my brain was giving me the heebie-jeebies.

It's weird, but I remember it like it was yesterday, not 22 years ago now. We were munching on our usual Saturday night treat of Chinese takeout and watching TV when all of a sudden, Carol came back from the toilet saying her water just broke, so it was time to drive like a bat out of hell up to Carol's workplace, Aberdeen's Royal Infirmary. Again, in line with my life, it was not your typical in-and-out deal. No, it lasted 42 fucking hours, a marathon birth, if you like.

Carol had this girlie all-natural deal that I will never comprehend. Fuck it—after watching the ordeal unfold almost like an outside observer, if that was me, give me the best drugs possible and schedule the C-section every time. That looked damn sore. We went through the on-bed, in-bath, back to bed. I even called my mates to get me a McD's carry-out before the scary stuff started. Our baby was breach, and that combined with Carol's small pelvis led to an emergency situation whereby after more than 35 hours of hell, all of a sudden our baby's heart stopped.

I had never felt so helpless in my entire life. I'll admit it, I'm kind of a control freak, and that's the reason I'd never taken drugs, because I hate being out of control of anything—especially my unborn baby girl. It was just like a real-life episode of those female orientated ER-type shows whereby all of a sudden, from being at my sweetheart's side, I was banished to a far side corner of the delivery room, with Carol surrounded by all these white-coated doctors and nurses.

Once they got the baby's heart going again, Carol finally caved to all the medical advice to have an epidural and a C-section. I couldn't agree more. I'm not the type not to have words to describe any situation, but watching your baby being born, especially with us almost losing her, was simply indescribable. Only one word can come close: *wonderful*. It was so much more spiritual than anything I had ever experienced, on a level all by itself, easily surpassing anything money can buy. This blood-drenched screaming baby was, in the strangest way, possibly the most beautiful thing I had ever seen. When she's yours, you get past all the gross stuff and just concentrate on *Wow, I helped create that, and even if I die tomorrow, this kid will leave a lasting legacy of both my and her own life in this world.* God, here come the tears. Breathe!

You know that feeling when the world carries on around you just like it always does, but in a weird way, you are in slow motion, with all kinds of thoughts and chemicals bombarding your brain? The only way I can describe that unique emotion was that it was just like when Hammy in the *Over the Hedge* kids' movie drinks a caffeinated pop beverage. Absolutely hilarious. That's another cracking animated movie that I love, as my nickname in school was Hammy. With my ADHD, I shared many of that squirrel's traits.

As with most things, the euphoria of the initial arrival was soon tempered by the reality of having a newborn baby. Apart from possibly stopping smoking, I don't think I have ever been so grumpy in my life ever. Try setting your alarm for up to four times a night, and no you can't go straight back to sleep, instead you have to stay up for the 30 to 60 minutes in order to feed the wee one. This was an absolute killer for me, as unlike Carol, I could never catnap. It always takes me an eternity to get to sleep, but once asleep, I go into REM deep sleep, which didn't work too well in the feeding regime.

We needed the money, so Carol went back to work. My flexible self-employed status meant I had more than my fair share of looking after new baby Michelle. As if that wasn't enough to deal with, after about two months, during a 3 a.m. feed watching mind-numbing TV, all of a sudden Michelle stopped sucking her bottle and went limp. Her skin went from pale to white to this colour I had never seen human take on: almost like the intense arctic blue you see at the heart of glaciers. It was super scary.

I did the only thing I could think to do, as although I knew CPR, I had no clue how you did that on something so frail as a baby. I ran through to the bedroom and woke up Carol. She immediately knew what was happening: basically, infant death cot syndrome, where babies literally forget to breath. Praise be, it didn't happen when she was alone in her cot. Carol started the necessary emergency action as I called 999 (911 in North America) and got an ambulance dispatched. I ran down to the street to wave down the ambulance and save as much time as possible.

It felt like time stood still, as I was all by myself on the pavement in the middle of the night with no idea what was going on upstairs. My new baby was on the verge of death after only two months of blessing this world with her love. Damn, it brings tears every time even after all these years. Yes, I can say time and again how unlucky I have been. I have walked down every rough road, had every sucker punch, hit ever speed bump, ate every curveball in my life. But yes, I need to thank God for being there the few times I really, really needed help.

After the drama that night. Michelle proved that just like her old man, she was a fighter. She pulled through when most would have perished, partly because of Carol's training but also something I like to call tenacity. Somehow my kid an inherited my survival instincts.

After a couple of weeks in Aberdeen's Sick Kids Hospital, undergoing every test in the book, she was strong enough to return home. Phew, thank you, Lord! Unfortunately, almost unbelievably, she ended up back there with a separated shoulder that was entirely my fault. I have always absolutely hated the sound of a baby crying, so after watching this TV program about how Russians bundled up their babies tightly in the blankets to help them sleep, I decided this was the bomb and an ideal solution for the sleep we so desperately craved. Only problem was, Michelle rolled over in the middle of the night and somehow hurt her shoulder joint.

Damn, I never in a million years thought I would ever be scared of babies, but quite honestly, after that, I was literally scared to touch her. Sometimes I don't know my own strength, and I have never been good with delicate things. Thankfully, I never killed her, but yes, I was going to love my little miracle child with all my heart and soul. There was no way I was ever going through that ordeal ever again. Yet another *Don't kid yourself, Andrew!*

After a few years stuck in my new retail operation, which was not too far removed from my days in the car accessories aisle, and after watching countless videos that highlighted Whistler as a mecca for snow sports, I decided we needed to go check out Canada and Whistler just to see if the place could live up to the hype, but this time in the summertime. With hindsight, unknown to me at the time, I had subconsciously decided that if it did, I was going to move there, as in truth I was tired and bored of Aberdeen.

I contacted the local British Columbia snowboard guru Greg Daniels— Cheeseball to all who knew him as he was, quite honestly, apart from being a decent rider, the cheesiest guy ever. All I cared about was potential career openings, so he directed me to the local rags, the *Question* and *Pique*. He also told me he'd heard that the job of manager of snowboard operations for Whistler Mountain was available. It was the absolute dream job for me, but I was torn, because I had recently been elected head of the Scottish Snowboard Association, completed my British Association of Ski Instructors level 3 snowboard instructors certification, and also enjoyed an all-expenses trip to Austria to become a fully certified freestyle and halfpipe judge. If I took this job, it might be construed that I had shafted them, which in many ways I did but not intentionally.

I did feel bad, but sometimes you have to be selfish and put your happiness before anything else. I was so desperately depressed in my role as Mr. Freedom Sports because in reality, the shop was only just breaking even, which left very little in terms of pay. It was like being on 100 percent commission but worse, because if you fail, then everyone will know and consider you a loser—at least in my head, anyways.

Have you ever worked a whole day and sold zero, thus making absolutely nothing? In reality, it's not nothing. It is in fact negative, because a retail enterprise is heavy on capital investments and fixed costs. You go home and all you do is worry about everything. Having your own business is not too far removed from having a pet or even a child. It is your baby, and it is with you every waking minute. All I knew was I needed a break, as after five years I could see clearly that if I was going to get back to a real salary again, I needed to move on. As such, I finally accepted one of our shop's most loyal and best customers, Gregor, as a full-fledged partner in the shop.

Then I booked our North American adventure. We flew into Seattle and checked it out, and to my surprise and relief, it was far different from Florida. I loved the Space Needle and the quaint fish markets, but my favourite was the dancing fountains of water just around the corner from Carol's favourite, the humungous Nordstrom's department store, kind of a Seattle equivalent of London's Harrods. Then we hired a car and made our way up the highway past the Peace Arch duty-free shops and the 49th parallel and finally entered supernatural British Columbia (BC), or what an American we met in our Seattle B & B so perfectly described as God's country.

You can definitely bring up many downsides to Vancouver, but no one can question the simply supernatural beauty that is BC. It really was love at first sight for me. Vancouver seemed to have everything I desired in a city, as unlike my folks—who were more into the manmade sights and sounds—I loved the astonishing beauty only Mother Nature can truly provide. And BC had it in droves.

Here was a city where you could work all day and afterwards hit world-famous ski slopes, follow mountain-bike trails or go kayaking—basically everything an outdoor sports enthusiast like me holds near and dear. After a couple of nights in cheap hotels (which in BC are never cheap) and B & Bs, it was time to say goodbye to Vancouver and hit the Sea to Sky Highway 99, which was just as fun to drive as it was in the video game *Need for Speed*. The natural beauty of the road was simply staggering. It was then, even before we reached Whistler itself, that I realized this was a place I wanted to live for the foreseeable future.

The village was smaller and more modern than I expected. In some ways, it was just as picturesque as its alpine counterparts. As much as I was trying to focus my mind on everything but my upcoming job interview, I simply couldn't, as the verdict was so crucial to me. I went over it again and again in my mind to perfect my answers to the questions I guessed I would be asked, but at the same time look as if it was not rehearsed, instead more impromptu and quietly confident.

The day finally arrived. After I met this very European boss called Wolfgang in his office, he decided he was hungry, so we left for his local sushi joint. *Could it get any worse?* I thought to myself. I had never even heard of sushi, and what I ordered turned out to be more like something Luke would have in *Star Wars*. I tried my best not to make it obvious I was not enjoying the food as he bombarded me with cold and calculated questions. To my absolute amazement, he stood up after about an hour and, with a firm handshake, stated he wanted me on his crew and the job was mine for the taking. Obviously, I had no choice but to accept.

In a bizarre way, there was a big part of me that was hoping I would not get the job, as I could avoid all the cans of worms and conflicts it would bring from both our families. I was going to go back to being the hated, never-fit-in-anywhere black sheep—a role I seemed to migrate towards far too many times for one lifetime.

CHAPTER 5

I WILL WALK 1,000 MILES

After my interview, I returned to Aberdeen to make easily the hardest decision of my life. Could I really leave my hometown and move to a foreign country? What made it especially hard was my self-employed status of owning the Freedom Sports enterprise, with its personal investment of five years of blood, sweat and tears and financial investment of 25,000 pounds.

I had made my friend Gregor a partner in the business. I had resisted the idea for a long time. He was one of the biggest risk-takers I'd ever met—yes, even more so than myself, which is saying something. We used to go on road trips all the time up to the Scottish ski fields, and he would try to overtake me on blind corners. God knows how I survived, as with my highly competitive nature, I was one of the fast and furious myself, armed with some amazing pocket-rocket cars. At least I had some brains cells, and I knew a head-on would kill us all, so I overtook him on the straights and he would take me on the switchbacks. That was so dumb-ass I had to back out. It was the ultimate in chicken-run, pedal-to-the-metal racing.

But if I was indeed going to escape to live out my dream of doing a season, partnership was my best—no only—option. Despite my worries, I brought Gregor in as a full and equal partner. Unfortunately, my fears came true. Greg's risk-taking caught up to him in his very first year as boss when he decided, quite rightly, that there was more money in renting equipment than selling it. He brought in a big rental fleet, but unfortunately for us, the incredibly inconsistent Scottish winter brought pretty much no snow that season. Like so many times when you own your own business, one wrong move can make you lose it all, which is exactly what happened. Freedom Sports was no longer.

With that, I decided that it was my destiny to go to the world's biggest mecca of skiing and riding. But not only did I have a battle on with Carol about this move, everyone from both sides of the family 110 percent supported her and said I was crazy to leave the old boys' club in Aberdeen, as with raw oil prices through the roof, it was a real hip and happening place from an employment standpoint. I knew deep down they were right; I could have commanded a six-figure salary, and that was probably an understatement. So why the fuck was I leaving my comfortable life in Aberdeen and dragging my entire family—wife, cat and newborn baby—halfway around the world for a seasonal position of at most six months?

To be honest, I knew it was an insane move from a financial and career perspective, but I never did a gap year; I went straight to college after my time stocking shelves in Fine Fare. It really was me against the rest of the world. It never struck me until years afterwards why my old dear was so upset—after three boys (bearing in mind Stuart was supposed to be a girl), she was over the moon with her granddaughter. She was besotted, and what do I do? Fuck off to Canada with a less-than-six-month-old. I think you have to be female to really comprehend the drama that ensued. I was cut off by my entire family, but in reality, it was my mum. The reaction from Carol's side was a bit less predictable.

It was kind of weird, but the only one who actually wasn't making me out to be the black sheep of the family was the one I despised the most: my mother-in-law (or the wicked witch of the north, as I would later call her). I think most married males hate their mother-in-law, as you will never be good enough for her wee daughter. Carol was supposed to marry her childhood sweetheart, a young farmer I later found out she lost her virginity to. His name was Allan, and it comes as no surprise that we more than disliked each other. Because her parents had split up in an acrimonious way and she was somewhat ostracized from her mum, Carol blamed the breakup entirely on her mum moving to England and remarrying Fraser's dead brother's widower, which I could never fathom out. Kind of incestual, if you ask me.

THE HOOD

It was almost a bonus to see her go to Canada with me, as it broke up the immensely strong father-daughter relationship, and her mother could get back in her good books. Isobel was as crafty, devious and conniving a female as I have ever had the privilege to meet. The bitchy side of females has always been something I found difficult to understand, as it flies in the face of my heart-on-the-sleeve character.

After much deliberation and enormous fights, I decided I had to follow my dreams and try a season in the world's snow-sports mecca. We packed up our flat on 546 Great Western Road and set out to fulfill my destiny. I wasn't like most graduates who believed that to be successful, we have to be lawyers, doctors or at least wear the work suit of some kind of white collar "professional"—a word I've never fully understood, as can't we all be professional? If you consider its true definition, it means we are more than proficient in whatever we choose to be.

My mum always quoted the old Special Air Squadron motto to me: "Who Dares Wins." To this day, it is one of the most important slogans in my entire life, because it is so true. With that motto in my head, I went against every single person who was anything to me and left the country to pursue my dream. Talk about animosity: you have never seen anything like it, especially from my old dear and Carol's dad.

We had agreed to make the move and stay for at least a year—but always in the back of my mind, we were moving there for good. We were living in a rustic cabin initially in Black Tusk, which was about 15 kilometres from Whistler. It was a cool pad that even had a sauna, but trust my luck, as soon as we arrived, the biggest and longest downpour I have ever seen commenced. It rained for two months straight, and every night, we heard the rain pound on these weird metal roofs that they have over here.

We were kind of isolated from the rest of the world, so I was actually fairly pleased when we got a phone call from the landlords saying they had changed their minds and decided to rent the cabin to one of their friends. Whistler fills up every fall, and if you haven't figured out your accommodation by then, you are well and truly screwed. Thankfully, I asked at a meeting, and the director of marketing said I could move into his family home over Christmas and New Year's, and then I had an in with this guy who worked in the race department and owned a small rustic A-frame to move into at Creekside for the rest of the season. It was all far from ideal, but hey, beggars can't be choosers. We were more than desperate, as we were homeless come January 5.

It was in Whistler that I encountered the most bizarre weather phenomenon ever: this freezing rain that turns everything into an ice rink. Not much fun when you're driving up the Sea to Sky Highway, which in those days was a death trap—so much so that it even appeared on a EA sports *Need for Speed* driving game. The most fun bit was the canyon, a real narrow single-lane twisty section where you throw in a heavy dose of black ice and it's more than a bit treacherous. It was really fun, to be honest, but Carol wasn't too impressed.

We moved to the original Whistler, which is now referred to as Creekside, and before I knew what was going on, a loyal customer from Freedom came over to see us—and was he a piece of work. Believe me, when you live in a place like Whistler, you gain so many new "friends" who want to couch surf. We sarcastically nicknamed him Double-0 Dave (as in 007). He was the biggest nerd you have ever met. He was the type of guy you would have picked on at school, a true git or punter, as we like to say in Great Britain. For example, he thought that disposable razors could only be used once, and then he discarded them in the trash. He was a true numbskull. Carol also noticed we went through a crazy amount of loo roll whilst he was with us. Then when we splashed the cash in the pizza restaurant, he ordered a pizza with only the cheese, no base tomato sauce—the weirdest order that the server had ever heard.

After a few seasons of travelling extensively in my youth, mainly around France and Italy for one-or two-week ski holidays, I had realized that if I did a season before getting my degree, I would never go to college. That thought was reinforced when I arrived in Whistler and met all these lifers who moved here and were stuck in a rut with no qualifications, no nothing except living the dream. They woke up and smelt the coffee 10 years later and realized they were going nowhere fast and they would never be able to afford their own house in this millionaire's paradise. Sure, they were amazing riders, skiers and bikers, but in Canada that doesn't mean very much compared to the four sports that still dominate North America: American football, basketball, baseball and ice hockey.

THE HOOD

I first noticed this when, on an evaluator's course in Silver Star, we turned on the news and the main news story was Wayne Gretzky, or the Great One, returning "home" to Edmonton for the first time. It took up almost 20 minutes of the newscast, and afterwards they merely touched on the Air India devastation. *Bizarre* is the only word that comes to mind.

When you move to Whistler, even if you are the king of your local hill, you can't hold a candle to the local rippers, as the standard there is on a whole different level. It was the most humbling experience for me at that time. I had competed in the Scottish and British snowboard championships with more than decent results in every event I entered, and I had been a partially sponsored athlete and a fully qualified instructor, but I got schooled every time I rode with a posse of riders. Worse still, I couldn't even keep up with unsponsored chick riders like Heather (a real cool girl I would have made a move on if I wasn't married).

When we went to off-piste black-diamond tree runs like Harvey and Robertson's, I hadn't ever been in trees, so they smoked me big-time. I had never been beaten by a girl at something that was my passion, except possibly in martial arts sparring, as I couldn't hit them because of my upbringing. But you know, it was the best thing that ever happened to me. I soon learnt how to keep up with Heather, and it sure light a fire up my ass.

It's real weird that when you go to Europe, they have these all these massive non-pisted (or ungroomed areas) that don't get tracked out like they do here. It is crazy how much terrain gets tracked by the swarm that goes up for one reason only: perfect powder. They actually have a 10-centimetre rule in Whistler that if you get 10 centimetres of fresh snow overnight, you are allowed to take the day off. It was the best rule I've ever heard, unless you're the boss. It blew me away that when you are the boss, these Muppets would take the day off to go up the hill and pouch the powder. They never got the plot that there is bar code on every season pass, which sends a message to me that they bunked off work!

To say I was the most hated rider in Canada was the understatement of the decade. With so many snowboarders in the country, why the fuck would they ever give a Celtic snowboarder from the other side of the planet what was the absolute pinnacle of snowboarding careers? I never really figured it out either. Suffice to say, I do really well at interviews.

To be honest, the whole world being against me has been the story of my life. When I was at university, I was ostracized by my fellow students because of my lack of proper school qualifications coupled with my intensely competitive nature. I just used their actions to make me work harder than everyone else. I never ever quit. I really believe you have to lead by example. That is the only way you will gain anyone's respect, not through empty words but inspiring actions. I believe wholeheartedly in the phrase I heard somewhere along my travels: "Don't aspire, rather inspire."

It's just like when we were competing latterly in the mountain bike arena. You had these fat fuckers of helicopter-parent "coaches" who hadn't dusted off a bike in decades devouring their XL hamburger pizzas with extra cheese and their guilt-comforting Diet Cokes while screaming at their kids to tear up these brutally steep, seemingly never-ending climbs they couldn't even walk halfway up. To me, great coaches have to do the thing they are teaching—maybe not at the same level as their elite athlete, but it's best if you actually make a reconnaissance of the course, whatever sport it may be, so you can give the right feedback as you have actually experienced it yourself. It's just the same as life, really. If you haven't experienced something, you can't really, truly comprehend it. End of story! It's just like me watching ice hockey: I suck at skating, so I can't really fully enjoy it, although it's almost a religion up here in Canada.

After my record season of 165 days on both mountains, even though according to all the locals it was a pretty crap season, I didn't care: I was in heaven in my white paradise or white gold as they call it in Whistler, as the white stuff is the basis of the economy. Although Whistler now has almost as many visitors in the summer as it does in the winter, their spending is way lower in the summer months, mainly because of the ski lift and rental incomes, but also they inflate all the prices in the winter because of the simple demand-and-supply equation. Summer can never make up for the loss of a bad snow season.

When all is said and done, Whistler really is a utopia for anyone who loves snow sports, but if you aren't at least an intermediate, I personally would go and check out some of the cheaper smaller interior BC resorts like Sun Peaks, Big White, Silver Star or my personal favourites, Red and Fernie. They are tremendous mountains and are more geared towards the beginner and anyone who prefers to cruise the blues in search of the perfect arc on the groomers. For the powder hounds, the champagne powder there is drier and doesn't get tracked like Whistler does. These resorts are also considerably cheaper than Whistler, but they can't compete with Whistler's après-ski village and electric nightlife.

Whistler remains the mecca for anyone who loves steep and deep, but with so much terrain, you only see a fraction of it when you are there for a week or two. Trust me, if you're coming from Europe, make it later, as you are only getting your snow legs and getting over the jet lag by the time you have to pack up your gear again. Also, take a lesson. I'm not making a sly plug for the Snow School here; honestly, it really is one of the most professional yet fun schools, as they will not only take your skiing or riding to a whole other level but you will get lift priority, an enormous plus if you are planning to come over on kids' breaks, as the lines are gigantic on the popular chairs. Regardless of your ability level, you will learn something that is way different than what the typical Euro instructor will give you in that the emphasis is on being an all-round free-skier/rider rather than the search for the perfect arc on the piste. This is way more fun and is actually how the best skiers and riders train themselves.

One of the very few lessons I ever had in Europe was a powder lesson, as I could never master how to ski powder. Let's face it: powder simply does not exist in Scottish skiing. They even have these wooden fences to stop the snow flying off the runs because of the blow-your-socks-off wind, and believe me, those fence posts hurt like a bitch when you impale yourself on them, as I found out on my first ever ski day—which, I tell no lie, I absolutely hated in my wet jeans and sponge-like jacket. I will never forget going up the most extreme black run's chairlift, the Tiger, a single rickety old conveyance. I tried my best to duck from the frozen hail the size of golf balls blowing directly in my face.

Although I live with minus-30 temperatures here in Canada, I have never been so fucking cold in my life than the wet, windy winter weather in the Scottish Highlands that seems to soak into your very soul. Don't get me wrong: Scotland really is wonderful country. But skiing there is pretty damn hard core. All the instructor said was, "Go fast and copy me." Yes, everything is fucking easy when you know how to do it, fool!

As instructors, we are all trained to take you places you would most likely never ever find yourself. This doesn't mean you'll be directed to the super-secret stashes that are the domain of the locals, as those are kind of a "I could tell you but then I'd have to kill you." The locals get pissed, and quite rightly so, if you take tourists to the killer spots that are the refuge of the lifers who give up so much to get to their fix on their favourite sweet spots.

There is nothing worse on your day off than getting 20-plus centimetres of fresh and heading over to Crystal, Glacier, Harmony or Peak to find it dominated by the Snow School getting lift-line priority to hit your favourite face-shot areas. Kind of like braving the masses on your search for your Boxing Day sale item treat, only to find out everything you were going to get has already sold out.

Nearing the end of my dream season, I witnessed one of the worst ski-hill disasters ever, with the Creekside chair going down. It was like coming home to a Hollywood movie set. There were TV helicopters in the air and tons of spotlights. We later found out that some clients lost their lives and others ended up in wheelchairs.

Right after that catastrophe, Carol and I had a hard decision to make. I was totally addicted to the lifestyle that they take full advantage of by paying you a pittance compared to European instructors, which is something I simply cannot fathom, as we do the same job. Actually, I truly feel we go above and beyond. I had many client feedback forms that said the standard of coaching was definitely higher than they'd ever had before.

Carol desperately wanted to go home, and I wanted to stay. Try to find the compromise there: there isn't one. Talk about fighting like cats and dogs. We were at loggerheads like never before, and there was no middle ground.

This was the potential end of our marriage, with the chips stacked in her corner, as everyone in our family wanted us to return. But there was no way I was ever going back. I had found my winter paradise, and I wasn't going home. I laid it out very simply. "If you want to go home, go. I am staying here, and that is the end of it." Believe me, I almost never use the "my way or the highway" ultimatum, but this was something that was very near and dear to me, and I was willing to fight as hard as any other fight, be it physical or verbal.

Somewhat acrimoniously, she relented and promised she could handle another season. On a return trip to the UK several years later, she turned to me on the flight back to Canada to reveal that even she admitted our new home's standard of living was way better than we would have back in Scotland. That left me speechless, but it gave credence to my decision to remain in Canada.

We went back to Aberdeen and sold everything. Wow, what an ordeal that was. I had been ostracized by both sides of the family. I couldn't give a fuck about her side of the family, as I had never liked them anyways, and the feeling was mutual. I stuck the middle finger up to pretty much everyone as we lifted off from Glasgow Airport. Fuck you all—this was my life, and I was going to do it my way.

All I can say is, despite the loss of her mum and her dad having a very serious stroke and now being very old, Carol is still in Whistler to this day. It was still a nightmare of a move, though. It is hard to decide what you are going to keep and what you were going to sell or give away to charity. I had one last boys' night out with my mates at the London Red Bull Big Air and Style event in Earls Court. Oasis's classic "Champagne Supernova" will always take me back to that stellar night.

CHAPTER 6

BAD

Before we left for our initial six months in Whistler, we had applied for the Canadian Permanent Residents visa. That was an ordeal in itself, involving an expensive trip to London, where we found out to our detriment that Canada didn't need nurses—which was Carol's background. Neither did they need midwives. When it came to me, even with a really diverse résumé, they still weren't going to let us in, as we hadn't achieved the 70 points. Eventually our interviewer decided he would call me a garment salesman because of my experience with Freedom Sports.

I replied, "You can call me anything you want. Trust me, I've been called way worse."

Emigrating to a different country is simply not the same as moving within a country, no matter how far the actual distance. It is so much harder. There is some kind of finality in leaving your roots, clan, culture, heritage and traditions for a new people in a new land. In your mind, you know that the country you're leaving will brand you forever as a traitor and never truly welcome you back or forgive you for leaving. On the other hand, your newly adopted country will be overprotective of its own and never really accept you as one of theirs, always treating you with suspicion.

Even armed with this knowledge, I was determined to prove everyone wrong and make a success of it. But first, we had to sell almost everything we owned for a pittance, beginning with our first real home. Then my pimped-out Renault Clio Williams pocket rocket of a car with a trick

THE HOOD

Alpine stereo system had to go, along with our furniture. It's almost impossible not to get sentimental over these things, as the memories they represent you're never ready to give away. But we did it, even though Carol really didn't want to leave.

Finally, we had every piece of the puzzle in place, and it was time to get down to Fife to spend our last night in Scotland, possibly forever. *Forever* is a very big word—just ask anyone trying to stop smoking, for example. The finality was so striking, it would make anyone anxious and second-guess whether you were doing the right thing. Was I doing this out of sheer spite and selfishness to prove my droves of disapproving doubters wrong? The way I saw it, Freedom Sports was now gone, and the world was a much smaller place because of the commercial airline business. If you never took a risk, you'd never get anywhere in this life.

I will never forget the feeling of sitting at Glasgow Airport after the big tearful farewell with Carol's dad before boarding our KLM flight to Vancouver with a stopover at Amsterdam. Despite our best efforts, we were ridiculously overweight, but thankfully, when we got to Holland, we were told the connecting flight was cancelled so we had to have an overnight at the airport. As such, the airline decided to let us off with our excess baggage that was over double the limit. With our lives in our hands, including a baby girl less than a year old and our cat, Cayman, we made the most of the inconvenient fluke and picked up the grand finale leg in our voyage to the promised land.

It was a blessing, as my ex took everything but the kitchen sink whenever she left to go anywhere. She started packing weeks before and then ended up taking shit out of her cases that she needed for everyday use. All I can say is that in marriage, you sometimes have to go with flow. Only thing was, it wasn't her who had to lift all the shit she packed.

This was easily one of the most emotional sagas in my roller-coaster life. Before I knew it, we were in Vancouver and heading up Highway 99, back to my beloved Whistler. It was almost like a life cleansing. It time to start from scratch. Thankfully, I didn't know then that it was far from the last time I'd have to start over.

We moved back to Creekside, and I started preparing for a whole new season as manager of snowboard operations. Trust my luck—it wasn't long before rumours started swirling around about an impending takeover bid from our biggest rival, Intrawest, which owned the adjacent Blackcomb Mountain. To be honest, looking back on my life back then, I was a bit of a tool. I was so determined to prove my worth, I went on a mission and became way too hard-nosed and a real stubborn git. It was hard *not* to be like that when, everywhere you go, you hear people talking behind your back.

For some reason, I wasn't a bit worried, as I thought I was doing a great job in my position, so why would I need to be? But as with most mergers, it is the management from the invading corporation that remains. Despite the absolute assurance from our commander-in-chief that my job was safe, by the end of another amazing snow season, I was informed that my biggest enemy, the head of the Blackcomb Snowboard School, had been promoted over both mountains, and I was out of a job.

I never realized how deep the hatred ran between us until I swallowed my pride big-time and met with him to figure out what kind of management or supervisory role I was to be demoted to. Well, the bastard stayed true to his hard-nosed reputation and approach to management, and I was left with no managerial opportunities, just an offer to coach for this Australian-based snow company called Yes Tours. I tried to put a positive spin on it; I had to, as the very reason for moving halfway around the world was now gone, and I had proved all my haters right. Maybe I could finally do what I came to Canada for: ride my board as opposed to sit in management meetings. I would lead by example in the rain-sodden beginner zone they ironically call Olympic Station with no responsibility and no real pay cut. Bliss, right?

I decided to make the most of it, and I did. Finally, I could just have fun riding almost every day for an entire season. The customers were an absolute hoot, and riding took precedence over coaching with pretty much every group. I remember I had these guys for almost a month solid who only wanted to ride as hard as possible, so that's what we did. Obviously, I was a much better rider than any of them, but that didn't hold them back. Like most Aussies, they were super-competitive, so after some of the biggest slams ever, they just kept coming back for more.

It wasn't until the course-ending party that I found out the real deal, when their wives and partners accosted me saying, "What the hell did you do with our guys?" Unbeknownst to me, they would go back to their accommodations every night so beat from the day's riding that after some grub and a couple of beers, they would crash, much to the horror of their significant others.

I decided from the outset of that third season that I was going to learn the one thing I always sucked at: catching air/freestyle. I always was secretly jealous of my mates who could spin to win and slay the halfpipe. It was something I would regret in the biggest way possible. But at that point, I had a very close friend called Andrew who was one of our sponsored riders from Freedom Sports. He was decent at freestyle and offered to help me out. Finally, after so many sore bails learning flips and spins, I managed to stomp my first front and back flip, spin 360s and even get a few grabs nailed.

Andy was a real chill teenager who had also found his heaven here, and he was one of the very rare riders who was as passionate about snowboarding as me. One night, we were chatting about the sport, and he told me he saw a local legend, Kevin Young, on the hill. Not wanting to name-drop, I told him to name any of his Whistler-based heroes. He would pluck a pro from his head, and I said I knew them, because I did. The simplest way to hook up with them was a look at the local phone book. For well over four hours, Andy very endearingly hunted through it with the aim of finding another one of his iconic riders.

I have never understood the urban legend that bad things come at you in threes, but it was proved true in this case. I still point to this time in my life as the start of my demise. It really shouldn't have been, as Carol finally ditched her part-time nanny and house-cleaning work and scored a casual nursing position in the local ER. Because of this steady employment, which along with my pay combined with our paid-off apartment in Scotland gave us just over C$70,000 to make a deposit, we were able to buy our first place in a subdivision of Whistler called Castle Drive. This was one of my favourite cool addresses: 111 2222 Castle Drive. I just had this real strong gut feeling that Whistler, and in particular this lower-middle-tier price point of the market, was only going to appreciate substantially, as "normal" people could actually afford it.

Not long after I lost my managerial job, the most unbelievable news came from Aberdeen. Not long after his return home, Andy had committed suicide by hanging himself in an underground car park. To say I was absolutely devastated doesn't explain my emotional turmoil when I heard the news. Then came the question why. After spending almost three months with me in Whistler, Andy had gone back to the UK in a quest to get a visa so he could follow his dreams of making it back and did everything possible. Unfortunately, all of his applications were turned down, and a return to Whistler was not going to happen. Riding his snowboard was everything to my good friend. Faced with the loss of his dreams, he decided life wasn't worth living anymore.

At that point in my life, I couldn't understand it. Back then, I believed suicide was a loser's game. How you could not love this blessed life that the Lord had given us? I didn't know quite how fragile that beauty is and how it can turn so ugly when your dreams are gone. To this day, despite my efforts not to, every time I hear someone saying the word *hang* or *hanging* instead of chilling or whatever, my good friend Andy's image enters my mind. I look up to the heavens and take a minute to remember my long-lost brother.

I told no one except Carol about Andy's death, as I simply couldn't handle my mixed-up emotions. To overcome them, I decided to do what I always do: work even harder, not only in my chosen work as a coach but to become the best rider I could possibly be with my God-given athletic talents. Most of my close friends were amazing riders. If they were anywhere else on this planet, they would be sponsored, but the talent pool in Whistler for extreme sports is simply second to none.

I was invited on a casual photo shoot, as my friends knew I had started to improve my freestyle arsenal of tricks. I remember it as if it was yesterday: an absolutely gorgeous blue-sky day. We hiked out of bounds to a place going towards Kyber Pass, which for my money had some of the best off-piste/backcountry terrain on both mountains. We started to build this perfect jump. There was about 15 riders in our posse that day, so with the kicker constructed in no time, the guys started throwing down in front of a couple of pro photographers.

My intense, all-consuming competitiveness is only accelerated when a camera is involved. We call it in the trade *Kodak courage*, a phenomenon I later found out I was not the only one affected by. I was willing to push every barrier I had to get the glory of the camera. I had watched an ESPN exclusive on BMX legend Matt Hoffman, who was not only one of the gnarliest BMXers ever but, according to this program, the pioneer of big-air contests in all sporting forms. Just like him, I could go off when it's just me against my fears, but throw a camera into the mix, and we try too hard to steal the thunder and end up pushing it too far.

In a moment of total insanity, I decided I had perfected the front flip so well that I didn't even need a trail jump to test the new booter, as in my brain I could now land any flip on any jump no matter the size. This was easily the biggest jump I had ever sessioned. With the cameras flashing, I hit the lip of the jump, and I remember this internal warning-system voice going off in my head as I started to get airborne—*Holy shit, Andrew, this is a big mother of a jump*—and questioning my original decision to nail a huge front flip, because this jump was gigantic in comparison to any other I had landed a flip or spin off. But as usual, I decided to ignore the voice of reason, rather opting to get even more air by popping off the lip.

Instead of landing where everyone landed—they had created a crater where all the soft snow was now compacted down into a landing zone that was pretty much ice—I went off to the side to find a softer touchdown spot. Unfortunately, my brilliant plan backfired in the worst possible way. Even though I actually landed the jump with my board below me, the jump's landing had been built in a natural gully, and where everyone else had landed was the deepest snow section. To my horror, I landed on an area that didn't have the necessary snow depth. My board penetrated the snow layer, and its base stopped dead on this badass rocky section. I might have been all right if I was skiing, as you pop out of their binding systems in such a scenario, but on a snowboard, you don't have that luxury.

I can only remember very vaguely what happened next. I landed with more weight on my back foot. as I would rather over-rotate the flip than under-rotate it. But the sheer momentum of the flip combined with the 25 to 30 feet of serious airtime equalled a massive force that had to be channelled somewhere. That somewhere was my left, back leg. I remember the worst pain of my life starting to radiate immediately from my lower leg as I hit the rock garden underneath the snow, and it buckling as I rag-dolled down the hill. When I eventually came to a stop, all I can remember is this colossal pain taking over everything that I was.

I have never been the type to show pain through tears, I think as a result of going to an all-boys school where crying would only give your rivals a sniff at your weakness, which was ultimately very exploitable. But every person has limits when everything you are feeling takes over and you set your pride aside and give in to your body's natural instinct to cry. When in such intense pain, that response takes over automatically.

It seemed like a lifetime before any of the patrollers and on-hill medical staff got to me, as we were a ways out of the ski-area boundary. I remember my close friend Trent trying everything to manufacture a supportive snow pocket that would immobilize my smashed lower left leg. Every time it moved even the slightest bit, a pain from deep inside my leg that resembled a knife impaling my flesh and twisting would flood every thought from my head. When the doctors finally arrived over 30 minutes from my original crash time, they gave me a huge dose of morphine. It was my first-ever encounter with heavy-duty painkillers, and as such my first taste of their immense power. Within minutes of the injection, the worst pain ever somehow magically disappeared, to be replaced by this mellow, laid-back happy place where nothing could ever be wrong. I went from crying like a little baby to cracking my favorite comedian Billy Connelly's jokes and waving at everyone, especially those with a camera.

The next big hurdle was how the fuck we were going to get me off the hill to the ER. When you're that far in the backcountry, the usual evacuation was by heli-vac, costing around C$2,000. That was way more than I could afford with the loss of my managerial wages, so mercifully, everyone on the shoot grabbed my stretcher and pulled it manually to a point where the patrollers' snowmobile could drag me back into Whistler's official area boundary. I was met there by another patroller who was going to ski my blood bucket down to the collection point for the ambulances. I remember so vividly the ride down the hill. With my morphine trip in full effect, I was so pumped to be in the stretcher, I would wave at anyone looking until we came to rest at the bottom.

Although this was my third season working for Whistler, I was ushered to a place I never even knew existed in the treed-off accident area fairly close to the main bus stop at the base. To my amazement, there were six other unfortunate casualties writhing in pain there. When the first ambulance arrived, I somehow jumped the line and was placed in the back. In most situations, I would have felt guilty, but as the paramedic explained, it is the severity of the injury rather than chronological order that dictates your place in line.

I went from a no-pain drug-infested fog to absolute killer pain as the morphine started to wear off. I remember I wouldn't let them cut off my boots and board pants. It always amazes me how your decision-making thoughts and priorities get so messed up under the influence.

It didn't take them long to give me the season-ending news: I had totally smashed my tibia and fibula. This really came as no surprise, as my wife's face (of course she was working that day), my intense 11-out-of-10 pain level, and the totally unnatural way my leg was contorted had already given it away. There was nothing to be done except get me to a Vancouver orthopedic department ASAP. But of course, I had to do this on a long weekend when the ambulances were beyond their limited capacity. Instead of waiting hours for one, Carol drove me down to Vancouver General Hospital herself. It wasn't until I returned home after almost a month at VGH that I realized I had now become the worst kind of fallen rock star. Everyone seemed to know the terrible story of my crash.

I never ever do a half-assed job at anything. I didn't just break my leg: my bones were shattered. The specialist told me he could see at least 23 breaks in the space of a couple of feet of my already battled-scarred tib/fib bones. At that, Carol wished me the best and headed back to Whistler to look after Michelle and Cayman. It is hard to access this drug-driven filing-cabinet drawer in my memory banks, but I can remember going through an excruciatingly painful surgery where they inserted a titanium rod through the middle of my smashed tib. Instead of providing the ultimate fix for everything, it actually intensified my pain, and I spent a horrific night pleading with the nurses to give me more morphine.

It wasn't until 6 a.m. that the resident doctor came in and, in no sugar-coated terms, told me I had sustained such a serious injury that instead of fixing the problem, my surgery had actually compounded it. My lifelong bad luck had somehow cursed me with this rare post-surgical complication called *compartment syndrome*. Despite being married to an ER nurse in Whistler, for God's sake, I had never even heard of this, so I didn't have a clue what it meant.

A few hours later, at around 9 a.m., a specialist arrived to give me the same diagnosis as his junior colleague. The real clincher wasn't the prognosis, it was the solution: they most likely needed to amputate my leg below the knee. I couldn't remember a time when my mind played so many tricks on me. Here I was, all alone in this strange hospital 125 kilometres away from my loved ones, up to my eyes in a bad morphine trip, freaking out about the all-too-real probability of losing my limb forever. I decided the worst thing I could do was share my overwhelming fear with my soulmate. What could she do apart from panic?

I took my second trip to the operating room in so many days, but this one was to alter my life forever. The last thing I can remember saying to surgeon before the anesthetic kicked in was that if he amputated my left leg, "I will hunt you down, as I can't face a life without my leg." I was scared beyond belief.

The next thing I remember is waking up to an inhumane amount of pain but more importantly, the indescribable realization that I could be staring at a stump replacing my otherwise fit and healthy lower left leg. After seeing my leg was still there, all I could do was look towards the heavens and thank God for letting me dodge that bullet. I simply couldn't imagine a life without it.

I appreciate and respect all the special and disabled athletes around the globe, and I still can't figure out why the IOC won't do the obvious and join all the athletes together. Wouldn't it make more sense to start every Olympics with the special and physically challenged games before the regular games? It would help the disabled athletes gain media exposure and hopefully sponsorship cash, along with the recognition they so badly need and deserve. To me, their resolve makes them even more worthy than any able-bodied athlete.

My unbelievably good news was soon mixed with a very big dose of reality. The surgeon came to my bedside and explained that the reason he usually opts for amputation rather than the open cut he made from my knee to my ankle was that the wound could get infected. If that happened, I would be right back in the OR, but this time they would probably have to remove my whole knee joint, meaning a much more complicated prosthetic and recovery time. Basically, what he tried to explain to me was I was most probably going lose my leg regardless.

In all honesty I have never fully understood what really happened. Because I did such a number on my leg, there was a great deal of internal bleeding, but with no compound fracture/breaking of the skin, the mounting pressure from the brutal bleeding had nowhere to go. As a result, the pressure had to go somewhere, so it started killing off the good muscle in my lower leg—in particular, the compartment muscle, which is at the side of your shin bone and is responsible for lifting your foot up in a leverage system in conjunction with your ankle. That's why they call it *compartment syndrome*. It is a very dangerous medical condition.

I was left with an open wound running the full length of my lower leg. It was probably the grossest thing I had ever seen, and what made it worse is that it was part of me. It looked like something off a biology experiment or a reality TV program. My life was in their hands.

I spent almost four weeks in Vancouver General watching Ross Rebagliati win the first-ever snowboard gold for Canada and doing everything in my power to keep my wound as clean as possible. I was obviously on a real downer with the knowledge that according to medical experts, it would take forever to walk again, most likely with foot drop. Any sporting ambitions were in ruins; snow sports, mountain biking and the like were going to be impossible with my injury, no matter how good my rehab was. For some reason, although I was certainly panicking, I had this voice in my head telling me I had heard all this before. Was it at school when people would challenge me to get on every sports team going, even the sports that I wasn't very good at, like basketball, volleyball and tennis? Was it when all the haters said I didn't have a chance to graduate at anything?

My mate Tony had given me a great nickname a few years earlier: Quiet Strength. It described the tenacious, feisty, fiery, passionate, wear-my-heart-on-my-sleeve, slightly mischievous character trait that was always inside me—in my DNA, if you like. I ain't going to lie; at first I didn't get it. It was like an oxymoron, two words you would never put together, as for most people they are conflicting opposites. But I grew to appreciate it, and for sure, it applied right here, right now. I had to harness all that silent inner strength and tenacity and apply it to my rehab with everything I had to prove everyone wrong and me right. This was quite simply the hardest thing I had ever come back from.

Praise be, I was eventually moved from the ward to my own private room to reduce the chance of infection. I spent the following weeks plotting my recovery strategy and watching the Nagano Winter Olympics whilst keeping a close eye on the internal workings of my leg out of a weird torturous curiosity. I have always wondered at the marvel of living creatures and how they work. If there really is life after death—which I'd decided not to believe in, as I want to make the most of my time on this earth rather than wait for my second, third or whatever life—I would love to come back and study sports medicine and/or psychology.

After two weeks of complete and utter boredom broken partially by the Winter Olympic coverage mixed with more than my fair share of pure pain, I had to return to the OR for what I was praying would be my last operation, this one to close over my wound by rather gruesomely taking a cheese slicer to extract a donor skin patch from my thigh and sewing it over my lower leg cut. As they had warned me, the donor site was actually more painful than the patched area.

I had been brought up to never ever hit a female, but when this nurse decided to change the dressing on my donor site in the middle of the night without waking me up, my natural reaction to defend myself kicked in. Thankfully, I realized what was going on at the very last minute and somehow restrained myself with just a warning not to ever do that again.

Obviously, I was hurting big-time on all levels. I remember this one day when I was allowed to leave the ward in a wheelchair. Boy, was that an adventure. As always, give me an inch and I'll take a mile. I decided to take full advantage of my newfound freedom and went so far I nearly never made it back to the ward because of sheer exhaustion from pushing a wheelchair for the first time. I finally found the hospital's main café, and just when I thought everyone was looking at me, all attention suddenly shifted from my plight to this obvious burn victim with a plastic see-through mask like some of the basketball players use to protect facial injuries. In a strange way, it was probably the best thing that could have happened to me, so I could get over whining and bitching about my worse-than-terrible luck. Here was an example of someone who was in a way worse place of hurt.

When I returned to my private room that night, although I couldn't physically go down on my knees, I still prayed for the first time in well over a decade with all my entire conviction. I thanked the Lord for saving me and my leg and begged for his support to give me the strength to take my rehab to a level I could not even imagine and not let this horrendous accident define me. I hoped to learn from its lessons and give myself the determination to return to as close to 100 percent as practically possible. Just when the tears were flowing, my nurse came in and gave me shit for leaving my room for so long and almost getting stuck on the ramp in the lobby as I struggled with my rookie wheelchair technique.

Another week passed, and all of a sudden, I started getting pains in my chest and running down my right arm. I put it down to the fact that everything was on the right side of the bed, but the doctors had other ideas. They were concerned about a possible heart problem from me being on my back for so long. In came this resident, and he wanted to take my blood, this time with a twist: he wanted the artery, not the vein, so he began putting this needle in my arm. He went digging through all my layers of skin, and I felt every movement, as he employed no anesthetic. Then he realized he had missed it and had to give it another go.

After three botched attempts, I told him forget it; I'd had enough. So a specialist came in to do it and scored the first time. I had a heart scan and a whole battery of other tests lined up. As soon as they ruled out the heart problem and gave me a sniff at going home, I was on the phone to Carol pleading with her to come down and get me, or I was going to catch the fucking bus, as I was honestly starting to believe that I was not going to make it back to normal life again. That's a feeling I would revisit many years later.

The honeymoon period of me being home was short-lived. I figured that this injury was going to be like the worst enemy I had ever faced, and as such, my recovery would require every single cell and molecule within me. Like all of my extensive sports injuries, it wasn't really the pain of the accident but the lengthy rehab process that challenged me. Not only couldn't I return to the sports I loved, I couldn't even have a shower without aid. Rehab blows!

My mission was simple: work harder than I had ever worked before. Every time I wanted to quit, I would go back to my reality wake-up call of the burn victim. Really, I was so lucky, as that guy would never be able to overcome his injuries like I had the opportunity to do. I vowed to spend every waking minute of every day mounting my comeback with a daily exercise program consisting of the following:

1. swimming in the morning, starting with 10 lengths and then increasing weekly in 10-lap increments until I got to my goal of 100 and adding in flippers/fins to increase the force on my healing leg
2. mountain biking in the afternoon, usually around two-hour rides, but with the knowledge that I had to fall off my bike on the right side, as I still couldn't bear weight on my left leg
3. gym at night, include the physiotherapists' instructed exercises, to rebuild the rest of my body
4. very painful physio visits five times a week with the owner of the practice, Sarah, a self-described Nazi dishing out the hardest and most painful but necessary manipulations and exercises, as the local doctors advised us that she was the only one likely to bring me close to my aim of regaining my athletic prowess to the fullest extent possible

It was Sarah who, after four months of full-bore rehab, noticed that the flexion in my left ankle was not coming back like it should. Everyone was so concerned about the major tib/fib injury, no one had noticed I'd broken my left ankle in three places. Although Sarah was a truly exceptional physio, and although I endured every painful stretching exercise possible, I never regained full flexion in that ankle.

I also had severe foot drop because I had lost two thirds of my compartment muscle and the remainder was not strong enough to lift up my foot. I got this big orthopedic contraption that slipped into my shoe and ran up my calf to keep my ankle at the ideal 90-degree angle so my toes didn't drag when I walked. Despite almost over-training my remaining compartment muscle, even to this day, if you watch me closely when I walk, I still have to lift my left leg a bit more just to avoid my toes touching the ground first in an almost limp—but I have become a master at disguising it.

The worst part of my comeback wasn't the extensive exercise and accompanying pain; rather, there was one break in my shin that wasn't healing properly, something to do with calcification, and I would need another operation to bone-graft it back together. Or so I thought—until on one bike ride, I had a rather stupid fall onto the wrong side but carried on riding for another two hours until I told my mate of the ache in my leg and then rode home. After Carol came home, like all women who know you as intimately as she did, she immediately noticed the change in my demeanour and whisked me off for yet another ER X-ray. It was confirmed that my fall had done exactly what they were planning to do in my upcoming operation: re-break my leg in the very place the bones weren't bridging the gap. My painful fall actually saved me a fourth operation.

It took more than nine months, but I finally did enough to rebuild my leg that I was strong enough to bear weight without crutches. This was a momentous achievement and one of those life-changing occasions you can never ever forget or even describe properly, as sometimes there aren't words. If everything went according to plan, I could gain strength on all levels for the rest of my life. It was reason enough to have a wild night with my good friends.

I had gone out clubbing with them with my crutches, which was the strangest night ever. When you drink, you notice how pissed you're getting by your movements to the bar or babe reconnaissance to the dance floor. But when you have a smashed leg, you just sit there and get drunk until it is an absolute must to hit the washroom. Precarious isn't a strong-enough word to describe navigating the alcohol-strewn floor and then the ice and snow outside. Fun times!

The only thing I was focusing on was being able to get on my snowboard the very next season and prove anyone and everyone wrong—except possibly my family, as they couldn't escape my determination, motivation and downright stubborn I-will-do-or-die-trying attitude. I vowed that if I could make it back from such an ordeal, nothing life had to throw at me would ever be too much or break me ever again. I had survived what I erroneously believed was the hardest and toughest road I would ever face. Wrong again!

My goal was not be ready and riding on the very first opening day the following season but to take a heli-trip I had always dreamed of but never had an excuse strong enough to justify the silly cost of such a day. My comeback coupled with the fact that my Australian best friends, Tracy and Shawn, along with a friend of theirs, a Kiwi called James, were all leaving Whistler at the end of the season to return down-under was excuse enough. Tracy had lived with us as KA's live-in nanny, and Shawn, her brother, was a terrific surfer and a blond bombshell the ladies loved. I had found out that I could get a local instructor rate of around C$600 for a heli-day. We decided, fuck it, some things are beyond money, and watched the weather forecast for the ideal perfect powder day.

It finally arrived, and after a week of storm after storm dumping copious amounts of powder on the local hills, the forecast was calling for a clearing day before we went back into another storm cycle. I headed off with my heart in my mouth—as I really didn't know if my weakened leg would be able to do a full powder day. Powder is not only a much harder workout than groomed but also you tend to put more weight on your back leg to keep your nose from submarining under the snow, causing you to bail every time.

As per the forecast, we were treated to the absolutely perfect blue skies as we boarded the chopper in Pemberton heading for its glacier. It was honestly like something off a ski or board video, like Greg Stump's or Warren Miller's ski masterpieces or the *Art of Flight* and *First Descent* board flicks. The only way I can describe what came next is spiritual, as in all honestly, it felt like I had come back from hell and now I had arrived in heaven. Despite being totally shagged, I was so pumped I couldn't sleep that night. So around 4 a.m., I wrote to my mates around the world telling them of the truly religious experience that only a perfect powder day via a helicopter could bring.

I know I will piss everyone off, but honestly, that was not only the best use of C$1,000 but simply the best day of my life ever, even eclipsing my graduation, my wedding or my kids' birth. Each run, we were gifted with this pristine white canvas on which, through our movements, we painted our own pictures. It was more than just an absolutely astonishing experience; throw in my past year and, fuck it, I deserved this one. I made the most of every single minute, turn, run, face-shot and helicopter ride. It was all pure magic.

I had booked us into the most expert group, knowing it would give us first descent and maximize our turnaround time. The original price of C$600 was for 10 drops, which we had racked up by noon. Our guide said its C$50 a drop from there, a deal we simply couldn't refuse. We doubled our original quota by doing 20 drops. It was such an awe-inspiring moment in my life that there really are no words grand enough to explain my emotions that day. Suffice to say it was so overwhelming that I intentionally turned down one drop. I was so close to tears I had to somehow be alone.

Here I was, celebrating possibly my greatest comeback ever with my closest friends in this winter wonderland. There really are no words to express the enormity of it. I was this tiny little speck on this most glorious of landscapes, all by myself, with the grandeur of everything that is Mother Nature. It was a moment that went on to define me and make me the man and environmentalist I am today.

Our guide—who I got really friendly with, as I gave him my camera at the start of the day—captured our euphoria in some glorious photography that encapsulated our perfect day. In a strange twist of fate, a few weeks later, his passion for mountaineering claimed his life in a large avalanche in Alaska. Even that couldn't dampen our exquisite memories of our best day ever. It did, however, offer proof, if I ever needed it, that this life is so precious. We all walk on a very thin layer of ice that could break at any minute. It was a lesson I would learn again in the not-too-distant future.

CHAPTER 7

THE GOOD LIFE

Now what? I had moved my family halfway around the world to take a dream job, and not only had the job gone, but so had my ability to do it because of my gimp left leg. I had no idea whether I could be a full-time snowboard coach ever again. Not only did I have titanium rod screwed into my left knee, which transmitted every impact painfully, but my shock-absorbing ankle had lost much of its flexion range, further amplifying the impact directly into my knee. Worst of all, because the compartment syndrome had left me with very limited ability to lift my toes, I had all but lost the vital biomechanical action of executing a snowboard heel side turn.

To further compound my troubles, my mum, out of the blue, decided to come over to visit us in Canada alone. As is usual for our relationship, everything was hunky-dory for a few days until she had her two wee glasses of wine, and then everything that she had built up animosity-wise reared its ugly head. She hit me with a verbal tirade so torrid that I think I would rather step into the ring with Mike Tyson.

It didn't take long before we got onto the "why did you ever leave Aberdeen" of it all. She pointed out that back home, I had an old-boys support system that would help me achieve my career aspirations; qualifications that were worth something tangible, as seemingly everyone and their dog has a degree in North America; and "we look after our own rather than in this foreign country, where no one gives a damn about you."

THE HOOD

My folks were never sporty, so Whistler was like being on another planet for her. Everyone's world seemed to revolve around outdoor sporting pursuits rather than a job, family, news, weather—the stuff the rest of the world deems important. It really is a resort town, a cocoon that's somewhat detached from the real world. She could never understand that her Tenerife paradise, which she practically lived in, was just a summer version of my winter paradise, as we mostly enjoyed opposite seasons.

After another huge argument completely centred around going home, I still couldn't get it through her thick skull that *this* was now my home. Despite all the obstacles, I was really happy here and had absolutely no aspiration to return to the auld country. As I saw it, all that really mattered to her was career, house, cars, clothes, and holidays—basically all the materialistic status crap that everyone sadly holds up as a benchmark of how successful your life's endeavours have been. I'm not going to say these weren't ever important to me, as this was all I had ever known from birth, but even then I knew deep down inside that all those things did not equal true, pure happiness. Rather, they were symbols we built up to prove our self-made worth and adhere to the hierarchical status these toys somehow stupidly grant you.

I was starting to learn, in the hardest way possible, that all these things can only give you temporary happiness. Just like every fantasy, once you have satisfied it, it doesn't take long for your brain (well, mine anyway) to concoct the next must-have pillar of success and wealth. What was always at the very core of my happiness was what I like to refer to as my three Fs: family, friends and fun. To be honest, there is another four-letter F-word that belongs there, but despite it being the most enjoyable and basic natural want/need, for some reason you're not allowed to put it there beside the other three.

After another blinder of a fight, she walked out, got a hotel room and left on the next available flight. She just couldn't see that I was no longer the red-headed stepchild, just an ordinary guy who didn't follow the mass's beliefs. I wanted to do it as good old Frank so boldly stated back in the day: "My Way." I wanted to do the things I had always loved more than words and make a life around them. This was far more important to me than salary and status.

Her answer to this had remained the same since I was in primary school: "Andrew, sports are hobbies. They are not going to pay your rent or give you trips around the world." These things were near and dear to her, but I was more than willing to put up with ridiculously low pay as some kind of Whistler lifestyle-choice premium that one had no alternative but to accept.

Before I knew what was going on, she had gone, and I was back to the "us against the world" deal. I had secured work again with the mountains. This time, somewhat ironically, I was back on a shop floor selling snowboards in the Intrawest-owned Showcase Snowboard shop. It was an incredibly hard pill to swallow, as I had gone from kingpin snowboard dude to a minimum-wage snowboard bum on a shop floor. Although I didn't have use for many of my parents' values, they had instilled one very clear core belief in me that unfortunately the world has seemed to forget these days: treat your fellow humans with the utmost respect.

It is my deepest belief that we all came from the same place and will end up in the same place. As such, we are all the same. We are created equal and are equal. We all have been gifted by God with a unique set of strengths and weaknesses that make us who we are. This is something I hammered into my kids before anything else, as Whistler was full of kids with arrogant attitudes and adults driven by the worship of their peers, which I hate so much.

Another value my parents drilled into me was to treat everyone the same: your colleagues with respect and give no more respect to your bosses than the people "beneath" you (a term I hate, as if you truly believe in the above, whether you are Bill Gates or the trash collector, everyone has an essential role in this life and no one is ever above or below you). Despite thinking my life was always going to be onward and upward, it was only now that I realized these words were golden.

During my time on the shop floor, I struck up a really good friendship with this girl who, if I wasn't married, I would have gone out with for sure. I think she liked me, but only God knows. I have believed this before only to get a rejection; a lack of understanding of the opposite sex is a major downfall of going to a same-sex school. Anyway, she even introduced me to her father. It was another core value of mine that if you commit the rest of your life to someone in front of God, you have no choice but to be faithful—or if the worst-case scenario happened, you left but never gave in to the temptation of cheating. In 23-plus years of marriage, I can proudly say I was never ever unfaithful, even when times got rough. I had so many opportunities, as being a ski or snowboard coach elevated your chick appeal, similar to that good dancers enjoy; why, I will never know.

If I'm going to stick with honesty as the best policy, there was this girl called Emily, before Carol and I were married or even engaged—we were doing the long-distant relationship deal. I got friendly with this hot chick on a trip up to my favourite ski hill. She decided to make her move after we'd been flirting with and teasing each other for a few months. Ever had a blow job when driving? That was a first for me too. Fuck me, it is almost impossible to use your feet on the pedals when that is going on, I can tell you! How the fuck we didn't crash before I eventually pulled over is beyond me to this day.

With Carol a distant thought at the time, I let Emily invite me back to her place for the best sex I have ever had. After going long and hard for the entire night, as she decided to use every piece of furniture as a sex aide and had toys out the wazoo, I literally found it hard to walk for a week afterwards from my friction burns. As much as I hate to admit it, that girl turned a boy into a man and taught me more about sex than any porno, kama sutra or other female ever did.

Closing that stellar sex file drawer and returning to reality, my employment fortunes changed thanks to Tom, an ex-hockey enforcer who found another career after his sporting days were behind him. He worked for this cleaning-chemical firm called Ecolab, and after a few meetings, he offered me the chance to take their sales personality and mechanical proficiency tests. His Whistler representative had just quit, and if I passed, he would push my name forward as a potential replacement.

For once, I was in the right place at the right time. My high work ethic combined with good old Lady Luck actually shining on me for a change to help me pass both tests with flying colours. I did particularly well with the sales personality traits, as I knew I was a much better salesman than serviceman.

Before I could blink, I had left the retail job and was on a flight to St. Paul, Minnesota, for management training weeks. I had an absolutely titanic learning curve in front of me. It was an ideal job because although the product line was soap, a very dull thing to talk about, I can sell ice to Eskimos as long as I believe in the product's worth and quality and I would buy it myself. On the other hand, the job was a nightmare because I had to be a chemist, an electrician and a plumber, as we had to service everything we sold. And it wasn't just in one area of expertise, either, as we serviced mainly the hospitality industry, which the resort town of Whistler is pretty much founded on, including laundry, housekeeping and stewarding, with these not-so-basic computer dispensers and pumps.

After a probation period of six months, including a total of three weeks of Minnesota training sessions, I had passed and was now a full-fledged territory manager. It's funny, as the final test was this taped sales visit where we had to pretend we were entering a new account for the first time and sell a particular product to our trainers, who had to put up some resistance. By this time, I had befriended this super chill guy Mark. He was also from BC, and we just hit it off. After a very long test day, we got the results back, and both me and Mark more than passed—but the summary of our sales presentation was, they thought we had smoked some sweet BC bud before we went in. Little did they know we had partied the night before, and it was the lingering effects of a big night that they were witnessing.

In hindsight, I should have known that this new career really was stretching and testing me to my very limits. Ultimately, it relied more on my weaknesses than my strengths—namely, mechanics. In fact, I had inherited a sales region that was very urgently falling to pieces, as my predecessor was guilty of the lazy, do-just-enough-to-get-by way of operating, as the role was almost akin to being self-employed. If I woke up and decided not to go to work that day, apart from emergency calls, I didn't have to. It didn't take long for my common sense to figure out that the more you did that, the further behind the eight ball you would get, the more super-stressful emergency calls you would receive, and the worse your life would become.

I decided that, as with everything else, I was going to do everything in my power to be as successful as my limited mechanical ability would let me. After almost a year of chasing my tail trying to save so many accounts, I became very jaded with Ecolab's overly ambitious customer-service claims not coming to fruition because of the useless previous manager and my rookie status. I had inherited one of the largest and key sales territories with next to no help from the head office, and I was on call 24/7/365.

Then they decided to expand my territory even further to include Squamish, Pemberton and even Lillooet. Please feel free to look these up on Goggle maps. It was totally unrealistic in terms of distance, number, sheer value and volume of its customer base. I'd had enough and was really starting to lose it. So after much ado, the bosses granted my wish to dump my emergency pager every second weekend. I grew to hate that thing, as I would live in literal fear of the noise it made any time of day and night. It was always to fix something that I wasn't even sure I could fix. Every other weekend, I left my hated pager and some equipment with the local fix-it company, Alpine Mechanical, as I needed some time to myself and my family.

I had an unadulterated desperation to gain a real job and prove to everyone, especially my parents and even more so my wife, that I wasn't some kind of sports douchebag and could actually do something that had absolutely nothing whatsoever to do with my sporting addictions. I had to break my number-one rule of life: work hard to play even harder. It was a reversal; it was all work, and even when I got to play, invariably my pager ruined that, as I could be called back to work anytime.

I had met this guy through Alpine who not only blew me away with his almost magician-like I-can-fix-anything skills but was a real diamond in the rough. Every day, he looked like he had just dragged himself out of bed after yet another heavy night. But the maxim "Don't judge a book by its cover" was truer of Gord than anyone else I had ever met. A nicer, kinder, truer mechanical wonder, just a dead-on guy as the Irish would say, you would never meet. I was determined to get him on-board with Ecolab, as we would make an absolute dream team. I could sell anything to anyone, and he could fix anything.

The bosses took one look at him, and all they saw was that he did not fit the perfect suit-and-tie businessman they would usually hire. This always baffled me, as you spent more than half your time upside-down in a dish machine (and there can't be many more gross places in the world than the inside of a non-maintained dishwasher) replacing very hazardous laundry chemical lines and pumps, repairing housekeeping dispensers, etc. Actually, the worst thing about the job was that it's damn hard to get pumped about cleaning solutions, especially because when you finally left work, people would ask you for advice on how to clean shit—for real!

Subsequently, they introduced this auto-flush dispenser system for urinals and toilets, which I sold a ton of, but again, I dreaded the labour-intensive installation, as sitting in a washroom listening to and smelling the grossness for days on end was not fun. But it paid the rent and then some, so suck it up, Andrew.

Well, after a few close calls, they relented. I had already devised a plan to turn the territory around that involved Gord. He said it was the longest, hardest and dirtiest work he'd ever done in his 50-plus years on the planet. I did what I always do when facing a seemingly impossible challenge: work as hard as humanly possible. Then no one could ever blame me if the unimaginable happened and I failed.

My plan started off with a combination of prioritizing the most in-danger-to-lose-to-a-competitor accounts and the biggest-dollar accounts. I took Gord along and replaced all the old equipment with new dispensers and the promise of unrivalled customer service from here on in. It worked: after almost a year-and-a-half of non-stop 14-hour days, we had turned the territory on its head and become the most successful district in BC and top three in Canada.

I managed to turn my dreadful C$37,000 basic salary into an almost six-figure salary-and-commission job. It was really hard but worth it. I was on top of the world. It was not the ideal job, but it was a hell of a lot easier than when I started. It gave me the life I had before I left Aberdeen, only better.

I had decided back in childhood that if I ever had kids, I would raise them so much differently from how my folks raised me. In particular, I would encourage them in whatever career paths and hobbies they wanted to pursue. I always wondered how good an athlete I could have been if my parents had supported me more in my sporting exploits. I went exactly the opposite and followed through on a master plan that I had developed for myself if I could do this life fresh all over again. To raise the perfect athlete, out of all the sports, I chose the following for my first daughter, Michelle, as soon as she was old enough to commence:

1. *Skiing*—I even lied about her birthday to get her started as soon as she could walk at around 18 months old. Heck, if she loved snow sports as much as I did, we were mint.

2. *Swimming*— I was a pretty decent swimmer in my day, and I knew it was the ideal sport to gain an amazing cardio base and super-diverse muscular definition. But more importantly, she loved it. It also taught her the work ethic needed, as let's face it, as amazing a workout as swimming is, doing the extraordinary number of laps needed to be a serious competitor makes it not exactly the most fun sport in the world

3. *Gymnastics and trampoline*—There is not a better sport to teach you biomechanics and air awareness, and it's the perfect cross-training for the three S's of fitness: strength, stamina and suppleness.

4. *Tae kwon do*—I remember all too well how mean kids can be—especially the physical and verbal bullying I had to endure until I learnt how to defend myself. Once you do, it somehow gives you the self-confidence, self-esteem and physical tools to overcome any intimidation, as well as crazy cardio and flexibility.

5. *Soccer and basketball*—These were 110 percent her choice, as although I also played these sports, I was much better at rugby and American football. They too were great for cardio, hand-eye co-ordination and killer foot movement

6. *Mountain biking*—This had become my favourite sport, and hey, regardless of its obvious crossover benefits like tremendous cardio, flow and fun, how better to build a strong father-daughter bond without any electronic and social distractions?

All of the above also gave her the physical, emotional and mental toughness required to succeed in this highly competitive world—and possibly some reasons to not give in to the ever-present temptation of drugs.

To say my plan worked well is the understatement of the decade. Within no time, her skiing was on a completely different level from not only mine but pretty much every one of her peers. Her success was beyond even my wildest dreams. To list all her accolades here would take way too long and just be bragging, but suffice to say, she became the youngest female member of the highly selective Next Snow Search Team, which earned her an award as the most inspirational athlete and a front-cover photograph on *Sports Illustrated*. The prize was a year's supply of Kellogg's Frosted Flakes, which to my immense approval, she donated to Canucks Place—a hospice for terminally ill kids.

What the hell is the Next Snow Search? After going around every major North American ski resort, they would select a handful of hopefuls and invite them to Colorado and Boston, where the 125 chosen were reduced through competition to the best 20 to be on the team. It was very similar to a Junior Olympics. The best thing for me was that because of the diverse competitions, ranging from traditional dual GS racing to skier-cross, moguls, big mountain/extreme, slopestyle expression session, half-pipe and finally a big air gala, it truly represented the best junior all-around skiers, snowboarders and telemarkers in North America—and my kid was one of them. *Proud* is not a big enough word to describe my elation. If once was never enough, we ended up going to three of those competitions, with good to unbelievable results, pitting her against the best athletes anywhere, a truly magnificent achievement.

On top of this, we decided at the very last minute to go to the Canadian Big Mountain Extreme Championships at Red Mountain. To my amazement, at the tender age of 14 (the junior division was up to the age of 17), she rocked up, and this rookie slayed the older girls' best run in her first run. I was blown away by the outright bitchiness of the female competitors, especially this one girl who, it later became apparent, was the three-year reigning champion of her division. After Michelle had won the whole thing, she could have simply walked away with the title, but she furthered her score in her glory run and earned yet another title and trophy for Junior Female Canadian Extreme Ski Champion, along with some killer media interviews.

With swimming, after an insane start (which included her doing an almost embarrassing 100-plus lengths of her 25-metre hometown pool when we were expecting a maximum of around 20) in Whistler's annual swim-athon when she was a mere 5 years old, we registered her into the BC summer swimming event in Squamish to establish whether that was just a fluke, and she walked away with not only wins in every discipline but records in her best events, backstroke and freestyle, which had been held forever by very successful Canadian Olympic swimmers. Every summer for nearly a decade, we spent every other weekend standing at the side of pool watching our child prodigy. To be honest, I hated it, but hey, for my kid, I would move heaven and earth. She ended up going to the finals twice and becoming one of Whistler's most decorated swimmers.

Tramp and gymnastics were always perfect cross-training, and as such, we never entered her in any competitive events. Same with tae kwon do, but after a couple of years, she pleaded with me to not have to do it anymore, as she simply didn't share my passion for that sport. It was a bit disappointing but also cool. In soccer and basketball, although she made her school team in both of these sports, I was determined not to let her do what I did and become a jack-of-all-trades and master of none. She needed to have sports she could do just for the fun of it.

I was so psyched that she loved my favourite sport of mountain biking almost as much as me; but yes, when she was old enough to compete, we travelled to the BC Cup races throughout the province, and in our second year of competition, we both won unprecedented category titles in the amateur downhill and cross-country disciplines. If you know this sport, it would be like Usain Bolt not only winning the 100 and 200 metres but also the steeplechase and marathon in the same year.

Because of all of the above, she was nominated and won the only Canadian Outdoor Sports Idol award, which involved an all-expenses-paid trip to Park City, Utah, to be treated like a rock star with numerous TV and media interviews and tons of free swag. Seriously cool!

Only problem was that—maybe due to a combination of my intensely competitive nature and the greed I believe is part of pretty much every human being—for every title, award, championship, newspaper and TV article, I wanted more, bigger and better. It backfired not just on me but my entire family in a major way years later. As much I hate to admit it, it wasn't a killer start in life dealing with competition, confidence and work ethic. Maybe I was living out my dreams of being at such a level in any sport through my child.

My dream was always to change the world with one great idea and/ or be an Olympian and serve my country with pride. Instead, I became one of those sports dads who focus more on the winning than the fun of taking part. I needed for her to listen and do what I asked or sometimes ordered. I used my intimate knowledge of physical discipline to achieve this. I regret both of these with everything I am as a man and a father. All I could think of was *what can go wrong now?* like it always does when I get somewhere in life. Nothing ever did, so I just ran with it.

Carol had scored a permanent position in the Whistler ER, so with our combined salary at around C$150,000, it was time to invest some of it before I spent it. Budgeting and finances were always a weakness of mine, as I did not fit the usual cheap Scottish stereotype. I loved spending my hard-earned money on all kinds of toys. There was this new subdivision being built in Whistler called Spruce Grove, and with the incredible doubling of our three-bedroom-apartment investment at Castle Drive, we could just afford one of the almost palatial single-family homes. It was unbelievable. I had come back from the dead and somehow managed to buy what is a fantasy to most people: a 2,700-foot single-family home in one of the outdoor recreational meccas of the world, complete with a 700-foot self-contained one-bedroom suite we could rent out to help pay a third of our somewhat scary mortgage.

We decided on the corner lot, and it was like the nightmare I had within three years turned into something beyond my wildest and most ambitious dreams. We would go there every Sunday to watch our new life take shape. Ecolab had also initiated an extension to their product portfolio to include a new pool and spa program that I fully bought into, as I knew it was a huge opportunity. There's hardly a hotel in Whistler that doesn't have pool facilities.

With my customer base intact, Gord and I had a field day, with me selling and then enlisting Gord's help with the very extensive installations. It was almost too successful; the only downside was it appeared from the outset that the program required more hands-on servicing. We both judicially decided how fast we were going to grow it, as we already had a great balance between being more than comfortable financially for the hours spent.

Gord also taught me a very important lesson, as he would temper my never-ending motivation, ambition and work ethic with a very simple: "Work smarter, not harder." Although it took me a while to really comprehend it, when I did, it was something I always adhered to, with my own twist: work smarter *and* harder. Another one my accountant taught me is that life is good, especially when you can make money when you sleep.

The new house cost us an arm and a leg and went against every cautious bone in Carol's body. However, for me, this major status symbol was an easy sell. Little did I know, my ambition was again setting me up for failure, and I was going to regret this decision in the not-too-distant future. I had watched my parents build up their net worth by buying and selling homes, and nowhere was this a bigger possibility than in Whistler. I had already won large in the real-estate gambling game with our apartment. Just like every gambler who has won big, I went back for more and more. At some point, you lose your logical side and greed takes over. As with every addiction, there is only ever one winner, and it's very rarely the addict.

But how could I ever believe anything else? I had found my Midas touch, and everything I touched really did turn to gold. My divide-and-conquer of the local real estate market got bigger and even richer while we were sleeping with the following properties:

1. Spruce Grove, Whistler single home worth around C$1.4 million (purchase price C$585,000), including a 700-foot suite that would bring in around C$900 a month to help pay for the high property taxes
2. Yaletown one-bed penthouse apartment with a killer view on the 31st floor, which we rented out for over C$1,750 a month and used as our weekend getaway when it was not rented; net worth well around C$550,000 (purchase price C$350,000)
3. Three Delta Village suites in the heart of Whistler Village, which I can't remember how much they would rent for but pretty much covered their mortgages; total net worth around C$600,000 (total purchase price around C$350,000)

Not bad for a guy who started out with nothing and everyone told him he would never amount to anything—and that he was crazy to leave his tribe for a foreign land. I had done what I had always done throughout my entire lifetime: proved all my doubters wrong, not with words but actions, as words are empty.

Credit where credit is due: I could never have achieved all this without my beautiful wife, Carol. But if she was being honest, she would have never taken the risks involved to win big. As gamblers know, the greater the risk, the greater the potential for rewards and/or failure. In reality, she never really understood how I managed to amass such wealth in such a short period of time. But hey, if Andrew's "who dares wins" attitude gave us a net worth of well over C$2 million and a life anyone would envy, who cares how, right?

We had a staggering lifestyle. Very hard work was rewarded, as it should be, with a dream home and lifestyle in Whistler; two top-of-the-range vehicles; an audiophile's dream C$7,000 home-theatre system wired throughout our home to satisfy my music fix; all the male toys, including a C$8,000 Ski-Do 800 Highmark Summit snowmobile, an enviable quiver of stellar skis and snowboards, and around 10 road and mountain bikes, most worth over C$10,000; all the best clothes, swag and bling any mortal man could ever have imagined; and, possibly most importantly, at least one but usually two exotic holidays a year, ranging from Europe to Mexico to Hawaii. Talk about living the dream. What could possibly go wrong?

Our favourite was easily Hawaii. We were enjoying it so much, I decided to extend our vacation to 10 days. While we were in Waikiki shopping for groceries, I decided I wanted to buy something else, and I left Carol in the cashier line. When I came back, I spotted Carol still in the queue, so I snuck up on her and pinched her ass. Only problem was, it wasn't Carol. After Carol, who was in another line, and I cracked up in laughter, the women involved took offence and started getting very upset, threatening to call the police.

I think it was also that holiday when I got Carol drunk, as when she drank she got really horny and a bit more adventurous in the bedroom. After leaving our pool bar, we went up to our room to get it on. I was so drunk, I couldn't really remember much from that night, and it wasn't until we got home I realized what had happened while showing our holiday video to not only our family but also the wicked witch of a mother-in-law. All of a sudden, from the usual scenery and playing by the pool, completely out of the blue it switched to me naked in the washroom masturbating, as Carol was so drunk she had fallen asleep, leaving me more than frustrated.

THE HOOD

All I can say is, I don't think I have ever been so embarrassed and blushed so hard ever.

It wasn't long before another of life's curveballs hit me squarely on the noggin. Completely out of the blue, Carol took me out for a slap-up meal, which she never did, and hit me with, "Andrew, I'm pregnant." Come again? How the fuck could this happen? She was on the pill, and we all know the effectiveness of contraception if used properly.

I could only hark back to the arguments we had every year when we did our annual garage-day clean-out and with it her blind insistence that she was not in the right headspace to get rid of all the baby gear. In truth, she had always wanted a second child, partly because of her body clock and her mum's pressure, but more crucially because Michelle and I were almost tied at the hip, as my mum remarked when she said she had never witnessed such a strong father-daughter relationship.

What could I say? More importantly, what could I do? As much as I didn't want another child, I had to accept it, but it left me with a bitterness that rocked me to my very core. How could she make such a life-changing decision without me? Was it revenge for me taking her to Canada years ago? I didn't have the answers, as even to this day Carol swears blind that it really was an against-all-odds conception rather than a sneaky and cowardly plan on her part.

I tried my best to muster a fake smile, but it left our marriage tattered and torn, as I developed a complete distrust for the person lying beside me. I struggled with what to do next but decided to follow my old dear's status quo advice: "When you don't know what to do, do nothing." Sad but true, but from my point of view, it was the first but easily the biggest nail in the coffin of our fairy-tale marriage.

As is always case with my crazy life, just as I was trying to make sense of that huge surprise, another sledgehammer rocked me to my very soul. I had always suspected, from as far back as I could remember, that my brother Ian was somehow different from other guys. I had, like everyone else, decided that because he was more than in touch with his feminine side, he must be gay and in denial. But he didn't just follow up on his not-of-this-earth joining of the Foreign Legion but surpassed it in every way with his coming-out party. Ian couldn't do it like everyone else; in Ian's world, everything had to be bigger and better than anyone else. From my folks across the Atlantic came completely unbelievable news that left me speechless: my brother Ian no longer existed but had been replaced by my new sister. At first I heard he—no, *she*—was called Jan, but later, I found out her new name was Abigail.

At first, I was floored, but then a light bulb went off in my brain, and suddenly I got it. He preferred men over chicks not because he was a gay but because he always saw himself as a female, so it made perfect sense for him, now her, to be attracted to the supposed opposite sex in her head. Trust me, to this day I get lost with trying to make sense out of this one.

To be honest, I cared so little for Ian, I really couldn't give a shit what he wanted to be. We had fallen out majorly years prior when he tried to treat me like one of his army privates and decided not to recognize my kids. There was absolutely no brotherly love left here. To put it simply, although I respected his decision to transform, I will never come close to understanding it.

As if our family hadn't been through enough, Ian took it to a whole new stratosphere by utilizing his PR contacts in the British army. He had been moved into a PR position because of his college diploma in media and television, which he got when he moved down south to England. It was a story from heaven for the paparazzi junk press in the UK to fall in love with. Here you had this highly decorated buff army officer who had served in every major conflict from the Falklands to Desert Storm, and more recently Afghanistan. To Joe Public, he was the epitome of a real-life action man and hero coming out on his terms and stating that he was born into the wrong sex. It was cheddar for the over-aggressive British media.

If it wasn't my brother, I would have agreed with everyone else and said I was cool with it—just part of the modern and supposedly better and more diverse yet inclusive world. But it is different when it is your own sibling who you spent the most crucial formative 18 years of your life with. His sexual problems landed at my door, with all my haters painting me with the same brush as my brother, which had spawned my homophobia from my early childhood to the present day. I was exactly the opposite, as I loved women, but my shyness with them combined with my lisp speech impediment branded me as a poof, which to this day drives me nuts.

Believe me, it is harder than you might think to get used to calling your brother your sister. Although in reality we were never tight, as we probably fought more than we played together, having never actually met the female version made it all the harder to digest. She had decided against my folks' advice to go to the UK press, the *Daily Mail* I think, and launder her story across the nation and latterly the world's media with his, now her, sensational story. To this day, I don't support her, not because of her transformation, but how she did it.

Why the fuck did she not accept my folks' cash of 100,000 pounds instead of the *Daily Mail*'s reward to pay for the surgery? No, Ian had to go out in his usual blaze of glory instead of preserving my folks' limited time left on this planet and letting them simply disappear into yet another sunset in paradise. The fucking tool opted for her own self-promotion in her drama queen constant search for attention, acceptance and, ultimately, fame.

When I confronted her with this question years later, she conveniently never replied, and we haven't spoken since. But truth be told, her false claims to garner sympathy to her cause that I was just like the rest of my family ostracizing him for his choice are completely untrue. I had stopped speaking to my brother, now sister, many years prior and it had absolutely nothing to do with her new identity. We were always chalk and cheese and really never spent much time together, as he was an introverted loaner who was happier playing toy soldiers and later obsessed by Dungeons and Dragons. Meanwhile, I hated being indoors, as I was an outdoor sporty type who needed social interaction as much as I needed air to breathe or food to eat.

Years of physical and verbal bullying (as Ian was not only two years older than me but also much bigger in every way) came to a head when we were on what proved to be our last-ever family vacation to Northern Spain, more than 100 miles from Barcelona in a seaside tourist town called L'Estartit. The holiday started as it would continue, with me getting badly sunburned with my Gaelic pale skin because being on the coast, I was lulled into believing it wasn't that hot thanks to the cool Mediterranean breeze. Follow that with the next day snorkeling and completely torching my back, and my whole first week was trying to get over the worst sunburn ever.

If that wasn't enough, we got hammered one night in the local discos and decided to steal a small wooden boat in the bay and paddle it out. Ian decided to christen the journey with a bottle of red wine. Before I knew what was going on, he had managed to scuttle the fucking boat. Well, having seen *Jaws* way too young, I swam back to shore with that movie's music blaring in my head. The next night we hit a different club, and out of nowhere, Ian decided, like he always did, that on his return to Scotland, he was going to hit on my best female friend, Jodie, who I had befriended very early in my teenage years. Although we had vowed it would never get sexual between us, we had hit the sack once when we were blitzed but woke up to decide it wasn't worth losing our friendship over, as we really were close.

Ian was always the golden child between us in the physical looks department and usually managed to score with his potential targets. He really was the asshole bad boy who treated the opposite sex like shit but so many women love. Why, I will never know; the only answer women have given me is that they see it as a challenge to tame them. Fucked up, if you ask me, but yes, nice guys usually finish last and end up heartbroken.

I can't remember who threw the first punch, but this time, he was encroaching on my life and friends, and I wasn't about to back down. After being thrown out of the joint by the bouncers, we moved our brutal battle onto the streets, and after taking some serious punishment, I decided to turn the tables on him once and for all. This was a fight I wasn't going to lose. You could have scratched my eyes out and broken my limbs, but I would keep coming until I scored the very crucial victory with a move he had taught me from his army training: a perfect elbow to his throat that decked him. He never got up. Just like my father before him that dreadful New Year's, I had more than made up for all the years I took a beating from that loser. Neither ever raised a hand to me ever again.

Despite the pain, I was literally on cloud nine, as I had finally got that monkey off my back with an emphatic KO of my army-hardened brother—fucking eh! Time to get another drink to celebrate. But as I walked through the streets, it became apparent that everyone was looking at me. I checked myself to get to the reason of why I was all of a sudden the centre of attention and felt that my T-shirt was wet. I put it down to fight sweat, but upon closer drunken examination, it was my own blood. After quite a while, I found the source: the fucking bastard had pulled his own version of Mike Tyson's legendary ear chomp out of desperation of not wanting to lose. Actually, my brother beat big Mike to it, as it was before the boxing incident happened. It was a version of his army-instilled dirty boxing.

I was rushed sirens blazing to Barcelona, where I was operated on. It was insanely painful, as I was so drunk they couldn't give me any pain meds. When dawn broke on the beautiful Spanish city, I was released with next to no sleep and more importantly next to no money, without a clue as to how the fuck I was going to make it back to our seaside holiday resort. After figuring out how to get back there road-wise, my next challenge was how on earth I was going to get anyone to stop, never mind pick me up, with a huge Spock-style ear dressing and blood-drenched clothes.

Thankfully, after hours of baking in the strong sun, I finally got a ride from a truck driver who took me all the way on the freeway and dropped me off at the turnoff. I fell out of his cab right into a ditch with all the roadkill you could ever imagine. Armed with an attitude of "Fuck, I'm going to kill him," I started my quest to get back to the village. Trust my luck, it was the straightest road on the planet, and after walking for seemingly an eternity in the sweltering midday sun, I finally got to the end of my horizon—only to find the same straight road extended to yet another point on my new horizon. All of a sudden, I started losing my energy. Although I didn't know it at the time, it was my first experience of heat exhaustion.

To this day, I have no clue how I managed to keep going. I guess it was because I had no other choice. Remember, it was before all the Internet gadgets and cellphones we all take for granted these days. I had to break into our apartment, as with my luck, they were all out hunting for me. So my injury put paid to any chance I had with the ladies for the rest of the holiday, but even more annoyingly, it meant I couldn't even go for a swim.

So please, don't believe Abigail's sorry-ass claims. There are a lot of open-to-interpretation subjects woven into her story. Trust me, she has always been a wolf in sheep's clothing. She is concerned with one thing only: publicity for her own vanity.

The surrealism of what was going on in my life was further protracted when I decided to check out the all-consuming Internet. To my amazement, the story was all over the Internet too. My brother-turned-sister didn't stop there; he, sorry *she*, was now on all the major TV news and talk shows, not just in Britain but all over the world, including face-to-face interviews in the North American media. Fucking crazy! She even had her own Wikipedia site. *Wow* is all I can say.

The worse one of all was written in this gay forum based in London by an old classmate of mine I don't remember. He stated that he always had his suspicions that not only was Ian gay but I secretly was too. Enough already, cunt. That's a word I very rarely use and reserve for things or people I want to destroy for being so judgmental to assume crap about me that was so far from the truth, you couldn't even fly there and get there in one lifetime.

It was actually my little brother, Stu, who gave me the heads-up in a mind-altering email, so I did what anyone would do and phoned home. My mum was beside herself. It sounded like she was having the longest panic attack ever. She gave me the goods on how Ian had called her up after his last tour of duty in Afghanistan and said he simply could not face another, from what sounded like PTSD. He went on to open the can of worms that he was born into the wrong sex and as a result had this DNA-driven gender disorder and had to listen to what everything his mind and body had been telling him since he was a wee boy. Put simply, he in every way apart from physical appearance was indeed a female in a man's body.

In a conversation I had with Abigail at a later date, she claimed to have tried to tell my old man years previously (a fact ardently denied by Dad), and that was the reason Dad kicked in the front window of our house in Aberdeen's very rich West End, and not, as I always thought, because I lied about stealing some of his precious booze. So the blame was shifted squarely on him. Abigail said that like most dads of that age, and just like my gay friend Colin's dad in the heated talk when he came out, my old man disowned him, as no son of his could be gay or, like my brother, a chick-with-a-dick transgender. With my old man's old-school upbringing and outlook on everything, he did what he always did and lost it, as he too has a brutal temper.

The whole spectacle brought my folks to their knees. Ian, now Abigail, was all over the news back home. It not only turned my parents into recluses but changed their personalities beyond belief, especially my mum, who became very guarded and withdrawn, a complete reversal of her usual extroverted and gregarious self. Little did I know, this was nothing compared to what was to come. My mum and I know just how remarkably true that song lyric "once bitten, twice shy" really is. Life's cruelest lessons bring fragility, frailty and humility that people who were born with a silver spoon or a horseshoe of luck can never achieve and therefore never truly understand.

To be 110 percent honest, Abigail is a big part of the reason I am not only an admitted homophobe but have even more of a problem with any word that starts with *trans*. There is nothing I or any of my psychiatrists or psychologists can do to mentally change that part of me. People say, "Get over it," but there is something deep inside my psyche from as far back as my childhood that simply won't allow it to this day. What amazes me is that because all these newfound sexual choices are now cool, I am a big bad straight square normal male.

Back to our new baby: as much as I tried to put on a brave, happy face, deep down inside I was in turmoil. As much as I didn't really want another kid, was it really that bad as to wreck our marriage? How could I hold it against the kid, when really it was Carol I despised for taking the biggest decision of anyone's life into her own hands? Like it or not, I was pissed, but I just did the man-up shit. The grandparents were all ecstatic, since this would still be only grandchild number two from both families' offspring.

This time, everyone agreed that Carol's pelvis was simply not capable of normal childbirth. Don't ask me all the girlie nitty-gritty details, but we finally agreed on a September 2003 date for a Caesarean section. My crazy life was moving towards another impossibly unbelievable coincidence. I will never forget that day as long as I live.

There we were, all psyched about our second kid as we drove my top-of-the-range Ford F-150 Lariat, pimped to the nines, down to St. Paul's to usher our newborn into the world. To me, finding out the sex of your baby in advance is like knowing what you are getting as your biggest and best Christmas present. I was on tenterhooks, as to be honest, this time around I really didn't care whether it was a boy or another girl. In truth, I probably favoured another girl, as quite honestly, I felt sorry for my folks having to raise this devilish, mischievous, rebel-without-a-cause Andrew. I was afraid of having to deal with a male mini me. After going to an all-boys' school and being one of three boys, I really wanted to see more of the other team and find out whether Michelle's tomboy nature was going to be repeated.

Finally, we were there at St. Paul's getting all prepped for the birth. I was shown where to go in the OR. Out of my well-developed peripheral vision (a must for every married man when good-looking women are around when you are with your trouble and strife), I saw all these doctors and nurses huddled around television screens watching what looked like a 007 Bond film. I had to completely ignore it somehow, as the urgency of the situation required my complete attention on the task in hand.

Straight up, if I was female, I would go for a Caesarean every time rather than the toil of the so-called natural 40-plus-hour fun-filled drama of the last ordeal. It was quite simply a breeze, but with the same result: a blood-soaked baby who looked like something off a *Carrie* horror flick. I am always amazed how women can find beauty in this hideous creature screaming at the top of its lungs. Get used to it, sucker, as this is the noise you're going to grow to hate more than any other in the history of noises. There she was, another baby girl. After much ado, we decided to name her Iona. Why, I simply can't remember; I think it was Carol's decision.

After a few hours, I wandered back to the Chateau Granville Hotel to tell my folks, who were visiting to greet the new arrival, the miraculous news. The second time around, I was for some reason more concerned about the baby's health. I think it was because one of our close neighbours had such a hard time raising their adorable kid who was stricken with some disease that was a 24/7/365 labour of love. Praise be, Iona was perfect, and as much as I loathed having to go through this all over again, especially as it wasn't my decision, it was impossible not to fall head over heels in love with this bundle of joy God had blessed us with.

Despite my eternal bad luck, when God had to be clutch, he was. It has taken me this long to realize that I have indeed been very fortunate when I absolutely needed to be. I just wish we had our grandparents around the corner rather than on the other side of the Atlantic. It would make parenthood a much easier job.

When I shared the amazing news of Iona's wonderful birth, despite the usual *wow* reaction, I could tell there was something going on behind my parents' smiles. I hardly ever use the word *unbelievable*, but there simply isn't another word that comes close to describing what was to follow. I noticed as soon as I walked in that my folks seemed to be watching the same TV program as the staff in St. Paul's. What gives? Well, you couldn't be a resident of planet Earth if you have never heard of the now infamous numbers 9/11. Yes, that's right: my baby girl Iona was born at 10 a.m. PST on 11 September, pretty much the same time planes were flying into buildings and it seemed like we were on the verge of World War 3.

For everything God giveth, God taketh away. In my mind, for the darkness of every lost soul, Iona and other babies like her born on that terrible day are a symbol of God's light shining brightly through the chaos to enlighten the world as to how far removed we have become as a race from our chosen destiny. I hope this makes sense. It was another example, if I needed one, of just how precious our God-given life is. In a strange twist of fate, it made me forget the circumstances of Iona's conception and love her with all my heart and soul. Although Carol to this day maintains that she did nothing to help this creation along, even my kids don't believe her on that one.

Years later, in another huge family fight, when my oldest daughter, Michelle, decided to drop the bomb, "You didn't even want her, Dad!" I replied with the most genuine answer I could, something like, "Yes, this is true. Actually, I didn't want kids at all way back when—yes, that includes you Michelle—so one was certainly more than enough for me. But ever since Iona was born, I have realized what an incredibly beautiful soul has blessed my life. As such, I have never regretted having another adorable and gorgeous girl. I love her with everything I am as a man, father and human being."

This is no lame-ass get-out-of-jail excuse, just the truth. I wish what happened next never did, because it created a rift that to this day I have yet to repair.

CHAPTER 8

IN SICKNESS AND IN HEALTH

My life wasn't, as you might think, on cruise control. I wish. Instead, it was a supercharged stress-filled thrill ride, working all hours and on call 24/7 to prop up our millionaire lifestyle. But like I said to my boss when I started, I work hard to play harder—something he fully backed me in. We had reclaimed the prestigious Whistler sales area, a particularly important feat given the news that Whistler would host of the upcoming 2010 Winter Olympics. Obviously, things were only going to get more prosperous for both Ecolab and my family.

It was my ideal equation: work my balls off to make as much money as possible, but on my hours away from work, enjoy our newfound wealth to the fullest. The best thing was that my boss was like a few-decades-older version of me. He enjoyed spending his time off on exploits like snowmobiling and riding his Honda Gold Wing on cool road trips.

I had really gotten into snowmobiling myself, or what most call sledding over here. It was a huge adrenalin buzz, as controlling a snowmobile in deep powder is way harder than it looks. I remember my second time out up on Black Tusk, my good gym-rat friend Greg, who had been riding for an eternity, coerced me to try a high-mark, whereby you simply pinned it up a scary steep hill. When you started to lose momentum, you executed an immensely technical 180-degree turn and headed back down at Mach 9 speed. As is usual for me, if you dare me to do something, I will do everything to prove myself worthy. Only problem was, I didn't have a clue what I was doing. After I hit this wind lip, my machine literally bucked me off and crash-landed about 10 feet in front of me. Then it started to roll towards me, and in deep snow, it was damn hard to avoid. It just missed me, but I was left watching my brand-new almost-C$9,000 sled roll down the hill with pieces flying off it.

Even worse was when I went up Callaghan Valley, the site of all the cross-country-skiing and crazy ski-jumping Olympic competitions. It was completely flat light, so even with the yellow lens in my Oakley goggles, I still could hardly see anything, as it ruins any depth perception or definition. That never stopped me; I had this weird skill of using my other four sharpened senses to make up for the lack of vision.

Before I knew what was going on, I was airborne, with no clue where I was going to land. To my misfortune, I was flying over a riverbed, and I landed on the up slope of the opposite bank—thankfully, in soft snow. Only problem was that all that momentum had to go somewhere, and it was to my wrists. I didn't even realize it until I picked up my shovel and started to dig myself out and I felt something was up with my wrists. You guessed it: I had broken both of them. But in the moment, I had no choice but to man-up, as there is no ski patrol in the backcountry to save your sorry ass if you bite off more than you could chew. Try life when you can hardly use both of your hands; not fun, I can tell you. I could still ride my board, though, with casts on both my broken wrists.

You might think fall in a resort town like Whistler would be a downtime, but my street smarts had shown me that if I resisted the huge temptation to slack off but instead went full bore at catching up with all the heavy-duty annual biggest and best maintenance of our equipment, it would pay me back large when the transient workers, tourists and white-gold snow arrived. I had, after all, come to Whistler for the snow, so the more I did now when it was crappy meant more smooth sailing and fresh-powder days for me.

Easily our largest and hardest client to service was Intrawest, which now owned both ski hills, with numerous large and small restaurants dotted all over each mountain. Greg and I were driving up Blackcomb Mountain in my company Jeep Liberty, heading for all the mountain's many restaurants. The dirt road was a mixture of deep mud, dirt and even snow up high, which was super hairy scary—and therefore mega-fun for me, the self-confessed adrenalin junkie. I had ordered all new equipment for all the locations on both mountains and had already completed all of Whistler Mountain's facilities. We had just finished off Blackcomb's biggest accounts in the monstrous Glacier Lodge and Rendezvous restaurants and were driving to pretty much the top of the mountain to redo Horseman Hut.

All of a sudden, my gut started to hurt. It was no time to panic, as driving up a snowy mountaintop road required 110 percent attention. I did everything I could to ignore the pain. The only thing I could think of was that the dreaded duodenal ulcers that had plagued me since my teenage years had somehow returned.

Problem was, the pain didn't go away. In fact, the dull pain only got worse with time. I did the usual guy thing and decided that if I could just ride it out, it would be okay in the end. After something like a fortnight of next to no sleep—as, like all pain, it got way worse at night, when there were no distractions—I relented and went to the doctor, hoping get my little purple pill called Nexium, which seemed to always make my ulcers vanish. Problem was, this pain felt somehow different. It was starting to get sharper, to a point that it would disable me from doing anything apart from curling up in the fetal position that seemed to help alleviate it.

I am not sure why, but Carol had the day off, so she came with me. I think with her nursing background and intimate knowledge of Andrew's don't-whine attitude, she knew deep down something really bad was going on inside me. I was ushered into the office of my favourite doctor, who asked the purpose of my visit. After a stomach exam, she concluded I either had appendicitis, severe IBS or Crohn's/ulcerative colitis. With that, to my total amazement, Carol starting sobbing. I was quite frankly shocked and gave her a big hug, even though I had never even heard of these autoimmune diseases and was totally clueless about their repercussions.

My thought process went: Hey, no worries. If I've never heard of them, they can't be that bad, right? Looking back, that fall day was the real start of my fall from grace. I reassured Carol that we had faced way worse than this in our time together, and it wasn't a big deal. If I only knew then what I know now.

THE HOOD

Before I could blink or think, we were on our way to St. Paul's Hospital for the first of God knows how many abdominal scans to find the cause of my terrible gut pain. Anyone who has had a similar condition will know that the necessary scans are not a like a simple X-ray, MRI or CT scan. They were much more intrusive. I still cringe saying words like *endoscopy*, *colonoscopy* and *enemas*, as in my world, my anal passage was for exit purposes only. This was reinforced by my GI specialist's joking words directed to my wife: "There's no doubt your husband is a typical Scotsman: a tight asshole."

It didn't take them long to rule out everything but the worst-case scenario. I had a disease that I'd never even heard of, which is saying something, as being married to an ER nurse I would always get a blow-by-blow account of her day. The last thing I wanted to hear was the potential consequences of pushing the limits, as I knew better than anyone that as soon as you started worrying about anything like falling or hitting something, you invariably slammed.

Crohn's disease was the verdict. I did what I always do in such a situation: learn everything about this frigging disease, as knowledge carried the power I needed to beat yet another one of life's speed bumps. After researching Crohn's in just about every website on the subject, it soon became very apparent why Carol was crying. This disease was just as horrible as its name sounds. Even though I probably now know almost as much about it as my specialist, it is one of those things that somehow defies words, except maybe a long overdue *why me?* Let's just say if you are like me back then, if you don't know it, you're better off.

I had what is referred to as an autoimmune disorder, which in layman's terminology is a messed-up turbocharged immune system that in some weird way falsely believes it needs to attack your very own body for nonexistent foreign cells. Crohn's was very similar to other autoimmune disorders like arthritis (joints) and MS (nervous system), but Crohn's and ulcerative colitis attack your bowels. All of them are not only very nasty and painful but most importantly incurable.

How on earth had I got such a disease? In fact, it was it passed down by my gran (my mum's mum). She always had a fucked-up gut, but it was never diagnosed and talked about properly. Around 30 percent of cases are contracted this way, so not only was I concerned about myself but crucially my kids developing such a terrible condition. My doctor advised me that my stomach ulcers from my teenage years were probably a precursor of the disease.

I wondered if my lifestyle had anything to do with it. I had piled huge stress on myself basically all my life. I genuinely enjoyed stress-related challenges, especially from my job and sporting accomplishments. A huge but often overlooked source of stress was the fact that we had no family support network to help us out with our kids in Canada. That one is squarely on me. Then there was our location: after countless hours thoroughly researching the disease on the Web, I found that Scotland and then Canada had the highest and second-highest incidence of my newfound disease per head of population in the world.

Like most things, it was probably a combination of all of the above, but hindsight tells me what I believe is the truth: the root cause was not external like food or coming to Canada (which to this day my mother erroneously believes is the answer to my question of *why me?*) but rather internal. I am convinced that my need to constantly push myself beyond what is human in everything I do is the source of the disease in me. When you do that, you bend and even break sometimes, then heal and come back stronger. Unfortunately, it took me too long to realize that sometimes the break doesn't heal. It's kind of like a river and pollution: nature has a way of naturally cleaning the water, but there comes a crucial point when healing cannot occur fast enough, and the river dies forever.

At least I knew what I had and was dealing with. However harsh the disease was, it didn't appear to be life-threatening, like stomach or anal cancer, so I had to count my blessings. That modicum of good news, however, did not bring me any solace when dealing with the tremendous aching pain night after sleepless night. It didn't take long for the consequences of having such a brutal disease to take their toll on everything I did, but most critically my work. Lack of sleep and inability to eat conspired to make me take time off, as I was a walking wreck and a mere shadow of my previous self.

Possibly my biggest concern was not for my health but for my family's financial well-being, as our heavily leveraged empire was built on both our salaries, and even a slight cut in either would make it hard to keep up with the huge mortgage payments. I tried everything to keep working, but it became impossible to cope, so I went on Ecolab's disability plan, which left me with 60 percent of my salary. I tried my best to hide my worries from my family, but I knew that the loss of 40 percent of my salary would make it impossible to prop up our house of cards.

My brain went into overdrive. How the fuck could I make up the difference? Something had to give. I decided we needed to give up our use of the Yaletown apartment and instructed our leasing company to find longer-term tenants. We also sold a couple of our Delta units for a decent profit—but even then, we were still behind the eight ball. I used some of the Delta cash to reno our home in a way that we could rent out the whole of our ground floor, including the girls' bedroom, to significantly improve our cash flow. The smaller rental suite only paid for our resort taxes, which had increased substantially over the years.

To my incredible relief, the rental idea worked. Although not ideal, it would be a stopgap measure to get us through until the doctors figured out what to do with me and got me better. Only problem was, Carol hated giving up part of our family home to strangers, and our arguments started to turn into full-blown battles. She too was not sleeping thanks to the noises downstairs and her worrying over our financial position and my rapidly declining health.

I wish I could describe the pain better than the lame 10-out-of-10 system all hospitals use. It eats at your very soul and core—so much so that the conflict not only takes over your body but dealing with the ever-increasing hurt becomes an unbearable psychological war in deciding what number to apply to it at any given time. A number is just so subjective and comes nowhere near to describing it properly. Was my pain worse today than yesterday, and even more profoundly, do I try everything to rough it out or at what point do you put up the white flag of surrender and pop some painkillers or, as last ditch effort to get rid of it, jump in the car and get even stronger, faster-acting IV painkillers in the Whistler ER. It was an option I despised; it was Carol's place of work and, in my head, somehow sacrosanct.

Picture yourself doubled over in pain and forcing your spouse to return to her place of work after a 10-hour shift to get painkillers. Worse still, sometimes we had to go for an enema to unblock impacted me, as the drugs were slowing and even stopping my gut, further intensifying my soul-sapping pain. Not cool.

As any couple that goes through a similar ordeal will testify, it irrevocably altered our relationship, as our husband–wife deal was now turning into an almost patient–nurse deal. As much as I hated it, for the very first time in my life, I was totally powerless. The pain was insane. I always considered myself a pretty tough bastard who could go toe to toe with anyone who threatened me or my family, but this was beyond anything I had ever encountered. Using willpower to defeat my disease only increased the stress and worsened the pain.

I had gone from a cut 225 pounds of gym beefcake to a 140-pound, skinny, disease-ridden shell of a man. I had developed the gaunt, more-than-chiselled face and sunken cheeks shared by most junkies (another derogatory word I try everything not to use, as it implies loser-ville instead of the real disease we call addiction). I was frail, fragile and feeble—things that did not sit comfortably with me but, again, were totally outside my control. Worse still were the psychological ramifications of not working and being weak on my self-esteem and confidence. I was unrecognizable from the me I had known all my life, and I started to hate myself. My brain was going a million miles an hour, as for the first time I was facing an opponent that wasn't another person. It was in me, a part of me, and I had next to no idea how to defeat it.

I spent almost four months living off the only things that didn't upset my gut—namely chicken noodle soup without the noodles and ice cream and jelly—before my GI specialist scheduled this high-tech scan whereby you swallow what looks like a large vitamin pill but is actually a miniature camera. It takes pictures every second to give a comprehensive internal look at everything from your mouth to your anus. This would help the doctor see the actual location of my ever-expanding ulceration and just how extensive it was.

Sounds simple, but it was an absolute agony for me. The capsule eventually got stuck to the most inflamed portion of my bowel, namely the juncture of my small and large intestine, around what they call the ileocecal valve. It irritated my bowel walls so much that the opening was reduced to a diameter of less than my pinky finger. After yet another excruciatingly painful ER trip, where they managed to get it to pass somehow (believe me, you don't want to know how), I was immediately scheduled for bowel surgery.

The only problem about gaining knowledge of any disease is that you know the consequences of all the possible treatments. Not only was it going to be at least as painful as my tib/fib surgery, it could leave me with a colostomy bag to shit in, something I desperately wanted to avoid. I knew all about that from my Rob, still the only long-lasting great friend outside my family I have told my story to.

Rob also was ultra-athletic and a competitive snowboard coach who had completely trashed his hips with an almost fatal crash jumping off Cafe Cliffs on Blackcomb and landing on a rock band underneath. He almost bled out on Blackcomb and was left with a temporary colostomy bag. He moved to Australia with his wife, Penny, and after a few very brief chats online when I opened up to him about my continuing struggles, he did the same with reciprocal issues like epilepsy and bipolar. Then, suddenly, he disappeared—nothing. About a month passed, and then I got the email I had been dreading. Rob had succumbed to his diseases and committed suicide. I was gutted. Even now, when I am watching or doing any of my snow sports, Rob's face appears in my head. He was quite simply the best natural all-around athlete I have ever had the privilege of calling a really close friend.

Back to my chronic Crohn's: I was prepped for surgery and pleaded with my surgeon to do everything within his power and skill to sew me back up minus any external bag. In reality, I don't think my words were quite that mellow, but as with my fear of possible leg amputation a few years earlier, I was more than terrified. I woke up to easily the worst pain I have ever encountered but nothing hanging off me, just a nasty scar running from my naval halfway down to my groin. Despite the excruciating pain, I was somehow content at having dodged yet another bullet. Thank you, Lord.

Just before I went into surgery, I had a tube inserted into my chest so they could feed me a total liquid diet (TPN). It hurt like a bitch going in and meant I had only ice chips to munch on for almost three weeks. It doesn't sound so bad, but trust me, it was yet another thorn in my side with this literally crappy disease. If you think about it, food is a very social activity, even more so in hospital. Your whole world revolves around it, as despite it being on par with airline food in terms of quality and flavour, those three servings a day are really the only highlight you have in a hospital ward to break up the boredom.

The worst thing, though, was the really intense post-op pain I had to endure. It was even worse than my smashed leg years earlier, and my only escape was a morphine pump that I could press as needed. Trust me—I used and abused it.

Reading the autobiographies of my then-hero Lance Armstrong, *It's Not About the Bike* and *Every Second Counts*, gave me the inspiration that no matter what else this life threw at me, I could, like him, come back from even the worst health problems. By the way, it amazes me that people hadn't figured out the truth behind his victories, but regardless, he wasn't the only one juicing himself up. In truth, they were all doing it, so in my world, you should leave the guy alone to enjoy his amazing recovery from life-threatening cancer (and he has put back so much with his cancer foundation) and his record successes in what I truly believe to be simply the hardest endurance competition on this planet: the Tour de France.

Don't believe me? Grab a flight to Lyon and drive a hired car around Albertville. Then and only then will you understand where I am coming from. Even at my fittest just before I caught Crohn's, with a resting heart rate of 30, I think maybe I could do one or at a stretch two of their 100-to 250-kilometre stages, but day after day for three weeks simply blows my mind. That's almost 3,000 kilometres in only 90 hours, which is just as crazy as it sounds.

When Crohn's kicked in, every time I ended up the St. Paul's ER, the doctors wanted to chuck a bunch of heart drugs down my throat, until Carol informed them of my cycling exploits. It was now my favourite sport but something I would never be that great at, as my heavy-set muscular frame is far from the ideal build, especially for climbing. But hey, I don't care. I love the challenge and pure freedom, with the wind in your hair and awesome views that you never see from a car. I can still hold my own at the race of truth (time trials) and even more so at sprinting, where I rarely lose. If you ever get the chance to watch *The Flying Scotsman*, the biography of Scotland's most celebrated cyclist, Graeme Obree, it highlights both his and my struggle with depression yet unadulterated passion so magnificently.

THE HOOD

What I didn't realize at the time was how my body was starting to become dependent and resistant to the morphine, and how the drug was starting to alter my personality. It was around this time that my severe memory loss kicked in. Although I remember a great deal of what happened, with some real big gaps, the order of events is a whole different story. I do remember doing some pretty stupid things while I was in St. Paul's GI, laced up to the nines on painkillers, like ordering a brand new C$75,000 Audi TT S-model, my dream car. I knew I couldn't afford it, but when you're that messed up on painkillers—which are pretty much the same as their street equivalent coke, crack, heroin or even alcohol—you somehow lose what I like to call logical reality and inhibitions. They're replaced by an overconfident invincibility and a belief that you can do anything without consequences.

Worse still was that because of my incurable illness, I felt I had to look at other possibilities of making my family financially secure. I had no idea of the length and severity my Crohn's curse. It was a very real possibility that I would never return to work, and how was our real estate empire going to survive without my salary? To this day, I simply don't know whether my realtor and supposedly good friend was touting this new hotel complex called Nita Lake Lodge, which was in the planning stages, for my or his own benefit before he left Whistler. Did he knowingly sell me a lemon to fund a very comfortable retirement in his millionaire's row in Victoria? Once again, if I only had the benefit of hindsight, I would have never risked everything we had built up for a one-hit wonder. The risk was way too high even for me. But it sure sounded like the best deal ever. Consider the pros:

1. It was going to be the first high-end boutique hotel in Whistler.
2. It would have its own rail station for the new Rocky Mountaineer train that, as its name proudly proclaimed, took its patrons right through the majestic Rocky Mountains.
3. It would enjoy exquisite views across spectacular Nita Lake.
4. It would be a stone's throw from the finish for all the alpine skiing events for the upcoming Winter Olympics.
5. As my realtor kept repeating, it was exactly this type and timing of development that provided the best appreciation, as history

showed getting in as early as possible was the ticket to making the most profit.

Of course, we soon discovered that the project had its fair share of cons:

1. A wealthy landowner who had a big mansion on Nita Lake decided to challenge the concept in seemingly never-ending cases all the way up to the Supreme Court of Canada to stop the development in its tracks. He only lost at the last minute because the government intervened.

2. The project was plagued by construction problems that substantially increased its build cost (why they don't have quantity surveyors, who are in effect building accountants, in Canada I will never know) and diluted the grandeur of the project.

3. The world was hit with the worst recession since the great depression of the 1900s. As a resort town dependent on people's disposable incomes, Whistler took more than its fair share of the incredible impact.

These unforeseeable factors collaborated to turn the Nita Lake hotel into a huge white elephant.

Looking back, I was no different from this old man Tom I met in the Las Vegas Airport years earlier. I was returning from my second trip down there and waiting for my flight with my family when I spotted him crying his eyes out all by himself on the concourse. I went over to try to comfort him in any way possible. It transpired that Tom had just lost his wife of over 50 years and had decided to drown his grief and sorrow by retracing his steps decades earlier where he and his beloved wife were married. Just audible above his sobbing, he told me he had got suckered by the palatial ambiance and free alcohol delivered by gorgeous waitresses, and before he could blink, in typical Lost Wages fashion, he had managed gamble away their entire estate on the blackjack tables. I now realize that the only difference between us was that my gamble was based on the somehow more socially accepted real estate tables. My courage was not fueled by alcohol but rather my new prescription drugs, especially the powerful painkillers.

As if I needed proof of their strength, artificial high and inherent boost to risk-taking, my daughter Michelle decided to experiment with some of my huge stockpile of pills. Fuelled by oxycodone (a drug I was addicted to for over 12 years), she decided to go out on her mountain bike and ride things she had never even attempted before. The drugs were like an invincibility cloak.

Armed with those drugs and my track record in real estate, plus a desperation to set us up for life, I took this enormous risk of buying not just one but three of the best suites in the complex for over C$1.5 million. For reasons I will never fathom, it seemed to make perfect sense at the time. I still am absolutely amazed that I and more importantly Carol couldn't see the red flags, as she had the clarity of a non-drug-infested brain. In fairness, I'm sure she would say there wasn't any telling me anything back then, an argument I have no answer to. I inked that deal out of my face on morphine in hospital. Now maybe you see why I have a major problem with any medical professional writing these prescriptions without proper knowledge of a patient's circumstances.

Surviving day to day took everything in me. The pure physical pain meant I couldn't sleep, eat or think. It takes you over, just like an evil demon does in possession. Crohn's disease did this to my life. It was part of my every thought, and no one could see the scars it was creating, only my ever-thinning appearance. I was now around 100 pounds lighter than I was before contracting the disease. It was like a silent assassin.

Or perhaps, as more and more people were starting to imply, it was no longer Crohn's disease that fueled my need for painkillers, as tests and scans suggested that the removal of 25 centimetres of my inflamed small and large intestine had got rid of most of the ulceration. Had I through no fault of my own become chemically dependent on these painkillers? Who really cared how it started; I was no different from any other common drug addict. All I knew was I was still incredibly sore, and something must have been causing it, because I knew I wasn't making anything up. I was still in fucking pain.

A wasted decade later, I finally figured out what was happening to me. It was a very rare and dangerous complication of Crohn's disease whereby the disease causes ulceration and inflammation in the gut that is so painful, the patient needs powerful drugs for the pain, but the side effects of the drugs bring their own pain. They cause the bowels to go into an almost emergency stop, as anyone who has taken any of these highly addictive painkillers can attest. This slowing of the gut causes its own pain from constipation, which believe me, in its extreme form, is almost as painful as the Crohn's disease pain the medications are trying to relieve.

I will save you the grotesque details and a blow-by-blow account. Suffice to say I couldn't count the number of times that, after getting my painkillers in the Whistler ER, I had to suffer through terrible enemas because I was so impacted with shit I was totally blocked. That in itself is a very dangerous medical condition. It was a vicious cycle called *narcotic gut* that goes something like this:

> Chron's disease → pain from ulceration and inflammation of your bowels → take painkillers to get rid of the immediate pain for 4 to 6 hours → slowing or complete stoppage of your bowels → constipation pain, so more painkillers to get rid of that pain and/or make the cleaning flush of your gut bearable, as sometimes that pain can be just as bad and even worse than the initial Crohn's pain.

Even when you completely remove the Crohn's disease from the extremely painful cycle above, you still get caught in this extremely painful condition where the painkillers become not only the cure of your pain but the cause of it.

The astonishingly real *Intervention* TV program is where I finally found out for myself that coming down from painkillers, especially oxycodone, can cause intense stomach cramps. It is still unbelievable to me that none of my so-called medical specialists, including GPs, ER doctors, GI guys, pain experts, rheumatologists, blood/testosterone dudes, naturopaths, Chinese acupuncturists and herbalists never told me about this. I only know now because of a TV show.

Unlike what all the juicy gossip merchants were touting—that I was just taking these drugs to get my fix—to my knowledge, I never ever took these drugs to get high. As a self-confessed control freak, and after what I did to my old man and my brother years earlier, I was scared to lose control of myself, regardless of what the fix is. I inadvertently became chemically dependent or addicted to painkillers because of the brutally painful cycle of narcotic gut.

I was going nowhere with my original GI guy, so I switched to one of his colleagues who eventually suggested that narcotic gut could indeed be the reason for my pain. After my long, traumatic and tragic road through this very real and dangerous complication, he shared with me that most patients with this condition commit suicide. I hope by now that you can see how this can take over a person's life. Suicide may feel like the only way to break the brutally painful, depressing and ultimately life-threatening cycle. He suggested, and I immediately agreed to, an intervention of sorts whereby I was admitted to St. Paul's and clinically supervised by my GI and pain specialist (the latter of whom I squarely blame for so many of my trials and tribulations) over a 10-day period.

It was one of the most excruciatingly painful things I have ever been through in my life. Slowly but surely, they reduced my painkillers, until by the end I was taking none. I knew it was going to fucking kill me, so as a backup plan, I took a small amount of my own stash in with me. When everyone refused me my much-needed pain relief, I went through to the washroom and took my oxycodone, which was for me the best longer-acting painkiller. Believe me, I only took them when the pain was so out of control I could no longer bear it. From all my sporting achievements and accidents over the years, I knew pain well, and I had developed some cool strategies to deal with it. But even armed with my very high pain tolerance, this was a pain that no man or women could stand.

When I was finally released from my agony after about a week, I was wrongfully thought to be cured and drug-free—clean. If you know anything about narcotic gut and drug addiction, even the very small amounts of painkillers I needed to take were enough to either keep the pain cycle going or continue my ever-growing chemical dependency. As much as I hate to admit it, as I thought I could never be that stupid, weak or lame, I ultimately became a drug addict.

Regardless of the cause, I was in effect no different from a common drug addict, no better than the alcoholics and pill poppers and crack addicts, people who range from shelf filers in our supermarkets to the CEOs of major companies and even high-ranking politicians right down to the street people getting their fix through needles, straws, pipes or whatever in the dirty alleyways on the dark side of towns and cities worldwide. Can we not all wake up and realize these legal and therefore somehow legit drugs (because they are prescribed by medical professionals) are every bit as dangerous and life-threatening as the medical conditions they are prescribed to aid? Prescription drugs have become the new street drugs, and until the providers of these substances realize the potentially disastrous consequences of their actions, we will continue to deal with their ramifications—possibly the most widespread, desperately sad, debilitating, demoralizing and defeating disease of them all, drug addiction in all its forms. The cure had become its own causation.

CHAPTER 9

SUICIDE IS PAINLESS

Have you ever had so many thoughts in your head, it's like constant feedback? Everything moves so fast, you somehow seem to be in slow motion. All your life experiences—good, bad and everything in between—flash past you, and apart from some key words and memories, they jump out at you for a millisecond and they're gone. You are numb on every level possible, and no matter how hard you try to ignore it, one loud voice somehow drowns out all the static: the one that tells you life is simply not worth living anymore.

You are convinced you've battled your hardest to defeat your army of demons, but no matter what you do, you simply can't win and have to raise the white flag. You have tried your best to right your wrongs, but nothing or no one will accept your heartfelt apologies or grant you the forgiveness you so desperately crave. You are so tired, but you can't sleep from all the flashbacks bombarding you. The harder you try to switch them off, the worse they get.

You are so hungry but can't eat, because you have no money to buy food or your emotional turmoil somehow makes your appetite insignificant. Your gut is so sore from the emotional crisis it has tied your insides into painful knots that no matter how hard you try, you can't untie. Possibly worst of all, you are so beaten and broken, you have no motivation. You can't move and just want to be still and sink into what feels like a self-inflicted concussion.

Even walking is hard, because it requires thought and effort. You are living off fumes or so numb from the cocktail of prescription painkillers, anti-anxiety/PTSD medications and antidepressants you don't even know how you are moving. Every step feels like climbing Everest.

The only other time I can remember visiting this place was when I was doing sports. You are so dead physically, you have to tap into your emotional, mental and spiritual strength to get you through. This was the case when I competed in my first-ever Test of Metal mountain-bike race, back when I was a 225-pound gym rat and my friend challenged me with "I bet you could never do that." I had to follow up just to prove her wrong. After months of training religiously and recreating the race in sections, especially the dreaded nine-mile hill I would kill myself climbing numerous times at night after work, I knew it was going to be my biggest hurdle, as my God-given physique was never meant for all-out cardio tests like hill climbing.

It wasn't until I actually lined up for the big race that I noticed I looked very different from my pencil-thin-upper-body competitors. To say climbing after two-plus hours of almost all-out effort was considerably harder than my hill repeats is a gigantic understatement. I had to work so damn hard, as I was put at the very back of the pack at the start and had to walk sections I could ride with ease because of the unavoidable bottlenecks going into the narrower single-track as 700-plus riders tried to funnel into a trail no wider than one rider at a time could go. As such, I had to ride the remaining sections at all-out effort or I was going to miss the two-hour time cut-off just before the intimidating nine-mile hill.

I got there just in time, but my legs were so burnt by then, and it was so hot outside, that I simply did not know whether I was strong enough inside to get up there this time. Armed with only a water bottle of flat Coke and a half-melted Snickers bar, I started the climb. It wasn't long before my head started playing games with me, very similar to the ones it plays when you don't know whether you are strong enough to face life's never-ending game of snakes and ladders. Leaner, less muscle-bound athletes passed me like I was standing still, although I was giving it all I had. At the other end of the physical and mental pain threshold, other competitors were giving up in droves and either walking or riding past me the opposite way to quit. Absolutely every single part of my brain—the devil in my head, if you like—was pleading with me to do the same, with phrases like, *You gave it a good shot, but this just isn't you* or *You tried your hardest, and there is no smear on your character if you are smart and quit while you're ahead.*"

Being passed by a one-legged rider—Phil Chew, one of the most inspiring, physically gifted and talented disabled athletes I have ever had the privilege of knowing—didn't give me any solace, so at that, even though I had no drinks left and I couldn't move my tongue in my mouth I was so dehydrated, I somehow dug deep. My pride kicked in, and I found the strength to pass Phil on the last steep grade of the hill and eventually make it to near the very top, where there was a water station.

I downed a whole pitcher of water, to the disgust of my competitors. Although I am very seldom like this, there are times when you have to be selfish. Your needs have to come before everyone else's.

After over an hour of brutal climbing, I finally made it to the top of the hideous nine-mile hill climb. Little did I know that in less than an hour, I was going to be right back in the same position, as after a long, fun and pretty technical downhill on the gnarly Powerhouse Plunge trail (as it had been raining hard the whole week prior to the race, making the wet roots and rocks very slick), my bike-handling skills ensured I caught back up and passed many of the more roadie/tri-athlete types who could only run down the technical sections of the trail, something I reckon should be a disqualification. Regardless, I could feel my legs cramping so bad that despite all my many years in so many equally gruelling sporting arenas, I really started to question not only my resolve but my pure physical limitations, and whether I would be able to complete the last, comparatively easy section called Crumpit Woods.

Anyone riding this section will tell you that apart from two semi-long uphill sections at the start and in the middle, it really isn't very challenging. It was a combination of my legs having nothing left and, possibly more importantly, my brain was bonking so bad I had gone into a zone of numbness similar to the one present in my many suicide attempts. I could no longer control myself or my bike. I tell no lie, it felt like I was riding a mountain bike for the first time as I clumsily barrelled into almost every single obstacle on the trail. I ended up doing the only thing left to me: I swallowed my pride and walked some of the sections that I would normally hammer through.

After all was said and done, I crossed the finish line with the rubber side down and maintained my never-ever-quit record on any sporting challenge or life hurdle. After over four and half hours of pure, unadulterated pain, I was pleased by the fact that I managed to finish and prove everyone wrong. But I was so spent I could not think, speak or do anything for hours—no, days—after the race.

Although I vowed I would never subject myself to that torture again, I went back, partly to prove to myself that it wasn't a fluke, but also to improve my time, as I knew I could have done better if I'd known what was coming. I did improve it, by well over 40 minutes, but that was still almost a full hour behind the top racers' times, which to this day I simply marvel at. This experience was so similar to the perceived escape from sheer pain that is suicide but more on a physical level. Instead of quitting by getting off your bike, you quit by drowning yourself in a bath, walking in front of cars, jumping off a building or bridge, cutting, hanging, switching on the car fumes or my chosen path, swallowing a large amount of pills to escape the intense emotional and mental pain you feel when you can no longer deal with anything anymore.

The only other way I know to explain this to non-sporty types is when you have too many windows open on your computer and all of a sudden everything freezes, then crashes. You are left hoping a simple ctrl–alt– delete or reboot by unplugging will be the solution, as it has so many times in the past. This time it doesn't work, and the computer goes into a state that only an IT professional can fix.

I simply don't have a clue whether other people have been pushed beyond what is humane to arrive at this point or not. Even getting out of bed is a like a monumental mountain that seems insurmountable, never mind actually leaving the house. You can't handle any more input— positive, negative or anywhere in between. You know emotions ranging from wanting to break someone's face to uncontrollable sobbing could come at any minute if you do leave the safety of your home. When you try to see the positive reasons to keep on living, everything is wrong. You start to believe stupid theories like everyone is against you and wants to hurt you—physically, mentally, emotionally and spiritually—through their words and actions.

THE HOOD

It's almost like your haters have found a voodoo doll, so they undo everything you have struggled to do to help not only yourself but others to feel better, do better and live better. And although you keep telling yourself things like *What doesn't kill you makes you stronger* and *Sticks and stones may break my bones but words will never hurt me*, they don't offer any respite from the feeling that you are slowly but surely drowning, and there is no one to save you.

My old dear maintains that everyone has indeed been to this place. We all have our stories that include such depths of depravity. But it is these very moments that, if you let them, can define your very being. If indeed everyone has faced the same thought that life isn't worth living anymore, how can you escape it? Are you strong enough to live? Or, even worse, are you strong enough to kill yourself? Why do I still feel so alone, stranded in hell with no way out? When the advantages of living are overshadowed by the advantages of not having to fight anymore because you haven't got any more strength to fight and are overpowered by all the advantages of making the pain go away in a simple, swift act of suicide, you keep asking yourself things like:

1. Why me?
2. What have I done this to deserve this?
3. When will this end?
4. Out of all the darkness, is there really going to be a silver lining this time?

You try so hard to tell yourself you have been worse or there are people in this world who are facing way more powerful challenges than you ever have or will, but even that doesn't give you any comfort. Your brain just spits out all the positive self-talk. It's like the harder you try, the harder the bad thoughts fight back until you are so tired, beaten and broken you simply have to cave; you have nothing left inside.

I ask myself, am I so weak? Have other people faced this, and if so, have they faced it as many times I have? I simply have no more answers as to why I keep arriving at this position. Is it my fault? Is it just bad luck? Or is it something I don't understand yet? I have no more answers; maybe some questions in this life do not have an answer. Somehow, I both care and don't care at the same time.

At times like this, you make even less sense than you usually do. So just as your stay-positive-at-all-costs defence mechanism starts to crumble, all of a sudden, all the negative thoughts flood in, like the following:

1. You're a grade-A asshole.
2. You're a deadbeat dad who dragged his whole family to places no one should ever have to bear.
3. You're the fucking tool of all time for pissing away every single penny of your C$2 million.

These hit you like a vicious uppercut and knock you on your ass time and time again, as you try in vain to pull yourself off the canvas and out of the ultimate depressed state you have now set up in camp in.

My only defence in such times of real desperation is probably the most important document I have ever received from a relative stranger. During my worst times in Yaletown, and after my eviction from there, followed by time in cheap hotels and then on the street, I found someone who to this day has had more of a profound impact on my life than anyone else, including my own family and friends. Her name was Celia Laval, and she was a free psychologist who took me under her wing in my darkest hours, while I was still attending a daily drop-in drug rehabilitation in Vancouver's downtown Eastside. She was a diminutive French Canadian female whose words honestly kept and continue to keep me alive, and I still to this day turn to her words when I honestly don't know if I can survive this all over again.

Like every good thing in my life, her lifeline of free counselling sessions had to end. Once she had finished her training, she moved into a fully paid private practice that I could not afford. The document in question was a two-page letter that she was in no way required to write. It was like an extension of her sweetheart personality that was filled by empathy, realism and, most importantly, the deeply felt love (on a purely a friend-helping-you level) she seemed to have for me. It does not happen very often, but put simply, sometimes someone's actions leave you speechless. Celia and the following letter represent one of those times in my life:

THE HOOD

October 27, 2009
Dear Andrew:

We've been working together only since July, and here are some thoughts as we near the end of our time together. As I sat down to write this, the phrase "test your mettle" was running through my head. It made me look up what *mettle* actually means. According to online Webster dictionary, it's "the quality of character or temperament; especially high quality of character; spirit; courage; ardour." Wow! Andrew, your mettle has truly been tested, and not just in the mountain biking arena. I imagine that the definition of "mettle" sums up a lot of what you have had to draw upon to withstand the onslaught of suicidal thinking and being in a high crisis situation. You have endured extreme levels of physical pain, mental pain and emotional pain. From what I understand, the intensity of that pain, and the different ways those kinds of pain worked together, have been incredibly brutal. To kind of sum it up, you have done the following:

1. Survived big-time pain, loss, crisis
2. Faced some of your worst nightmares
3. In the midst of it all, smiled at strangers, dressed your best, helped others, gone dancing!
4. Despite the tremendous burden involved, taken necessary action to move forward
5. Kept breathing one day/moment at a time
   Those are the reasons you are a hero in my books.

I wonder if your mettle and your will to survive have surprised even you. I mean, you have had your mettle tested in different ways before, but not like this! I would venture to say that most people have not had to endure so many stressors in so many areas of their lives, simultaneously. I wonder if you could have predicted all that has come out of these painful experiences.

Here are some questions that I wonder about for you to think about if they fit for you:

1. Have you found capacities in yourself that you didn't expect?

2. What new knowledge do you have about your own ability to handle the big trouble of life? How might these resources be of benefit to you in the future?

3. Have you uncovered new purposes and commitments as anchor points for your life? Including absolute faith in yourself and even in a higher power there helping you out?

From my perspective it seems that you have accessed new knowledge of yourself, new resources, and new understandings of compassion, new spiritual resources, new values, and new ideas. What do you think? I also wonder how this new stuff will affect you in the future, and who will benefit from some of this stuff.

I don't want you to think that I am trivializing or belittling the pain that you have experienced and the huge challenges that you still face by trying to put a positive spin on it all. However, I want you to know that I hold hope for you because of all the evidence I have seen of your mettle. I picture you shouting something like "bring it on" as you ascend an impossible mountain in the mountain bike Test of Metal race you described, especially the nine-mile hill. In my opinion, that same spirit is very much alive and well today, and in fact, I believe it has kept you alive despite huge adversity.

I believe that suicidal thinking can be powerful, sneaky, and full of alluring lies. It's a liar if it tells you no one cares, because obviously your girls do. I am personally very, very glad that you have been able to withstand its attacks so many, many, many, many times and taken action to diminish its power. When things get tough, and problems happen, suicidal thinking can get right in there. I hope you continue to see it for what it is. In my opinion, you have quite a few cool ways of handling the pain, either letting it wash over you (and curling up into a ball), fighting it out with music, relaxing into a hot bath, going to your happy place or calling the crisis line or mental health emergency line if need be. I hope you continue to use those and other ways to stand up to the force of that suicidal thinking, because I believe it is incredibly important for you and your girls.

In closing, if things get tough, I encourage you to invoke your own Quiet Strength and soak in your own words that you told me before this whole eviction thing went down:

1. "Fuck you, I'm a survivor."
2. "Money can't buy character."
3. "Doesn't matter how many times a man falls, rather how many times he rises."

These words are truer now than ever

Yours sincerely,

Your friend

Celia

How many times that letter has saved my life, I simply don't know. Way too many for one lifetime. It amazes me, but even going through the painful process of typing the letter into this Word format in my oh-so-slow and somewhat pathetic two-finger typing technique has again brought me back from the brink—from the no-hope fog I was feeling only a few hours earlier. That's even more proof, if anyone needed it, that the pen is mightier than the sword.

The first time I thought of committing suicide was very early in my life. To be honest, I had totally forgotten about until, on my recent trip back to my hometown of Aberdeen, my younger brother Stu reminded me. It was my first big school test that potentially was going to affect the rest of my life, my O Grades in grade 11. If it was going to go the way of my usual school tests, I would be lucky to pass any of them.

The only way around it, I thought at the time, was to either kill myself or get hurt so badly that I wouldn't have to sit them. I planned to jump out of my bedroom window, which would at the very least break my legs if not do more damage. The only reason I didn't go through with it wasn't lack of courage, but rather, I couldn't get over the thought that I might end up a paraplegic. That scared me way more than dying. I truly have never feared death. Why, I don't really know. Something happening to me that I had to live with—something I just couldn't handle, like the loss of a limb or a loved one—is way more frightening than death will ever be.

I thought I'd have no need to ever go back to that darkest of all places in my grey matter. Little did I know, I would find much more devastating snakes to fall down to put me back to where the black thoughts would be magnified to a point where I actually believed all the lies that suicide offers. It absolutely amazed me. The onslaught of negative thoughts are somehow amplified to a point where it's like having many different boomboxes playing different songs all at the same time, and they are playing the most depressing songs ever, like Simple Plan's "Untitled," Jeff Buckley's amazing "Hallelujah," Pink Floyd's "The Wall," Tracy Chapman's self-titled first album … you get the picture. Despite your best efforts, all of them somehow get past your psychological defences and eat you up from the inside out.

The next time I seriously considered suicide was when Carol and I had our last fight and I was forced into living out of the investments I still had at the Delta Village Suites in Whistler. I wasn't stupid. Whistler is a relatively small town, and I knew that our marriage breakdown was already public knowledge. Everyone who was anyone was waiting with bated breath for the thrilling grand finale, which we handed to all the haters on a silver plate. The vultures ate up every single morsel and licked their lips in satisfaction afterwards. We all now seem to get off on other people's misfortune in a way that makes us feel better about ourselves and our life. Quite how this works is still a mystery to me, because I honestly have never ever done that, even with my worst enemies. I get off on my own successes rather than on other people's miseries.

All of a sudden, I had lost pretty much every material possession, except my beloved pimped-out red Toyota Tacoma TRD truck (little did I know, it was going to follow the way of everything else, and I was going to lose that also in the not-too-distant future). Thankfully, common sense prevailed, as there was no way in hell I was going to let the gossip merchants have their way. I figured that getting out of Dodge was a better solution, and I would revisit the topic wherever I ended up.

To backtrack, I had intentionally done an expensive redesign of our downstairs and garage-entry door so we could, if needed, rent out the whole lower floor of our Whistler townhome. Problem was, I didn't take into account that a woman's home is her castle. Carol and I would fight like cats and dogs over the noises that kept her awake at night. Without that rental option, and with my ever-failing health, we had no choice but to sell our dream home and move to a rental house in Squamish to retreat and regroup.

Unfortunately, Carol still treated me like a no-good douche-bag drug addict, and in fairness, that's what I was—but she didn't understand that it was not a lack of willpower but a very real disease that can creep up on absolutely any and every human being on this planet. As my new psychiatrist put it so clearly, it's no different from Crohn's disease or a heart problem. You simply cannot fix it on your own, and when you try, that usually only fans the flames.

This is when I said "fuck it" to her and all my haters. You don't believe me that I need it for the pain? I'll go into hospital as part of the planned intervention. But unfortunately, that didn't work. The vicious cycle of narcotic gut started all over again, with a pill here and there until I was right back where I started. The body builds up a resistance to the drugs and needs more and more to make them work. Like it or not, I had either relapsed or maybe never got clean in the first place.

So here I was, in a town I didn't want to be in the first place, with the seemingly never-ending rain which earned Squamish the nickname *Squish*. When it snows in Whistler, it generally rains in Squamish. It's beside the water and at a lower elevation than its resort neighbour, meaning I got soaked every time I went out on my road or more usually mountain bike, as I hate riding the road in the wet. My disease had turned me into the kind of house husband I hated so much. My old dear always told me the person who brought home the bacon was the one with the power, and as usual, she was right.

This was not lost on Carol, who tried everything in her power to become the one who wore the trousers. With my old-school upbringing, I could not and never would let that happen. I remember Fraser Fyfe, Carol's dad, way back when I told him it is a crew that runs a ship, replying, "Yes, but there always has to be a captain," inferring it was the guy's place to be the head of the household. I only partly believed that, but the control freak part of my brain did almost subconsciously.

On clear days, I would pop a few pills, jump on my Trek Madonne road bike, ride the mainly uphill 50-plus kilometres to Whistler and crash in our old house's suite. Then I would ride back the next day. It was a place where I could just be myself and not do anything but what I wanted to do. I didn't have to worry about all the innuendos and fights that our relationship had become. In hindsight, it signified independence, freedom and ultimately the inner peace I sought after. Something had to give, and it did in the most dramatic fashion.

What I am going to tell you next is something I know most of you simply won't comprehend. You can't unless you have been there. It will probably make you hate me, stop reading and return my book to the store in disgust. In truth, it disgusts me more than it ever will anyone else. It is still easily the worst memory of all, and believe me, I have some dark, scary skeletons in my closet.

After enduring so many fights in Squamish, I had no option but to move out. I went to live in the one-bedroom suite in our old house in Whistler, which we decided to rent off the new owners. I simply had no choice.

For reasons I to this day don't understand, Carol decided to follow me. She was going to give up the Squamish rental and move back in with me, which I knew was a massive mistake. In less than a month, my horrible premonition had come true.

I had gone to the interior for a mountain bike competition with Michelle and a few members of the Epic Riders team. When I returned, Carol had decided to move back in and totally redesign the interior of my tiny 600-foot apartment, even though I had asked her to leave me alone. She had also moved all my pills, which by now I needed 24/7, as my body and brain had become chemically dependent on them.

I lost it, and despite my upbringing that hammered into me to treat women with the utmost respect, I wrestled with her when she came home that night after work. I told her to leave and get out of my life, because it was over, done, completely *finito*. I could no longer deal with her derogatory remarks about how much of a loser I had become.

What happened that night troubles me more than I can say. For the first and only time in my life, I physically hurt not only a woman but the very woman who had been there for me through all my highs and too many lows throughout my life's journey. My memories of what exactly happened that night are vague, but although I never hit her, we had a very real physical fight—a brutal wrestling match as I tried to physically expel her from my life once and for all. It got out of control and left me with only one option: move out and try to move on.

When you are a drug addict, as I had become, you transform into a monstrous beast. You will do anything and everything to get your fix, and if anyone gets in your way, you will go through them to get your drug of choice. I hate myself to this day for what happened that night. There aren't words to express my deepest regret and sorrow at hurting Carol and my kids, who witnessed this entire dramatic and traumatic event. Fuck, how low can you go, Andrew? Shit, here come the tears again. This is easily the hardest thing I have to deal with mentally, and it scares me so much I still have found no answer, except that I was wrong, and I admit it.

I think this is the fundamental reason neither Carol nor I has had any relationships since that fateful day. The memory is still so strong, I am scared to get close to any other girl, given that I was capable of doing the unthinkable to my soulmate. My only hope is that she and other people can understand it wasn't the real me who did that; it was the very frightening mind-altering drugs that made me into this monster. The drugs somehow bring out and amplify the most evil, darkest side of me.

You know when you have a real bad fight with someone and all you want to do is put a beating on them, but you know you can't or you're in deep shit? Well, the drug-induced rage makes you forget about your logical *I can't*, and you do it anyway. That was the kind of drug addict that I had unintentionally become.

It didn't take the police long to figure out where I went to: the ER to get my fix. This is where drug addiction to painkillers is so hard, as you are never sure at what point you will need those drugs to escape the mounting pain. Was it legit or was it a trick of your mind to convince you that there was a logical reason for taking these drugs—to alleviate the intense pain rather than feed your addiction? As I was getting my IV of morphine, in came two cops with handcuffs to escort me to the local police station and charge me with assault after showing me heartbreaking pictures of Carol and the bruising I had inflicted on her. In fairness, Carol always bruised very easily, but even considering this fact, it sickened me to my very core that I was now in a place that was so desperate, I would nearly kill to get my prescribed poison.

All I can say is that this ordeal stands alone. No matter how hard I try to follow all the experts' advice, I can find no reason for forgiveness, even if I got off all charges in court because she had tried to enter my new home, and therefore it was self-defence. My only solace is that Carol now realizes that the vicious beast was created by these super-powerful drugs rather than an inherent personality trait of my own. Even though I admit I got my old man's fiery, feisty temperament, without the absolute need for these drugs, I would have never crossed that line.

Before I knew what had hit me, and after a very temporary stay in our Delta Village hotel room (which we still owned as part of our real estate portfolio), I had moved to and was living out of our pimped-out Yaletown penthouse pad in the heart of Vancouver. We had acquired it by leveraging our other investments and rented it out mainly to Hollywood North film executives and their casting people. To say I loved the place doesn't come close to describing my serious attachment to this cool penthouse stud pad in the big city. It gave me panoramic views of the downtown core, which was especially eye-catching at night; the water of False Creek and its marina; and over to the snow-capped North Shore mountains.

Whatever you say about Vancouver and its downsides—like homelessness, a stark contrast of immense wealth and poverty, and North America's worst drug problem—it is truly is one of the most beautiful cities I have ever been to. That includes other beauties like Edinburgh, London, Barcelona, Paris, Rome and Athens.

CHAPTER 10

SHE'S OUT OF MY LIFE

Before leaving Whistler, and despite a restraining order not to go within a prescribed distance from Carol's abode, I managed to go back to get Cheyenne and Rori, our other ginger cat. Although the cats were more Carol's thing, it had been my decision to get Cheyenne from the local animal shelter, and I had grown very fond of him also.

I was so messed up by then, I can't even remember which time this was on highway 99—the very road that ushered us to our new home decades earlier—but I do remember it was night-time, and thankfully the pets were not with me. All of a sudden, I was pulled over by the boys in blue—the Squamish RCMP. They forced me head-down onto the tarmac while they searched my vehicle and eventually impounded it. In all the chaos that had become my new reality, I had let the insurance expire only days earlier. A convenient coincidence? I don't think so. I was now a hardened wife-beater criminal, and they were out to get me, pure and simple.

Although I went to the police complaints committee about their excessive use of force, and the timing being within weeks of my assault charge, this was an internal police authority in effect being run by the police for the police. Good luck getting any kind of positive judgment against them. With nothing else to do, I grabbed a cab to the nearest Stagecoach terminal, where I took the bus back to Van, riding in pain, as with the stress and pure anger of what had just happened, I was so freaked out I had stupidly left my painkillers in my truck. It was one of the last times I ever drove my beloved truck before the Toyota credit agency came to take it away.

I wish I could figure out when that was. All I know for sure was that it was early 2010. Thankfully, it didn't happen sooner, as I needed the truck for a couple of trips to Squamish to meet up with my criminal lawyer. Carol, the witch, had decided to press charges. I know I would not have done the same if the roles were reversed. In retrospect, I think Carol did this not only out of spite (and yes, she was more than justified, but again, I could have never done that to someone I loved for 23-plus years) but also, more importantly, to make sure she kept custody of the kids. The sheer dread of getting a criminal record and possibly spending time behind bars scared me more than anything.

Even in my manic state, I made damn sure that I did everything my lawyer told me to. After a few incredibly scary trips to court, the case was thrown out. As Carol had in effect broken into my new Whistler home, I was within my lawful rights to remove her. I just wish I had found another way than through a physical confrontation.

Back in Vancouver, I was living a lie, and although I knew it, the drugs somehow numbed all my worries, leaving me with a feeling that I was immune to everything—most notably mail and never-ending phone calls from creditors. All I could do was isolate myself in my beautiful apartment with my animal friends around me. I had to go to court on the civil divorce side, and yes, the first date went in my favor. Like it or not, I could always kill Carol in pretty much any verbal debate, and the judge sided with my visitation rights. I was allowed to see the girls every two weeks, alternating once in Whistler and once in Vancouver with me.

Only problem was, I had lost my wheels to drive up there to satisfy my end of the bargain, and right afterwards, Carol hired one of the most successful and therefore most expensive divorce lawyers in the province to take me down. In my delusional state, I decided that if I ignored things long enough, they would work themselves out or simply go away somehow. Don't ask me how, though.

I remember listening to M's newly released *Relapse* album along with *MJ* over and over while I tried to figure out if I wanted to remain on this earth any longer. Then completely out of left field, on 25 June, my hero died—killed by his doctor's overzealous use of prescription drugs. His death had a profound effect on me. He had inspired everything in my life, and his music was my soundtrack and my rock every time I hit rock bottom.

I was so upset, I couldn't watch his funeral concert. It took me two years after his death, on its anniversary, to finally watch it. It was like I had just taken the hardest uppercut, round kick, Glasgow kiss (head-butt) ever, and it did what next to no man had ever done: floored me.

I needed to do something to mark the passing of my icon. After much debate on which picture would encapsulate his life and commemorate his passing—it was between his black-and-white tiptoes Billie Jean pose or his last almost Zorro-like one promoting his upcoming concert series in London—I decided on the latter and went to a tattoo parlour on Granville Street that I knew had an artist who could do it justice, as invariably tattoos of people wind up looked nothing like the original picture. I didn't pop any pills that day, as somewhere in my mind, I knew that prescription drugs had killed my idol and I needed the pain to prove how much his death had genuinely impacted my life.

After almost five hours of pure pain, the tattoo was completed—there on my right calf for all the world to see. It couldn't have turned out any better. It was my statement to the world that I couldn't care less what anyone thought of either me or him; he meant everything to me then, now and forever.

Although his fame, wealth and pure talent dwarfed anything in my life, I somehow related to his lifelong struggle with haters who made up shit about him to press all his buttons and get under his skin—all to make him out to be the bad guy, a polarising figure you either loved or hated. That was and still is my life, with way too many very loud haters making up BS about me. After exposure to that sort of thing day in and day out, you started questioning their authenticity, acting out just to satisfy their little minds. It is easier to give them what they want than show them they are so far wrong.

It's called group think: someone pretty much manufactures lies about you based very loosely on tidbits of erroneous information, and before you know it, the rumour becomes a storm in a teacup, especially about those topics that hit the hardest. When the juicy gossip merchants and rumour mills get going, they escalate out of control, like a snowball turning into an avalanche. They gain so much momentum that if you try to stop them, they will envelop you and drag you to your inevitable downfall. All I can say is, for fuck's sake, before you judge and attack me, make damn sure your own house is in order. Humanity should go by the rules of any court case: innocent until proven guilty.

Back in my apartment, the only way out of severe emotional turmoil—no, full-scale mental breakdown—was to eat more pills while watching Michael's remarkable HBO "Live in Bucharest" concert every night in my king-size bed, looking out on Vancouver's downtown skyline with the ever-more-prominent voices in my head asking *Why me?* and telling me life was no longer worth living. It was around this time that I found both Johnny Cash's and John Denver's music. They perfectly described how the love of my life turned cold after so many years together, probably the hardest of all the bitter pills I had to swallow over my life.

How a love so strong could turn into almost hatred was something I could not comprehend. It was such a contrast. I was so used to being in a loving family. Apart from a brief time in university when I was living with a group of guys, this was the first time I had been truly alone without the loving aura only a family around you every day and night can deliver. Twenty-three years of the best and worst years of my life were now in my rear-view mirror, and I was on every level horrendously lonely and hurt beyond belief. If you've ever listened to Barry Manilow's song "Mandy," then you get it. I was the man in that song, and Carol was my Mandy.

I remember sitting for hours on end trying to make sense of how the fuck this fall from grace had happened. Was my new life even worth surviving? The emotional pain was excruciating. Even with my unbearable physical pain from so many injuries and diseases, I now realized that mental and emotional pain took things to a whole new level. There was absolutely no escape from it. It was part of my every breath, deep inside my very being, with time as the only possible healer. Believe me, I was hurting bad, totally gutted, despite my use of all kinds of drugs, painkillers, happy pills, sleeping pills and anxiety pills. A list of drugs as long as my arm were all meant to temporarily ease the pain by numbing my brain.

I had become, for all intents and purposes, a functioning drug addict. In truth, I had been for well over a decade, but with the pure amount of chemicals I was putting in my mouth and through an IV, the "functioning" part was starting to be open to interpretation. The drugs were starting to take a terrible toll on my body and soul. I was now walking the 20 minutes up to St. Paul's for my IV of morphine almost every other night to cure my physical pain and numb my extreme mental and emotional pain.

I had found out by now from my daughters that Carol's dad, Fraser—a guy I didn't have anything in common with but somehow, despite our immense differences, had a decent friendship with back in happier days— was now funding Carol's ridiculously expensive civil lawyer fees, which at a ludicrous C$650 per hour were adding up to the tens of thousands of dollars basically just to fuck me as payback and revenge for leaving her. My folks quite rightly had decided they were not going to grant me the same, instead going back to their tried and tested tough-love equation. They sent me only a fraction of what Carol was spending on civil lawyers. The eventual tally for Carol, if my daughters are correct, was in excess of C$110,000, compared to my almost C$10,000 (some of which was my own personal money from selling my investments). It's no surprise who came out on the winning side. This only fueled my hatred of lawyers and their completely over-hyped professional position, with our hard-earned green paying for their lavish offices and lifestyles.

To get my former father-in-law back for funding this fiasco, I would walk around to the payphones to hide the caller source and call him in the middle of his night, wake him up and then hang up. My everyday thoughts were taken up with how to give at least as good as I got in our bitter love war. It was a triangle of pain and hurt—very sad after all those years of pure love.

In the beginning of my stay in Vancouver, I was like a rock star who had finally found his freedom, and just like the celebrities, with all my drugs on board, I started to live the single life all over again. You have to take into account that Carol and I had gotten together in my early twenties, so I was now hell-bent to party like a superstar to make up for my lost party years. I would pop my prescribed pills, just like most do with alcohol, to give me the buzz I needed to overcome my intensely private, guarded and shy personality. I would put on my pimped-out wardrobe and head to the various nightclubs on Vancouver's' High Street.

Every weekend, I'd go to my favourite club, Gossip, which was less than 10 minutes from my penthouse pad. It had the biggest dance floor for me to bust out my old-school moves and gain the temporary relief dance had always given me to naturally deal with my struggles. Looking back on my clothes back then, I was dressing like a man more than 20 years younger, but to be honest, even when I'm completely sober, I have never accepted this super-judgmental rule that as you age, you need to conform to that decade's rules regarding where you live, your type of house and your brand of car, clothing and gadgets.

In my world, you are only as old as you feel. I was young at heart and hopefully always will be. From listening to music all my life, I could find a beat and rhythm through dance. I had many offers to take some hot girls home, but I just couldn't. Sure, just like my star sign of Scorpio, the most sexual of all the signs of the zodiac, I loved and missed a woman's touch, sex and company more than you will ever know. Yet something within me just wouldn't let me go there. To this day, I find it is impossible to describe. Was it my loyalty to Carol that somehow, even when our love was gone, made me felt guilty about being with another woman?

In a strange twist of fate, I somehow stumbled on this real cute, no hot, girl from the states called Julia. She seemed to have a really chill personality and to like me. If I remember it right, it was a connection that I made on one of the many dating sites like Match or the more sex-orientated ones like Fuckbook. She started talking about coming up to visit me. Yes, I know how dumb can you be?

Late in our marriage, Carol had offered up only rare, bad, predictable and frankly boring sex, because her pussy was as tight as her purse when it came to me, ruining one of the most important parts of a lover's relationship: the physical side. It was not the main or the only reason I left her but a very real reason. Call me shallow, but every man has his needs, especially this very sensual and passionate Scorpio. Throw in the hallucinogenic effects of the drugs, and maybe now you will understand my unbelievably stupid naive quest to have another woman in my life, as to this day, I genuinely miss the touch only a woman can give.

I fell hook, line and sinker for Julia's advances and story. Before I knew what was going on, Julia revealed that although she was American, her dad had taken her to Nigeria, and to get to me, she needed money to buy a flight. Christ, I am so embarrassed to admit this, as to my knowledge my oldest daughter, Michelle, is the only person I have entrusted with this part of my story. As a guy who prides himself on having more than his fair share of common sense and street smarts, it bewilders me how I ever fell for this. It was the fucking drugs. That's my excuse, and I'm sticking to it!

Before I knew WTF was going on, after our middle-of-the-night surreal sexual communications revealing all our deepest and darkest sexual fantasies coming true, I was going up to the nearest Western Union and sending her money to get the fuck out of Africa, totally embroiled in her web of lies to extort an ever-growing cash amount in an attempt to make my sexual dreams real and overcome my desire to have red-hot sex when we eventually got together. I can't remember who in my past warned me of the lure the "golden triangle," a women's vagina, had over us males. All told, over a few months, I had sent "her" (because who really knows what sort of person was really on the other end) over C$10,000 that I desperately needed to pay off my creditors and live.

Yes, I hear you. I have absolutely no defence for this. What an asshole! To no one's surprise, I never got near Julia's body or pussy. I was left in a worsening state of depression and desperation on every level possible. It simply blows my mind how messed up I was then.

At one point, there was a job as a sales rep for the Canadian bicycle company Cervelo available to me. All I needed to do was get my shit together and meet them in Vegas for a face-to-face interview at their booth. Michelle and I had gone to this enormous exhibition of cycling called Interbike for the past couple of years, but because of the shit hitting the fan with our dirty separation, this time I would have to make the trip alone. I knew deep down I could not afford the journey and was in no fit state to make it, but I was clutching at straws.

I packed up my bike and swag and booked the flights, and off I went in my totally space-cadet state, completely convinced that all I had to do was show up and the job was mine. I had already started dipping into my investments outside real estate, like insurance policies, GICs and even my substantial retirement savings. *Hey, fuck it, who cares,* was my attitude. I'd done it once, so I could do it again. I would repay it all. Yeah, right, Andrew!

I arrived in Vegas, which by itself was a minor miracle, as I was packing some heavy-duty prescription drugs. I was out of my box, and for the first time, I got the impression people were starting to notice—either because of my gaunt appearance of around 120 pounds or my out-in-space eyes and actions. I remember cycling back to the hotel every night; I literally had my life in my hands, as I was out to lunch and still don't get how I didn't end up as roadkill. So it comes as no surprise that I didn't get the job and had wasted even more of what little money remained on a wild goose chase.

Back in Vancouver, I would walk around the scenic sea wall and the streets taking in the vibe of the city. I had grown up a city slicker, and as much as I loved the outdoor ambience of Whistler, after almost 15 years I was getting tired of it and found myself driving to the big smoke on an increasingly frequent basis to exercise my need for retail therapy, as I was so exactly the opposite of the typical cheap Scottish stereotype, like Carol and her (and my) old man. I was more like my old dear and loved the temporary buzz spending money can give you. If you know anything about human psychology, it is a very well-known symptom of being depressed.

There comes a point when you are so low, I mean lower than you could ever imagine—desperate, depressed and flat-out lonely. Out of the legions of sayings imparted by my mum, this one stood alone: "If you don't know what to do, do nothing." All I could do was just focus everything on surviving every single second, minute, hour, when every single voice in my head had already thrown in the towel.

I remember it like yesterday. I would unplug the land line, as the only people who would call 24/7 were creditors. I had built a stack of their statements and warnings that "if this isn't paid by such and such the inevitable will happen." It was then I realized my incredible real estate empire was just like the house of cards I had built with their documents on my coffee table. Like any gambler, eventually I had to lose, and that time was now.

Despite my kidding myself that I had thought of every eventuality, and despite the feeling of invincibility drugs gave me, I had gone the same way as the gambler who loses everything in casinos around the world. The house is always the winner in the long term. I had come to the conclusion that the only way out of my fucked-up life was suicide, so I decided to walk around the city in my drug-infested state recording on my retro Sony mini tape recorder. To this day, I haven't had the balls to listen to those tapes. I know it will be very troubling listening.

THE HOOD

I stood on the middle of Lion's Gate Bridge and on my balcony on the 31ˢᵗ floor for hours, asking myself how I could muster up the courage to jump. But just like years earlier, although it might be an unlikely outcome, I could not face life in a wheelchair if I failed to succeed in killing myself. After giving up on the jump, I moved to walking out in front of cars—but again, the thought of surviving such a crash put paid to that potential escape from my painful reality of a life that no one in their right mind could bear. I decided that popping pills was the easiest and cleanest way to commit suicide.

Although I think my brain's self-defence mechanism won't let me access all the details of my suicide attempts, there is one I can remember. I had tearfully said goodbye to my gorgeous dog and best pal, Chi, and my cheeky-ass cat, Rori. I went into my safe, happy place—a hot bath—and after sending a kind of farewell email to my folks and my kids, I popped an insane cocktail of pills. Yet I somehow woke up in the back of an ambulance heading to hospital. I think, all told, I did this half a dozen times, both in and out of water. These were not cries for help, rather a very real death warrant, as in my mind, I was past my expiry date and could no longer face waking up to such a terrible reality each and every day.

I eventually gave up and decided that God didn't think it was my time yet. From there on, I simply isolated myself to my four walls, as I couldn't face the real world anymore. It wasn't long before the inevitable grand finale: Carol's lawyer sent me a warning that Carol had been given the rights to sell my apartment. It's a mystery how this could have happened without anyone consulting me. Carol's lawyer wrongfully claimed that she could no longer afford to pay the mortgage. I was told to keep the place tidy for viewing. I decided to spend money installing two Murphy beds in attempt to pay the mortgage myself through renting out the other rooms, but I never got the chance to.

How do I describe genuinely one of the worst days of my life? Regardless of what my future holds, I will never think of that day without the waterworks starting. It was a Friday, and I went out in the late morning to walk Cheyenne and get my java fix at my local Blenz. I returned around one in the afternoon and was met by a more-than-agitated concierge. He informed me that Carol and her lawyers had been back to court and gained the rights to my home, and I was officially evicted. I don't know how to explain my feelings—everything from the worst anger to deepest shock to purest disbelief that my life could get worse. I was completely dumbfounded. The only possessions left from my multi-millionaire life were now contained in two backpacks and one wheelie bag, along with Cheyenne and the clothes on my back.

You will never truly understand what it means to be evicted to the cold, cruel streets of an urban jungle unless you go through it yourself. Imagine, if you can, coming back from a long hard Friday looking forward to the upcoming weekend with your family. When you arrive at your lovely abode in suburbia, you are met by officials saying you no longer own your home and therefore cannot live there—and just to rub salt in your open wounds, they've had to impound pretty much everything, from your prized toys to the bare necessities. Everywhere you go to undo this massive injustice, you are met with cold, bland, I-don't-give-a-fuck smirks, as your many enemies message you, "I told you I'd get you, bastard. Here's your new life with nothing more than three bags and your pet. See you later, loser!" It was absolute rock bottom.

To this day, it is on par with losing my beautiful golden retriever back in my teenage years. There is a finality to death you can never reverse, and back then, at age 15 and having had Vharie since I was 2 years old, I was completely lost in this world without her. Now maybe you will understand how deeply I love all animals, but especially my canine friends. They are like and mean as much to me as my own children.

Now I had lost the only safety net stopping my decline into nothingness. There was no point crying over spilt milk, as I had no one to blame but myself. To be honest, I still was coming to grips with what Carol was doing to me. It felt like she wasn't going to be happy until I was six feet under.

I could call my folks, but it was too late for them to help me out financially, with the time difference of nine hours between Vancouver and Aberdeen. Time to suck it up and spend my first homeless night of many on the streets. Even being out of my mind with shock and the drugs I shoved in my mouth in the nearby Urban Fare supermarket washroom, I sat in my local coffee shop trying to formulate what was in effect a survival plan. The only thing I could think of was that as much as I hated hanging in my new hood of Yaletown without having a home there anymore, its affluence meant it might be a safer place to crash than the drug-and crime-infested downtown Eastside. There was a gazebo just outside the door of my former apartment that offered some shelter from the crappy wet fall weather that, trust my luck, had arrived in earnest.

Talk about the biggest contrast and irony ever. I had gone from a half-a-million-dollar stud pad in one of Vancouver's most prestigious hoods to sleeping on the streets less than 100 yards from its door. This was the most bitter pill I had ever had to swallow, and it got caught in the back of my throat for a long time afterwards. Thankfully, my time in the school army cadets and more than my fair share of street smarts helped me out, and I decided I needed to schedule my sleep to avoid the frightening times of around 1 a.m. to 6 a.m. That's when the street rats were hunting for morsels of scrap to feed off of and keep themselves alive.

My plight made me think of what it must be like to be an animal in an African safari, where the hunters and the hunted try to outsmart each other and stay alive. With no previous experience of the rules on the streets, if there indeed were any, I knew I would be rich and easy pickings. I had to muster all my strength, courage and common sense if I was going to survive this horrendous ordeal. I popped a few sleeping pills and got a few hours' sleep, if that's what you call it on a park bench. I was like a dog who sleeps with one eye open. I knew I couldn't afford the deep REM sleep, which would leave me vulnerable to attack.

Around midnight, I decided I needed to stay awake for the remaining hours by hitting the only Blenz that was open all night. I followed this new survival routine for a few nights until the inevitable yet unthinkable happened. I had done my trick with the Zopiclone sleeping pills, but by now with so little sleep, I was out on my feet and slept through my watch alarm. I was awakened around 3 a.m. by a street gang kicking and punching me whilst trying to steal what little remained of my life in my luggage. They even tried to pull Cheyenne away from me, as she was probably the most valuable thing I had left.

Although I had won pretty much every fight I got into, I didn't even have a chance to get to my feet. There were simply too many of them, and I was a disease-ridden 100 pounds if that. I somehow went into autopilot and did everything within my power to take their strikes in the least lethal parts of my body. I assumed the fetal position. I also was committed to protecting my dog before anything else, as she had turned into what resembled a wolf and was barking and biting anything she could. This is why, to this day, I tell people that my dog saved my life countless times, but probably most of all this time, as it was her barking that eventually made them split and saved my sorry ass from further brutal abuse.

It was impossible to protect everything. Within minutes, they managed to grab one of my backpacks and flee into the night before someone could call the cops. Although I was beat, sore and bleeding, I knew I had escaped with a "welcome to the ghetto, sucker" warning message from my newfound brethren and foes. Unfortunately, the backpack they stole had my wallet with all my cash, credit cards and, crucially, my Canadian citizenship card and my Canadian and UK passports—in effect, all my ID. I challenge you try to live in our modern world with no money and no ID. It is next to impossible.

I did the only thing I could: called my folks and begged them to help me out with money so I could get a cheap hotel. There was no candy-coating what had just happened. Tough as I think I am, I had to admit it: I was scared. Thankfully, they came through, and I found rooms in this cheap rundown hotel called Bossman's that was just around the corner from St. Paul's, well below my usual three-star-plus accommodations.

We spent a few nights there until Cheyenne snatched my bar of Cadbury milk chocolate while I was sleeping, and as a result, had the worst case of the runs I had ever seen all over the room. I smartly got up and disappeared as quickly as possible. We moved to the Sandman Inn on Davie Street, which Carol had often booked us in when we were a family. It was right in the middle of gay central in Vancouver. It was time to put my homophobic demons away, as I needed to try everything to forget my past. All that was important was how the fuck was I going survive on the streets, as I knew sometime in the not-too-distant future I would back there.

Reality struck very soon. My old man refused use of his credit card, and the front-desk staff started to stalk me for another form of payment, which I quite simply didn't have. I knew something had to give, and as I watched ice hockey on TV, I went through every possible solution. By then, I had spent pretty much all my investments. Because of this, my options were more than limited. I did what I always did: switched off the light, curled into my sweetheart Chi on the floor, and prayed to God for forgiveness for all my sins and to protect both me and my darling on the rough road ahead.

CHAPTER 11

MY PURSUIT OF HAPPINESS

Where do I begin when it comes to my four tours of duty in homelessness, on the streets and in shelters, primarily the Yukon and then the comparably easier time in the upstairs residency in the North Shore shelter? My memory won't let me access the file pertaining to how I ended up in there in the first place. The very last memory I have before waking up from my fog in room 11 of the first-floor Yukon shelter—with my dog, Cheyenne, and a very annoying know-it-all roommate named Pete—is lying outside on the sidewalk of Davie Street after being kicked out of my last cheap hotel, the Sandman just up the road, waiting for the ambulance to pick me up after another suicide attempt.

My father had finally cut off my only revenue source, and my world came crashing down on me yet again, with the hotel manager and his security guards banging on the door to get me the hell out of the room. I remember it like it was yesterday: I had a telephone in one hand and an almost full bottle of liquid morphine in the other, facing the literal life-or-death decision to call the crisis line or down the morphine, with my dog barking her head off, as she could somehow sense the finality of our predicament. I am not sure what happened next. I think I downed a massive dose of morphine and, before it kicked in, called the crisis line in the hope they would take care of Chi. I obviously got kicked out, and if I remember right, my dog was taken to the local shelter. I was locked up in the secure psyche ward of St. Paul's hospital.

To be honest, I only kind of knew what was happening. The memories are so vague, I would be lying if I gave you a blow-by-blow account of my time in there. One thing that stands out is that my usual armour against all things threatening, namely music, was confiscated from me. Time seemed to drag incredibly slowly. I looked around me in the ward constantly trying to figure out why the hell they were holding me there with all these wacked-out crazies. Little did I know that I displayed all the typical characteristics of a drug addict and became verbally abusive to what I felt were my captors. It wasn't long before my antics put me in a place I pray none of you reading this ever visits: the secure locked-down cells located in the back of the ward.

The tiny dull grey cell had a cold hard stone floor, a worse-than-useless super-thin foam mattress that offered pretty much no respite from the frigid concrete floor, and metal bars for a door. It was what I always imagined a jail cell to be like, but the only jail cell I have been in was like a five-star hotel compared to this.

The hardest part to deal with wasn't my physical discomfort but the disturbing screams of my fellow prisoners in the adjacent cells. It lasted all day and all night, driving me even more insane than I already was—and trust me, I was extremely messed up. I went back to my favorite self-help mechanism, namely music, to try not to lose it more than I already had. Three songs in particular I sang over and over:

1. the Corries' adopted Scottish national anthem, "Oh Flower of Scotland," which I had sung with so much passion at the start of the Murrayfield rugby games back in Edinburgh in my youth, a true happy place for me mentally

2. Michael's self-help anthem "Man in the Mirror," with its poignant, no necessary, "If you want to make the world a better place, take a look at yourself and make the change," which truly speaks for itself

3. one of my all-time favourite songs to put me in my happy place, Louis Armstrong's classic "What a Wonderful World," which is why even to this day I hardly ever use the word *wonderful*, as its mention in conversations triggers my worst of all memories: a locked psych ward

THE HOOD

The only relief from this absolute hell was the occasional unlocking of the bars to get some horrible hospital food that actually tasted reasonable because I hadn't eaten real food for so long. All my money was totally gone, and as any hard-core will tell you, drugs somehow quell your appetite. This was yet another cause of my intense Crohn's/IBS pain, which was now seriously requiring painkillers to reduce it from its 11 out of 10 intensity and growing.

I have absolutely no idea how long I stayed in that cell or even the ward—and, possibly more importantly, where the fuck I went to afterwards. All I remember is that when the drug-infested fog cleared, I had been magically transported to room 11 on the first floor of the Yukon homeless shelter with this rather large (in truth, I was now so skinny any normal-sized male dwarfed my drug-ravaged physique) and very annoying roommate, who turned out to be a compulsive gambler named Pete. I don't have a clue how I was still getting my newly preferred fix of liquid morphine, but my pain specialist, Dr. May Ong, was still filling my prescriptions without even seeing me. That's yet another part of the puzzle I have yet to come to grips with.

I would leave the Yukon at 9 a.m., when we had to vacate our rooms, and walk across the Cambie Street Bridge, usually in the pouring rain. I somehow endured the sting of walking right past the doors of my beloved playboy high-end Yaletown apartment and collected the morphine from Urban Fare, my previous local grocery store. To this day, I cannot understand why they would even give this man, a shell of his previous self, these drugs that were killing him from the inside out and leading him down a road that very few ever make it back from. I was so dependent on this chemical that I would literally be shaking and sweating profusely. I had to immediately hit the store's washroom and take a shot under my tongue.

I had been down the very same road with every other painkiller known to man, with wildly different trips—oxycodone, sufentanil, Demerol, hydromorphone pills and now the latter's liquid, which was my main drug of choice because that's what Whistler ER kept giving me in IV form. Previously, I had favored Demerol, but I'd attained such a level of resistance that while I was in Squamish Hospital, the doctor told me that if he increased the dose any further, he would most likely kill me, as my body's automatic breathing mechanism would become so numb I would stop breathing.

Literally within minutes of taking the liquid morphine, my cold sweats and uncontrollable shaking were gone. More importantly, I was in an artificially numbed mental state. In truth, the morphine was really for numbing not the physical pain but the incredibly intense mental and emotional pain I was going through because of all the bad shit I had encountered over the past couple of years. I had started to develop strategies for distracting myself from the physical pain, like box breathing (where you count to a number; my usual is 10 to breath in, then 10 to pause, then 10 to exhale, and finally 10 to pause again), looking at every detail of my surroundings, listening to music, dancing, meditating, having a bath, stretching or curling up in a ball and accessing my happy place.

After the hit of morphine, I appeared to be an almost normally functioning human being. You would have a hard time knowing I had just jacked myself up. Somehow this chemical altered my deepest core thoughts or even changed the very way my thoughts were being conceived. With the possible exception of the sufentanil, because of its greater potency, most of the painkillers didn't eradicate my horrendous past, but on a whole different level stopped me from focusing on the hell I had suffered and was still going through. They replaced these thoughts with an aura of contentment and happiness, almost a dreamlike state, which came with underpinnings that ranged from an "everything is going to be okay" trip to delusions that I was still living the dream of my multi-million-dollar life. This is highlighted by a few lasting memories of my drug-infested initial visit to the Yukon that, to this day, I still have the hardest time trying to comprehend.

I remember one night, I swallowed my usual amount of the morphine, and it somehow warped my thoughts to the point where I honestly believed I still was living at my 1033 Marinaside Crescent address, so I decided to go home. With 100 percent conviction that I was still the owner of my cooler-than-cool penthouse pad, I calmly walked up to the concierge and asked for my keys, as I had lost mine, rather than lost my sanity. To his credit, the concierge who was on that night remained professional throughout and tried his very best to reason with me, as we went way back. But instead of just going back to the Yukon, I was persuaded by my brain that this guy had somehow been bribed by Carol not to let me go home.

I decided to knock on the doors of some old neighbours who were on the ground floor to appeal to them to convince the concierge to let me enter. Suffice to say, that resulted in one of my way-too-many-to-mention police escorts. I found myself in the back of a Vancouver Police Department car wearing handcuffs so tight, they were actually stopping the blood supply to my hands. That is why, to this day I do everything to distract my brain from looking at any emergency service vehicle or personnel—police, fire or ambulance. Their sirens cause flashbacks and trigger some of my worst memories. They convince my brain that I will again end up in one in the not-too-distant future.

Most of my memories are not so detailed. One time, my gut pain seemed so out of control and I was in so much pain that I got the Yukon's front-desk staff to call an ambulance for me so I could get IV pain meds, which somehow worked so much better than the oral liquid or pill form. Unfortunately, by then the word was out that I was a junkie, so I ended up in Vancouver General Hospital with an IV of saline and nothing else all night long. By then, my veins had been so abused by IVs that it took even their IV specialist more than 20 attempts before they found one in my hand—no lie. To this day, I quite honestly can't tell you if I was in real pain or if it was all some form of excuse my brain concocted to get back to my numbed state. My new reality was just too hard a place to stay in for any length of time. I honestly think it was a combination of narcotic gut, IBS/constipation and painful abdominal cramping from withdrawal.

I eventually lost it, and around 6 a.m., I simply left, with the IV still in my arm. I later removed it myself with a rather large loss of blood, as I didn't have the proper medical supplies needed to close an IV site in the communal showers back in the Yukon. Even now, I'm amazed that I could still access my normal common-sense brain throughout, as I soon realized that this source of artificial high was gone. I never again tried to go the IV route.

Another time, after getting my ridiculously small government pension plan cash (C$627 per month), I decided to take a couple of black girls who obviously had a thing for me to dinner at my favorite Yaletown restaurant, the Cactus Club. My loyalty to that place was not founded on the quality of its food but their policy of hiring the hottest waitresses in town. Then I treated the girls to the recently premiered second part of the *Twilight* saga, as I knew it was a chick flick, and I could move in for the kill afterwards. Problem was, I stupidly decided to tell them of my extreme paranoia and that I was more than convinced that everyone in Vancouver was somehow watching every step I took. (My new mental health adversary, complex PTSD, convinces me to this day that I am "the talk of the town"). After various useless attempts to sleep after I got back to the shelter, I decided to do my best werewolf impersonation, ripped off my shirt and ran around the neighborhood in the pouring rain topless—before being picked up by another cop car and deposited back at the shelter.

My rapidly worsening mental state and drug addiction were starting to take a real toll on every single part of me. When I took a larger than usual shot of liquid morphine in the bathroom stall of the Yukon and then more still in my local Blenz on Helmken Street, it took everything within my power to even walk. I always had a thing for this coffee shop, as I had gone there in my time in Yaletown. The owner, Brett, was so nice as to reward my loyalty with the occasional on-the-house cup of tea when I had no money. It had also become my port in the storm of every dreary wet day whilst I was in the Yukon. I stretched out the entire morning every day by walking Cheyenne around the sea wall past Science World and ending up with a pot of tea because it was half the price of my vanilla latte.

It honestly felt that my legs were completely useless, and I had to relearn how to walk one painful step after another in the downpour back across the bridge, where I stopped on the keystone (a good metaphor for where my life was back then) and debated every possible reason for staying on this earth or ending it all by jumping off into the cold water below. I swear, without my dog, Cheyenne, beside me, I would have done it. Looking deep into her eyes, I found the strength to carry on. After only just surviving that ordeal, I sat outside the Starbucks across from the shelter and didn't move until they closed, despite the freezing cold in my rain-soaked clothes. When I managed to get back to my room, I had so little energy I collapsed on the floor until I was awakened by my shocked roommate, Pete, who opened the door who knows how many hours later.

Although it is almost impossible to categorize my terrible memories in a chronological list, I think my worst was easily what I like to call my

THE HOOD

Pursuit of Happiness real-life experience. My birthday is 6 November, and if you want to really understand me intimately, check out the description of my zodiac sign, Scorpio, as it is uncanny how well it describes me. I arrived at the shelter on October 20, with the weather worsening from the fall rainy season that dominates Vancouver from October to April. To ease my troubles, my oldest daughter, Michelle, decided she would ignore my ex's pleas not to come down and see me for my birthday.

After going to see my lifelong icon MJ's marvelous *This Is It* movie for the seventh time in the Tinseltown Theatre, we returned to the Yukon and jumped into the not-so-comfortable but better-than-a-park-bench single bed and tried to get to sleep. The Yukon had very strict rules, like no drugs in the house except those strictly enforced by the front desk. But I wasn't stupid, and my bottle of morphine never left my backpack, which went everywhere with me. The consequences of being caught were something I could not face: namely, being turfed back out on the street, as I was sure they went through the tiny lockers in the rooms during their cleaning times. The other rule was no overnight guests.

Despite my best efforts at hiding my kid under the sheets, the midnight bed check witch caught a glimpse of this extra bump in the bed and quickly sent us outdoors. As you can imagine, the last thing I could ever have wished was for my child to live through a night on the scary streets of Vancouver in the pouring rain. My only option was to take her to my last line of defence: the only all-night Blenz coffee shop on the corner of Burrard and Robson. I packed up the flimsy duvet, and we walked through the rain, with me trying desperately to put a positive spin on the situation.

We eventually reached our destination, and with what little money I had, I purchased a pot of tea and commenced building a shackydoon (a makeshift bed) on the wooden bench seats in the coffee shop so she could bunk down while I stayed awake all night in her defence. It really was our own personal version of the Will Smith film. I still don't understand why they couldn't open a few strategically placed underground rapid transit stations for the homeless at night-time to give them some kind of free shelter; probably because it might draw attention to the scourge our modern-day lifestyle creates. No one is willing to deal with this ever-growing problem. All I can say is, I pray you never have to go through the same ordeal with your own children. It makes you feel like the biggest deadbeat douche dad and worst parent ever. I questioned my own credibility and worth as a father.

That ordeal is actually the last memory I have before I ended up in Richmond's psych ward. Sharon has told me so many other stories that were equally disturbing, like the time I organized a party for my fellow Yukon "friends" with some of the green my father sent over in a hotel room that we trashed. I have absolutely no recollection of it.

I remember some of the Yukon's residents better than my actual experiences there. They ranged from pretty decent people, like my mate, Chris, a gambler who like me stood out like a sore thumb. He too was sucked into spending his winnings on big-bucks branded clothes and kept himself most of the time.

One of the most memorable residents was an older lady, Rowena, a recovering alcoholic who seemed to be in an even worse place than I was. Because of her tales of how many times she had flirted with suicide, I felt an affinity for her. She rekindled my awareness of the magical bond between dogs and people in crisis. Somehow, just stroking Chi made all her tears and fears subside and turned her frown upside down.

The most notable residents were the two Dereks: roommates who were like night and day. The evil one was a tall, white, middle-aged dude who was one of the most deceitful and sneakiest wolves in sheep's clothing I have ever met. That bastard took me to the cleaners with a one-liner that I dumbly fell for, as it mirrored a very similar sentiment my mum had hammered into me: "Don't ever beg, lie or steal from me." I decided to trust him, and my naivety cost me my entire C$6,000-plus iTunes library. I gave him my password when he promised he could hack into iTunes somehow and access all of its rap music, which I wanted not only for myself but also for my oldest daughter.

I am still confused as to how he did it, but he also managed to steal not only all of my pills from behind the front desk but all of my clothes, including my quality mountain-bike wet-weather gear. I was left with nothing but the clothes on my back, which included no waterproof gear except a beige water-resistant Oakley hoodie Michelle had bought me years before.

THE HOOD

The last I heard from Chris about evil Derek was that he ended up in the psych ward himself. Payback, motherfucker (a term I reserve for the lowest scum of the planet, as its literal meaning disgusts me).

The other Derek was the complete opposite in appearance and everything else. He was an elderly black gentleman who, to this day, is one of the nicest, most genuine and most honourable men I have ever had the privilege to meet in my life. He only looked after himself and avoided confrontation until there was no other option, as you had to on occasion stand up for yourself; the consequences of not doing so were far worse than the possible physical or verbal fight threat. After my usual sussing him out with my street smarts, I decided to talk to him, as he seemed like a rare trustworthy type. After a few pleasant chats, he revealed some of his past to me, as he had similarly figured out I wasn't like some of the blood-sucking vultures in there.

It transpired that he was a military person in a small South American country, the name of which eludes my memory for some reason. He had risen through the ranks of the military to a point where he became the president's personal bodyguard. After a rebellion that overthrew his employer, he fled for his life to Canada and had fully utilized his survival skills and training by spending the last decade camping in Stanley Park, Vancouver's version of the more world-famous Central Park in New York. For 10 years, he had been camping and sleeping under the stars with only the raccoons for friendship—a feat that blew my mind and made my however many weeks on the streets look pitiful. It was just him, the animals of the forest, his aging red Ford pickup and his most important belonging, his Bible.

I just could not fathom how anyone could manage to survive and live that way for so long. He was the ultimate urban version of *Survivor* in my books. I always wondered why that TV show never did a city-survival episode; probably because it was too tough. I knew from experience that, as the great Australian naturalist Steve Irwin often stated, it is our fellow humans, not animals, that we need to fear the most.

The impact of Derek's immense hardship was evident in his physique. He was riddled with very noticeable arthritis. But even if I didn't genuinely like him as much as I did, he was one of the very few guys I would never ever challenge, as he knew his shit when it came to fighting on any level, be it physical, verbal or whatever. He was like a Gandalf or Professor Dumbledore out of *Harry Potter* to me. This old man taught me self-defence moves that I was glad to accept at the time but now almost wish I could unlearn, as this combined with my extensive martial arts and my brother's British paratrooper, SAS and French Foreign Legion techniques mean I have to be extremely careful not to land myself in prison.

Derek shared my passion for music, and we traded CDs and DVDs. He would play me Bob Marley's "Redemption Song," which encompassed everything I sought from the world, on his harmonica and a borrowed guitar. A better person you would never have the privilege of meeting anywhere. He even dropped everything to come and see me in the Richmond psych ward but was refused entry. I had somehow managed to call him from the pay phone on the ward and ask him to bring me the all-new Chevy Camaro. My brain had somehow dreamed up that I was getting free sponsored wheels from GM.

At least, I don't think he made it into the actual ward. I can't even remember two of the three visits from my own daughter and none of Sharon's visits. She told me I managed some fucked-up small talk but didn't even know their names or how I knew them.

I do remember meeting this older woman who claimed she was an ex-veterinarian who had helped me with Cheyenne's sore paw. Later, she claimed she was one of the founding members of Supertramp. She claimed to have written "Everybody Hurts," one of my suicide defence anthems because it reminded me that I wasn't the only person in the world at any particular time feeling as low as I did, so man up. She went on to try to convince me that all lesbians were modern-day witches, which I knew was total crap, as I had known very many gay and lesbian people. Although I had to battle through my homophobia, they were some of the nicest people ever.

This other older street woman, Mary, was the spitting image of Nanny McPhee and lived under a loading dock at the back of the shelter. She absolutely loved Cheyenne. Almost every night, we and her other street clan members discussed life, the universe and everything while out walking my dog around the block. My brain will never let me forget that, as they were my escape from the madness that was the Yukon shelter. All I can say is it reversed my lifelong political beliefs, changing me from a true-blue rich-and-getting-richer conservative to a very red socialist.

Last but not least was this bisexual guy, Ryan, who had hit on me thinking, like many, I was gay because I avoided any woman in there, fearing my dick would fall off if I gave way to the normal male temptation of an easy lay. His girlfriend, Marg, was a recovering-from-everything addict and someone I hated to begin with, as she was very loud about everything, including her public admission that she had never worked a day in her life. When she wanted something, she would simply steal it. We had the common bond of dog ownership, which was both a blessing and a curse in that place, but I ended up liking her once I got used to her very loud in-your-face personality. Marg was very loosely married to this mellow junkie called Jim, but she was still a prostitute at heart, so it was a very open relationship. She fucked pretty much every male she wanted to in the back alley and was far from subtle with her moves towards me.

Other notable people included a very moody and aggressive female Inuit bitch who hated my dog and got in everyone's face. She turned out to be a convicted serial killer. An old Austrian bugger called Olaf kicked my dog in the face after she took his pastry off the floor. To this day, I don't quite know how I managed to show the immense self-restraint not to kill him, as if you hurt my pal, I'm going to hurt you. Problem is, the Yukon had a rule that if you have a physical fight on their premises, it gave them grounds to remove you and put you back on the streets, a place I knew I could never survive long-term. So I swallowed my pride big-time and reported the incident to the front desk. He paid for his crime and left not long afterwards.

The best person by far I met in there was not of this earth: a social worker, Sharon Bard. After being through the wringer—and in so many ways, I was still there—I had decided my stupid male pride and independence were going to get me killed. I had been through stress and tackled distress but couldn't deal with the crisis that had become my life, so I plucked up the balls to knock on her door. I should have gone to her as soon as I arrived in the shelter but couldn't because of the way-too-proud independence my tough-love upbringing had helped to mold. But finally, what was left of the logical side of my brain knew that without help, I was either going to die in the Yukon or get booted out of the shelter. As they kept telling us, it was a short-term facility and could put you back on the streets with next to no notice.

Sharon worked for the Lookout Society, an organization whose primary mission was to help disadvantaged homeless people. After so many wrong turns and life snakes I had fallen down, finally I did something right. It was a decision that, along with my dog, saved my life. In reality, Sharon was the only person who really had my back through my hardest times. I truly believe that without her, I would be dead by now, no bull.

The thing that truly scares me more than any man, animal or weapon is being pink-slipped or anything happening to my family, including my best friend, Cheyenne. Only now can you understand my intense dislike of the color pink. It is honestly not rooted in my admitted homophobia, which I truly hate and try everything to change. Nor is it a flashback to my childhood memories of being bullied because of my diminutive size; the colour pink in North America now represents a support mechanism to eradicate this troubling bullying trait that still haunts way too many kids and adults lives today. Rather, my reaction to the colour comes from the jargon for being deemed certifiable and committed to a psyche ward. I genuinely don't think I could cope with revisiting that horrendous ordeal ever again, but hey, I said that about revisiting the Yukon shelter for a second time, and I managed to do so, along with a third and hopefully final time. Truth be told, I only survived by the skin of my teeth.

Something had to give, as my health on all levels was in a downward spiral. One of the final stakes in my heart was losing my top-of-the-range 15-inch Sony Viao laptop when I stupidly left my backpack in a corner while I hit the washroom. The mere minutes that it took me was enough for it to be snapped up and most likely fed to one of the local pawn shops. That laptop was home to years of family photos and videos. With my crap computer skills, none of them were backed up on anything. Although it was too painful for me to view any of them as a comparison between the then and now, the loss of the pictures only deepened my worsening depression.

I don't quite know when my brain had had enough and went off the deep end. My very vague last memory was almost getting into a fight with my roommate, Pete, and then going down to the Yukon's living room and, in front of everyone, busting out my MJ moves as "Billie Jean" came on the radio. No matter how strong, tough, mature or experienced you think you are, everyone is human and has a breaking point.

I still don't know why I have such severe memory loss around this particular time. I will leave that one to the brain experts. I have to believe Sharon that after almost a week of trying to go behind the counter in the local Starbucks to help them out, I decided I had to escape Colditz. I packed up my Dakine bag, jumped on the SkyTrain, and headed for Vancouver Airport with no money, no ticket, no passport and, most of all, no dog. This reinforces my belief that I truly was as insane as they come, because I would never leave my best friend in a fucking homeless shelter where her full pedigree and sheer beauty could be converted into cold hard cash to fuel any addict's fix in a heartbeat.

I'm just so glad I didn't do anything stupid like attack someone. It is an issue I struggle with, because if you really are as far gone as I was, would I have ended up with prison time if I did? At any rate, it didn't take long for the security and police presence to notice my mental state, and I was cuffed and taken to Richmond.

I remember being dispatched to what seemed like a general medical ward, which was very well-furnished and even had its own flat-screen TV. Problem was, it didn't take me long to hit withdrawal city, and with all my belongings gone, I had no option but to use my distraction skills to take my mind off the intense pain in my gut. When I went to the rehab clinic, I had learned the strategy of massaging certain areas of my face and other strategic spots, which somehow amazingly reduces the pain to an almost bearable level. My antics made me the centre of attention as I writhed in pain and pleaded with the nurses to give me something for the excruciating abdominal pain.

After the usual protocol of doing every test in the book, the doctors could find only a small amount of Crohn's ulceration and therefore refused to dispense any painkillers. What they didn't understand was that I needed those drugs to keep me alive, just like breathing. After hours of traumatic pain, I unfairly started losing it on the nearest caregivers: the nurses.

Somewhere in all this turmoil, I received a phone call from my mother in Tenerife. After what I think was a huge fight, I slammed the phone down on her—something I had never ever done with my mum. It just wasn't an option. I really had very little control of my actions back then. I simply cannot fathom why my parents were not there for me in my darkest hours, except for their reasoning that they were scared of the monster the drugs had turned me into. Before I knew it, I was leaving that ward and going upstairs to a completely different ward that would be my troubled home for the next five months.

CHAPTER 12

WILL YOU BE THERE

In our darkest hour, in my deepest despair,
will you still care, will you be there?
In my trials and my tribulations,
there are doubts and frustrations
In my violence, in my turbulence,
through my fear and my confessions
In my anguish, in my pain,
through my joy and my sorrow,
In the promise of another tomorrow,
I'll never let you part
for you're always in my heart.
—Michael Jackson, "Will You Be There"

I simply cannot count how many times I ran those lyrics through my mind over one lifetime, but they only really made sense when my world collapsed around me. Everyone loves a success story, but too many real friends are there for you when it all goes wrong. Sad but true.

After a quick ride along some corridors and up in an elevator, I was introduced to a place I never thought I would ever see in my lifetime: a locked psych ward. This easily offers my worst memories and triggers my complex PTSD. Before I knew what was going on, I was surrounded by Providence security guards (even over four years later, the sight of their logo immediately transports me back to hell on earth). When I refused to follow their demands, they crudely dragged me by the arms to the lockdown cell for an undefined period of time. Once there, I had to strip in front of them, and then they slammed and locked the metal door, which was covered with engravings from past inmates. It ranged from pure genius to drivel. but it was the only thing to concentrate on to pass the time. Trust me, time stood still in that godforsaken place, and a night felt more like a week.

I will never ever forget the sound of that door slamming. It still haunts me to this day. It was only years later that my psychiatrist explained it's the reason I jump when I hear any door close, but especially car doors because they too are made of metal. Somehow, my brain makes this connection and transports me back to that locked cell.

I can't tell you how much I hated that place, more than any other. It was just so degrading, as not only did you freeze, the solitude made you even more insane. Apart from my periods of must-have isolation when I am too low to face the world, I need human interaction, no matter how mental it is. I've always hated isolation more than anything. In my younger years, when my folks or teachers wanted to punish me, they realized way too late that corporal punishment was easily my choice, as for me, the pain soon vanished, and I could be back doing whatever I wanted to. Detention, on the other hand, deprived me of my beloved outdoors and, with it, social contact.

Although my mind was in another galaxy, I still could access my consciousness and figure out that this was a place I didn't want to frequent. I had to surrender to the orders of the medical staff. I was in a total no-win situation: they had all the power and I was, for I think the first time in my life, completely powerless.

I beg you to try this: put yourself in a place where nothing you have or wear gives you any status. Going to prison is the only similar circumstance I can think of. In this environment, fight (ending up in lockdown or badly injured) and flight (not possible) are off the table. Freeze, the hardest one of all, is the only option.

My initial memories are wild, vague and random, but one of the first people I met in there claimed not only to be one of the main producers of CNN but managed to persuade me of his God-given gift for controlling human energy, or *chi* as he called it. He befriended me when he noticed my super-hyper ADHD personality. I can explain a lot of things that have happened to me, but quite how he did this with only a mere touch of his hand is beyond me. Was it a mind trick or was it real? Let's face it, I was in no state to challenge its authenticity. Quite honestly I didn't care, as I had much more pressing issues on my mind—like how to save the world, the universe and everything. But it worked, and possibly more importantly, it gave me the chance to listen to my beloved music on his iPod. The music somehow transported me to another place and time, allowing me to escape my terrible confinement for a few minutes.

There was this other middle-aged dude who was even more gone than me called Steve. He would, out of the blue, at any time, shout at the top of his voice, "The Russians!" Even after a few weeks, he could still make me jump every time. There was also this super-mellow blacker-than-black guy called Dreamer who looked like he had just arrived off the boat from Africa. No surprise, he had actually just come from Nigeria. Last but not least was this skinny younger guy who for some strange reason, my brain convinced me was Britney Spears' bodyguard. I can't explain why. I always thought she was really hot, especially as she could throw down on the dance floor with the best of them.

To this day, one of my favourite TV moments was when Britney joined Michael for his 25th anniversary concert in New York's Madison Square Garden on probably my favourite all-time MJ fast track: "The Way You Make Me Feel." I have watched it way too many times to admit to here. I think it has something to do with the fact that I borrowed from the ward's magazine collection this *People* magazine with a huge feature on both Michael and Britney that I kept in my room. I read it over and over again during my six-month stay to celebrate my hero's life and try to escape the boredom of the ward.

Then came my fellow tae kwon do martial artist, Jeremy, who never stopped speaking about how he knew the system and was hell-bent on not only getting the fuck out of his capture but causing as much trouble as practically possible in the most childlike way. Any attention, even bad, was better than none, which got extremely annoying after a while. On the few occasions he wasn't locked up in the slammer cells in the back, he retaught me some of the tae kwon do katas, a very welcome relief from the boredom of the ward. He also helped me revisit the happy and serene time and place, not only in my childhood training but throughout my life, that this underestimated (so it fit me like a perfect glove) martial art took me to.

The next person of interest was a middle-aged Asian guy called Tom. He was all about Chinese proverbs and the yin and yang tai chi stuff. He almost became the dad I never had and really needed now. We did have a rocky start, as I called bull on his attempts to calm me down. I really was bouncing off the walls in there the first month, as again, I hate being detained anywhere. Little did I know it was probably one of the worst places on earth. Even the homeless shelters had nothing on this place. I checked everywhere to find a way to escape my prison, but everything was locked down. Even the large outdoor garden space was covered in wire mesh.

I can't describe how it troubles me to explain my mental state at that time. How can you describe something you don't understand, even after reading just about every pertinent article on the subject of psychosis and schizophrenia on the Internet? Although you know your feet are on the ground, your mind is in a completely made-up world controlled not by the usual external inputs but by the deepest and sometimes darkest corners of your brain. You are in your own world with its own unique set of variables, beliefs and rules. You genuinely believe you are the biggest rock star, movie star, superstar and celebrity on planet Earth, and as such, everyone is looking at you, following you and wanting a piece of you.

My only source of music was the television set, and I spent pretty much every minute of my waking hours in front of it, watching and listening to Much Music (Canada's version of MTV). I would get these messages from the broadcast that somehow all related to me, because I was the centre of the universe. I truly believed there was a camera installed in the TV and cameras all around the ward. When I was watching something as basic as a TV advert for Tim Horton's, in the most bizarre way possible, I was convinced they were filming me to star in their next advert. This was also true of all the Chevrolet and GMC adverts, I think because of my love of *Transformers* and the pimp daddy car of all time, the Bumblebee bright-yellow new Camaro. My brain decided it was only a matter of time before I would receive my brand-new top-of-the-range Camaro, all decked out with a stylish *Starsky and Hutch* red and white arrow paint scheme.

While watching TV, if a song came on that I liked, regardless of who was there—fellow inmates or their family and friends during visiting times, which I hated because no one ever came to visit me—I would get up and dance my ass off without any inhibitions. There was this real cute chick who would occasionally join me. I still have no clue why I didn't move in on her, as she freely gave me her email address when she was leaving, which really upset me cause she was a first-class sweetheart. If you're still out there, girl, and ever get a chance to read this, please get in touch, as I'm still smitten.

When we occasionally went out for a walk around the scenic gardens, complete with a small lake and tons of ducks, I could not step on any lines in the concrete path. I even walked to a beat I made up in my mind. This was also the case on the multicoloured tiles inside the ward. Yes, it was just like Jack Nicholson in *As Good As It Gets*. I had somehow developed all these crazy habits that, at the time, seemed to make sense. As to why, I simply have no answer. I think the lines somehow presented a threat to me, but I can't be sure. My brain won't let me access that file.

Every time the word *premier* was mentioned on TV, it was translated in my brain that I was going to be offered the premiership of Canada. In line with that, every female-oriented program somehow meant they were chasing me, which kicked me into my shy zone, which was further heightened by the fact that my soulmate of 23 years, Carol, never even came to visit. Even though we split under the worst-case scenario, without a doubt, if the shoe was on the other foot, I know I would have gone to see her. That and the fact that my folks were also no-shows still bites harder than probably anything else.

I would not only sign my name for the masses on the visitors' book like someone really wanted my altered-ego insane autograph but believing somehow that when my folks halfway around the world switched on their BBC news, I could somehow get messages to them if I watched the same channel. Over and over again I would find out the telephone number of the ward and write it down along with a short message and put it face down on the actual TV screen.

When this black nurse with an American accent every so often filled in a shift, the message to my messed-brain was that President Obama was checking me out. He was planning to groom me for a major political role within his administration. I had to be on my best behaviour.

I would try to rhyme all my words, playing games in my head where I would come up with a random word and then list every word I could think of that rhymed with it. Unfortunately, that game followed me into my supposedly sane world, as to this day I can't stop it doing it. Its origin was a game I would play with my youngest daughter, Iona, whereby we would alternate picking a word and the other had to come up with a word that rhymed and go back and forth until one party couldn't come up with anything. The last person who had a rhyming word won a point. Iona was the best competitor in this game that I have ever come against. Why hasn't anyone come up with a cool rhyming application so we all can all access our creative artsy side making poetry and lyrics?

Every time I went into the bathroom, before I left I would position the garbage can under the sink's U-bend. Don't ask me why! The angled mirror obviously was hiding another camera. I could never escape my fucked-up brain's thoughts.

Almost like clockwork every day, I would draw a compass sign on the staff signage board and re-arrange the table soccer games score beads into 5 for the Jackson 5 and the five senses; 9 for my scrum half rugby number; 10 for my years of addiction and Bible commandments; 12 for AA and NA serenity prayer rules; 18 and 21 for my coming of age.

I talked to myself constantly with complete crazy garbage, writing down words that somehow had become crucially important for me to document my journey to insanity. Why I did this and all the rest—really just the tip of my insanity iceberg—I to this day have absolutely no clue. I was so far beyond the realm of normal thinking, I sometimes wonder how I ever came back to reality. Suffice to say my new home for such a long time has had a profound effect and impact on me.

After about a month—again, my memory is so vague that I can't be absolutely sure—all my pleas for a pass to go visit reality were granted. I was ecstatic, especially because they somewhat stupidly let me go on my lonesome. For some reason, this episode is clear to me, as I knew the area well. We used to shop in Richmond Mall regularly when we came down from Whistler, so that was my first stop. Problem was, I had no money, so straight to the ATM I went.

THE HOOD

Because I was still lost out in space somewhere, my primary focus wasn't the C$400 that I took out but the transaction slip. I was determined to find out the real date, because for a reason unknown to me, I simply did not believe the nurses or the staff board. I was so focused on that, I forgot to take my cash. I left before I knew what the fuck was going on and started thinking about what I was going to buy. No surprise there: I headed straight for the Sony store to buy MJ's *This Is It* DVD, which had just come out. It obviously didn't take me long to figure out I had no money in my wallet. *Fuck.* I ran back to the ATM and, praise be, somehow no one had stolen it. After a bit of hassle, I reclaimed my cash.

So I got my beloved DVD but was so dumb I bought the Blu-ray version, even though I knew they only had a regular DVD player in the ward. Then it was time to find my favourite fast food chain, Wendy's, where I stuffed a bacon cheeseburger meal down my throat. As soon as I left, I was met by another police car, handcuffed and ushered back to my temporary home, the secure ward. It is so hard to explain what the world is like when you have severe psychosis. Your brain believes everyone is watching your every move and the world revolves around you. I had stretched my one-hour day pass to over five hours. It was not intentional; I was in a world of my own, quite literally. But I screwed myself and was never extended a pass again.

Our day would commence with breakfast at 8 a.m. Sometimes I spoke to my friends; other times, I kept to myself. I had met this elderly lady called Joy (another trigger name for me now) who was in there for almost as long as me, and we just clicked, as she shared my passion for dance. We would compare notes when watching our favourite program, *So You Think You Can Dance*. Then around 9 a.m., we had a group meeting that was 100 percent voluntary, but I usually went, as what else was there to do? Then, depending on the day, there was a morning activity like going for a walk outside, art therapy (where you either drew or built stuff) and cooking classes that I loved, as I knew so little about cooking and there were always sweet treats at the end of the session.

No surprise, my favorite was music therapy class, where this Asian piano player with a list of songs gathered a bunch of us to play instruments like bongo drums, tambourines and other stuff I can't remember. Even now, when I hear Simon and Garfunkel's classic "Bridge over Troubled

Water" or John Denver's epic "Leaving on a Jet Plane," I automatically revisit the ward, as these were the songs I would invariably choose.

How on earth did I fall to such depths of depravity? Somehow, it didn't bother me, as all I was interested in were my chaotic thoughts of artificial grandeur, which were way more fun than accepting the truth: instead of being on top of the world, I was pretty much at the bottom, along with possibly people in jail. I could write a whole book on my time and my fucked-up thoughts of being there for over five months. Maybe that will be the content of my next book, with an appropriate title like *Psycho*, *Paranoid*, *Madness*, *Crazy* or *Disturbia*.

In truth, my memories are so sporadic and random, even now I have a very hard time differentiating what actually happened from the many troubling videotapes my brain spits out. The fucked-up and somewhat harrowing flashbacks can turn me into a crazy man, especially at night, when I have no distractions. I finally fall asleep, but the peace and quiet I crave only brings more and more messed-up flashbacks from my past.

I believe it wasn't until around Valentine's Day, four months into my stay, that I actually started to come out of my fog, regain solid memories and allow almost normal thoughts to enter my brain. All I can do is thank God there was the hometown Winter Olympics on TV to pass the time. I would be glued to the TV for pretty much every event, apart from maybe ice skating (which despite their immense talent was a bit too girlie for me) and curling (I find the slow-motion replays faster than the real-life action). In retrospect, I would have loved to go to some of the events, especially if I was still living in Whistler—but that life was so far removed from where I was at the time, the irony never really hit me until I was released.

This wanting was further exacerbated when I saw my oldest daughter in the Much Music hot tub at the base of the mountain. As soon as I started to think semi-normally, which coincidently occurred at the end of the Olympics, my time in there started to drag so badly, and I started sussing out what they classified as sane thoughts and behavior. Problem was, I was in this halfway-house state where I would have a period of sanity laced with insane thoughts, as my brain had started to figure out the real ones from the seemingly never-ending mind tricks, but the more subtle ones that could be believable still remained.

THE HOOD

Once a week, I was summoned into the main meeting room and bombarded with feeling questions from my main psychiatrist and her male resident. It didn't take me long to catch on to the reasoning behind their leading questions. Even though I knew their innuendos to be true—like hearing voices in my head and getting messages from media like the TV, magazines and papers—I lied because I knew it was my only way to get the fuck out of this place. It gets real hairy when sanity starts entering your mind.

The resident would then ask me a bunch of questions, test my brain with a picture test of what I could see on these cards and check my reflexes. Then he would weigh me to see how much I had gained since my frailer-than-frail 87 pounds when I first entered the ward—quite a difference from my 225-pound muscular physique a few years earlier. My daughter will testify to anyone who is interested that I had every bone, muscle and rib showing. To overcome this, they fed me a diet high in protein and carbohydrates along with a meal-replacement fluid called Boost with every meal.

With my improving mental health, it made sense not to try to push my luck. The way to get out of this place was to act like you were as normal as can be and remember there was no point in arguing with the nurses, as that just sent you back to the locked ward. Thankfully, I found out that when you accepted your position of no power and realized it was useless to argue with them about anything, you'd never be escorted back there. I was moved to a single room and got to go on bigger accompanied treks—even once to the Richmond Mall for another favourite junk food, New York fries with gravy. It was like entering heaven for me after being locked up for so long.

From my new single room's window, I could see the car park and had a bird's-eye view of planes taking off and landing—something I always loved to watch since I was a child and going to the air shows at RAF Leuchars. My childhood dream wasn't to be a fireman, train engineer or James Bond; it was to be a fighter pilot, like Maverick in *Top Gun*, still my favourite action flick. Unfortunately, my asthma precluded that dream. I used to sit for hours watching all the planes start their landing and taking off in the desperate belief that someone who loved me would come for me or at least come to visit me.

QUIETSTRENGTH

Tears are running down my face as write this, it hurts so bad. To this day, I simply cannot comprehend how I was left for dead by everyone I loved. In my mind, it meant no one loved me anymore. Why, I simply do not know. My brain somehow conned me into believing that if I watched long enough and prayed hard enough, one of those cars or planes would finally contain some of my family to either visit me or, even better, get me out of my hell. But no one ever came.

Sorry, that's not entirely true. Michelle did come down against my ex-wife's orders, as she inherited my super-rebellious, don't-touch-the-red-phone-and-now-you-have-no-choice-but-to-touch-it attitude. She supposedly came down three times, but I was so insane that not only did I not recognize her, even calling her various wrong names, I still cannot remember any of her visits except for the last one. We went to the mall, but because of my mental state, I think she was mortified to be with me. I was dancing in this female clothing store and generally acting completely weird. We promptly left and went to this Chinese restaurant just around the corner from the hospital. But before we got a chance to eat, I was met by yet another cop car, handcuffed behind my back way too tightly (why cops do that I will never know, because it hurts like a bitch) and escorted back to the locked ward.

Coming out of my psychotic state wasn't as simple as waking up one day and you're back to your previous self. In fact, I have never returned to my old self, as what I have been through has made me question and challenge every value, belief, faith and hope. My perspective of the world has changed, and I realize what is important in my life. My trip to sanity was a very slow and gradual day-by-day progression. It was accelerated by the planned gradual removal of all of my painkillers, which they believed were responsible for my mental state.

When, after months, they ceased my Cesamet (which really was just a synthesized man-made version of chronic), as much as I protested that I really needed that stuff to take the edge off my living hell, the removal turned out to be the catalyst I needed to completely come out of my fog. They also used an ever-decreasing time-release fentanyl patch to keep the necessary painkiller but reduce any potential for addiction, as you never get that initial hit through an IV procedure. This was probably the single most effective technique. The immediate and considerable high of this drug was taken away by the time-release method, and it probably brought my brain back to almost sane, although still a million miles of being cured.

The last few months in the ward dragged like no other time in my life. After my Winter Olympic TV vigil of spending every waking minute of the day in front of the tube, there was nothing to take my mind off my dire circumstances. We should all learn from the lessons history teaches us, both from a micro and a macro point of view—especially our mistakes, so we can avoid them in the future. In general, we don't; we convince ourselves that somehow this war, this accident, this pursuit is somehow different from the last one that bit us in the ass. Our seemingly incurable scars, for good and bad, mould us into something unrecognizable.

I know the phrase "born again" usually refers to a person who has seen the light and taken the comfort religion offers, but for me, it is so much more than that. I learn some of the most important things, like humility, compassion, empathy, frailty, belief, hope, faith, loyalty, forgiveness, integrity and, most importantly, that there is nothing more important in this world than true love in its purest sense. It is ultimately life's greatest prize.

Trust me, being a lifelong hard-ass, badass alpha male, appreciating these qualities was like learning a whole new language. It's much like the excellent Robin Williams movie *Patch Adams*, in which his psych-ward adventure made him quite rightly challenge the medical professionals' attitude and start treating patients more like customers or even friends rather than being an almost inhuman professional with zero bedside manner who only concentrates on the diagnosis and treatment of another poor soul with a medical condition. It's quite honestly the most valuable lesson for me to treat people differently from what I used to, as an equal human being. Even if you are a star of the silver screen, music, business, sports or whatever gives you fame and holds you in high esteem these days, we all came from the same place and will ultimately end up in the same place.

Same goes for the street people in every city in this world, caught up in so many diseases, from addiction to mental illness, poverty to starvation, and barely hanging on to this way-too-short and precious thing we call life. Check out the music video for "Streets of London" by Ralph McTell. Its images are very powerful, especially with the number of multi-millionaires and even billionaires always on the rise. I wonder why.

Whether you are a practicing religious person or a complete atheist, we can all learn from the core values religion offers us, like the Ten Commandments and, most critically, treat others the way you would want to be treated. Contrary to what I used to believe, there are only a very few black-and-white clear-cut topics. Most are in varying shades of grey, and we all must come to our own conclusions; but instead of sticking with our opinions no matter what, we should constantly open and seek information to either confirm or even better change them. As one of my biggest sporting heroes, Mohammad Ali, cleverly stated in a recent BBC interview despite his crushing Parkinson's disease: "If a man of 60 believes and thinks the same as he did when he was 30, he has wasted half of his life."

Regardless of what you might think, I make no claim to being some Mr. Perfect know-it-all. I am only human and as such far from perfect; as my past makes clear, I am as inclined to make mistakes as anyone. But I have a hunch that the next few generations, with the use of the Internet, social media and public gatherings, have a true and very real chance to change some of the injustices in the world. Most of us live in ever-shrinking high-rise tiny boxes, and the rich just keep growing their wealth in pharmaceuticals, energy, cars, banking (including stock markets), data, real estate and international trade. They're the ones who really run this world. In their belief, the only way this world can change is if the "angry peasants" (I believe that's how we are referred to by our leaders) rise up with demonstrations, marches and voting. At election time, every vote is the same, regardless of whether you are Donald Trump or a street person.

There is just so much proof it is the companies that rule this world, with crazy rich middle to high corporate management executives—or maybe it's just easier to say I'm still crazy. People living the life project it back to Joe Public to sell the capitalist ideal that in North America, if you dream big enough and work as hard as you possibly can and take a few calculated chances with investments, you too can be all be pimped and blinged out like you see in most music videos and movies. All of this is could be yours? Good luck on that one.

Widespread corruption is not just a problem with communism. Look at North and South America, Africa and India—all the same. As Bono from U2 said in his last concert, "The power of the people should be greater than the people in power." Yeah, right; maybe one day. Hopefully all this new information at a tap of a button might just give us the ability to reclaim some of the huge monies of rich people like the self-confessed tax-evader Donald Trump and the many like him who never pay their taxes. I'm the crazy one? He has five bankruptcies and millions of dollars lost, and he still penny-pinches the small-and medium-size businesses he intentionally used so if it doesn't work out, they can't really sue one of the richest and most powerful men on their meagre budgets.

What the fuck does anyone really need more than a million dollars a year for? Growing up in an upper-middle-class home, followed by private school and being top student at Robert Gordons University, I can say with full conviction that everything I worked so hard for all my working life disappeared, and I had to adapt to a completely new life in a completely different social strata, from the top 1 percent to the bottom. It's been a monumental shift in lifestyle, thoughts and actions. Let's just say I never knew how much living from paycheque to paycheque really bites. I'm always worrying about money, because I know I cannot go back to the streets.

If you learn nothing else from this book, check out Vice News and the very real movement that is going on today. Something has to change, pure and simple—hopefully without the blood and death other revolutions have required. A real new world will indeed come to pass that truly makes things better for everyone. It will happen only when these severe injustices are corrected. We still stand back and watch the homeless problem reach biblical proportions all over the world. More than 30 percent of the homeless are families struggling in cars, in cheap motels or sometimes on the sidewalk. They suffer from not only physical ailments but mental ones like PTSD, traumatic brain injury and addiction. We lose an astounding 22 veterans to suicide every day in the United States. It's simply staggering, if you ask me.

My apologizes for the political rant. It's just that when you've really been there, done that, your view of life changes forever. And yes, most if not all politicians are the scum of this earth.

CHAPTER 13

YOU ARE NOT ALONE

After saying goodbye to pretty much everyone who had been in the ward previously, I couldn't figure out why the hell I was still being kept in there. Compared to my mental state when I entered the ward, I might not have been totally cured, but I was in a much better head space. With the benefit of hindsight, I was still far from being 100 percent mentally when I left. I now realize that they probably kept me in there not just because of any lingering psychosis but because of my addiction to prescription drugs, especially painkillers, which they had so dramatically weaned me off over the five months I was in the hospital. I later learned that was close to the maximum stay in a local mental facility; they would have had to go to court to further confine me.

As compared to most private rehab centers, my recovery took twice the normal 90-day program; but in all fairness, you couldn't get any more addicted than me. Couple that with my drug-induced psychosis and/or schizophrenia, and it makes perfect sense I was in there for close to the maximum. Because my life had been put on hold for half a year in this prison-like lockdown, I was not only kind of shell-shocked but extremely anxious about being let out into the cruel world with all its temptations. I had an all-encompassing feeling of being totally and completely lost. It's weird, but my new mental state was purely fight, flight and freeze. The outside kind of scared me. This safe cuckoo's nest felt like my only "home."

THE HOOD

Unlike every other time I left hospital, and unlike everyone else, no one came for me. Tracey, the superb social worker I met in there, took me into her office to give me the great yet scary news that I was being let out in a few days. To where and with whom were a complete mystery. I was ecstatic to be finally leaving but at the same time overcome with emotion and gratitude to the nurses and doctors who basically saved my life. Now it was going to be up to me and my willpower to stay clean. Willpower combined with my inherent traits of stubbornness, tenacity and never giving up were exactly what had saved me from a certain death.

I found it impossible to verbalize my thoughts, as how do you express your unbridled thanks to the people who saved your life? Sometimes there simply aren't words big or deep enough in meaning. I did what I always do in such moments: let my actions do the talking. I broke down in tears and hugged everyone I could get my hands on.

With that, I finally got to go through the locked doors I had stared at every day of my incarceration, wondering if I was going to be locked up in here for life. I boarded the elevator I had previously believed was going to bring me to some television program to be heralded into a life of fame and fortune. I thanked the Starbucks staff in the lobby who had been so kind during my darkest days.

No sooner had I stopped celebrating my deliverance to the real world than I was informed that no one was there for me, and Tracey would be driving me to the Yukon homeless shelter. How can explain going from the natural high of being released to the lowest possible low, with all my hopes and dreams of going back to a normal life shattered. I was leaving one hell to go back to another that had been one of the biggest catalysts for putting me away in the first place. Somehow, I had believed I would be magically transported back to million-dollar world. Instead, my new reality of hopeless homelessness hit me like a Mike Tyson right-cross punch, knocking me flat on my back emotionally. The only thought I had was that I was alone in the world. Not being met by anyone after five months of imprisonment meant no one loved me, right?

What had I done to deserve this? Had I no real friends left in the world because of my pill-popping manic state? Don't get me wrong, my family is everything to me, but I will never ever understand or forgive my parents and Carol for not coming for me then or, ideally, before then. I know I would have been there for them and my two beautiful daughters regardless of what any of them had done to end up in such a dreadful place. I had some pretty intense feelings, thoughts and emotions for sure.

I tried my best to keep my brave face on and exude relief when every cell in my body was crumpling with pure astonishment and grief. I was devastated but tried everything to keep telling myself I had made it this far on my road to recovery alone. I was not going to let the shelter life do what it had the first time around.

Once again, I sat in Sharon's office trying to collect all my thoughts and, I'm not going lie, very real fears for my future. I knew my mental illness was actually a blessing, as it had convinced me none of this was real but rather a kind of surreal nightmare that I was going to wake up from any minute and be transported back to my glory years in Whistler. Both Tracey and Sharon assured me they were behind me and everything was going to be okay. I just had to take life one day at a time, sweet Jesus.

The only positive I could take from my complete disbelief this was actually happening to me was that my beloved dog, Cheyenne, was fine, and she was coming down real soon to join me in the shelter. As such, I could avoid the dungeon where 50-plus men lived and slept in a large dorm. Because of my dog and most likely my indescribable friendship with and respect for Sharon, I was again privileged to get a shared double room upstairs.

The other thing I clung to was the knowledge that I had survived this place before, even when out of my face on all kinds of prescription pills, so I could do it again clean. My biggest worry was relapsing, as you could get any drug in there in a heartbeat in return for next to nothing cash-wise—or the other currency that ruled in that place, a few smokes. I was one of a very few who didn't smoke anything.

I don't like repeating myself, but I just could not comprehend how none of my family or friends was there to pull me out of this pit, as I knew I would have been there for them. Was it because I had burnt every bridge during my craziness? If I did, could they not realize that wasn't the real me but the fire-breathing beast the drugs had turned me into? Despite what you might think, it wasn't a lame-ass excuse. Just look what alcohol does to perfectly sane individuals every weekend around the globe, like the angry or sad drunk. Drugs can do the same mind-altering tricks, and like alcohol or weed, it affects everyone differently.

My only guess was that because they had never been there and done that, they simply couldn't understand what can happen to a person riddled with addiction, and they believed erroneously that it was in fact the real me, and all the wealth had turned me into a cocky asshole. Believe one thing: despite being told on countless occasions that I was the epitome of self-esteem and confidence, I actually hated most of the old me too. I just went back to the theory that I had been misunderstood all my life, so this experience was no different—just an extension of my past, present and future.

As I cried myself to sleep that first night with all my heartfelt remorse, my brain took over with this montage of videos and images of my life that are just so hard to grasp even now. I committed myself to coming back and being a very different person than I had been before. I would focus my life not on what it was before my fall from grace—all greed, money and power—and replace it with the drive to be as good a person as I could be. If I managed that feat, then no matter what happened from here on in, I could find that inner peace I craved so much more than anything else.

It wasn't long before I was hugging the best friend I have ever had, human or animal: my adorable guardian angel, Cheyenne. That put my mood in a slightly better place than before. Life in the shelter was pretty much a routine, starting with waking up around 7:15 or 7:30 for breakfast at 8 a.m. (with the exception of the weekend days, when you got an extra 30 minutes in bed). I could never understand why they were being so cruel, as no one in that place had anything to do all day, so why not let us sleep in? I guess they were trying to put us on a "normal" schedule, even if our lives were so far removed from normality. Plus, they probably needed to clean the rooms.

Every morning, I would wake up from my only real escape from my terrible reality, namely sleep, to be smacked in the mouth with the fact that I was still in this dreadful place and had fallen so far in such a short period of time. Depending on how much actual sleep I got that night and how awake I was, I would hit the communal showers before or after breakfast. On many occasions, I simply could not face the anarchy that was breakfast, so I would have an extra-long shower when everyone else was eating.

I remember how much I hated opening the bedroom door to be faced with the hallway that I dubbed my real-life Green Mile. I hoped I would meet no one and avoid any games. Trusting no one was the only way to go. I still have major trust issues with every human.

I couldn't really even eat anything they had for breakfast, because most things on offer were super-greasy. I had to find something to eat, though, even if it was the worst lumpy porridge you have ever tasted in your life (this is why, to this day, I never ever eat the stuff, despite being Scottish and loving it in my youth). The other morning offerings included a choice between Rice Krispies or Corn Flakes with toast.

A couple of days a week, I allowed myself my favourite: hot sausage, bacon and eggs. My problem was I had to be super-careful not to upset my Crohn's-ravaged gut and be led back down the life-threatening narcotic gut road. My specialist had informed me I was one of a very privileged/tiny group of survivors of that particular complication of Crohn's disease. I tell no lie, it often precluded everything except dry toast, which I tried to put a positive spin on by remembering Dan Aykroyd's order in the cult movie *The Blues Brothers*. The only thing I could bear on my toast were the small cartons of blueberry jelly I tried to store up so I could avoid those dry toast and cereal mornings.

Worse than the diet was the intense psychological warfare that was always so prominent at mealtimes, especially breakfast, as they knew you were at your most vulnerable first thing in the morning. The basement crew were awakened almost a full hour before we were, and therefore they had a jump on us, as our brains had not yet reset themselves to the guarded mode required in the shelter. People would intentionally get in my face, get in my way and cut me off. They talked about shit they hoped would hit a nerve to try to gain a psychological advantage by bringing out any insecurities and chinks in my armour, exposing those demons we all have. If they found your Achilles heel, they would exploit it to the fullest in an attempt to gain control over you. Trust me, I learnt more about human psychology in my four tours of duty in Vancouver's homeless world than I ever did in my 47 years on this earth, never mind the five months in a locked psych ward.

Christ, looking back on it, no wonder I developed complex PTSD. To say they were some of the sharpest minds of any opponents I have ever faced in sports, school or business does not come close to describing the situation properly. When you haven't got money, power, family or material possessions—all those things we hide behind—you are in effect naked and vulnerable to attack. These ultimate warriors would test you to the limit every chance they got. I know it sounds lame, but honestly, the only thing I had to compete with these true survivors was my street smarts; mental strength gained through sports and my folks' tough love; physical gifts from God; and believe it or not, a love for reality TV. It was as if by watching those shows, I had subconsciously formulated my own plan of attack if I ever got into such a precarious position. It was like a dress rehearsal for my shelter ordeal.

Because of what I have endured, the human psyche fascinates me more than anything else. Brain wins over brawn every time, and if knowledge is power, imagination and creativity are on a whole different level. Ultimately, this is what drives the human race forwards (and yes, sometimes backwards). Of course, shows like *The Apprentice*, *The Amazing Race*, *Survivor* and *Intervention* paled in comparison to the psychological warfare that rages every second of every day in that place.

Among all my crazy out-of-the-box ideas on how we could improve this world we live in, one that is truly on my bucket list is highlighting the growing worldwide epidemic of homelessness. Don't believe me? Go walk the streets of our so-called capitalist heavens, Los Angeles and New York, and check out their homeless problem. From my real experience, I honestly believe a concept based around the worldwide homeless and poverty trap would easily become the best and most popular reality TV series ever, about capitalism's muffler/exhaust pipe for all those pursuing fame, fortune and greed as their chosen path for *The Pursuit of Capitalism*. This is something I am determined to complete, so Mark Burnett, watch out!

I constantly used to pretend to watch the television in the shelter. Most of the time, I didn't get my choice of program, as they watched shit. I was reluctant to use some my limited resources in a dumb-ass fight about the crap that is on our television sets these days. It was simply not worth the aggravation. Anyways, the unbelievable drama of the shelter was way more interesting. I pretended to watch but secretly used it as an information-gathering time to give me critical insight into my potential foes.

The absolute last thing I was going to do in there was watch my reality TV, as it might give everyone an insight into my secret strength and knowledge. It was like life had turned into the biggest game of street-style Russian roulette I had ever played, right out on the edge of human survival. You had to hold your cards as close to your chest as possible. I used the proven route of so many choice reality-TV competitors, like nurture potential alliances, fly under the radar as much as possible and keep your friends close but your enemies closer.

Back to the routine: After breakfast, I went upstairs to get myself ready for the mass removal at 9 a.m. I had already checked the seemingly pivotal factors, namely how much money I had left and the weather. These dictated how I was going to waste the three and a half hours until 12:30, when we were allowed back in our rooms.

It didn't take Sharon long to realize that I was, as she put it so eloquently, "a champagne lover on a beer drinker's budget." She persuaded me to agree to a very rigid budget. In my recent past, I'd been able to pretty much buy whatever I wanted, whenever I wanted it; now I was reduced to a semi-self-imposed budget of a mere C$10 a day. Please try it sometime, for not just a day or a week but six whole months. Only then will you see how far it goes. Otherwise, trust me: it's super rough but a necessity I needed to survive. I received only C$627 per month on the Canadian Pension Plan, with the remaining balance for special times like the all-too-rare occasions when my kids came down to see me. Understandably, Carol used the excuse of shielding our kids from the danger and evil of the homeless shelter.

Sharon also coined the description of this three-hour daily time-wasting exercise as my "marathon dog-walking time." I had the choice of walking around the sea wall past Olympic Plaza, Science World and my favourite dance club, Gossip, which I used to frequent when I was a Yaletown resident out of my tree on prescription painkillers. Then back to the park where I used to walk Chi and on to my favorite Blenz coffee shop on Hemlecken, where I would usually buy my C$3 pot of tea that lasted the longest and was the cheapest item and therefore gave me an excuse to spend as much time as possible, often pretending to read the daily papers and attempting their crosswords until about noon, when I would take the most direct route over the Cambie Street Bridge back to the shelter.

THE HOOD

This was my chosen route when it was raining. The coffee shop would be my shelter, as I had no wet-weather gear except the water-resistant Oakley hoodie my daughter bought me. That fucking tool Derek had stolen my wicked Fox mountain-bike rainwear.

On clear days, I would go the opposite way and head to a great dog park with Chi to give her some much-needed social time with other dogs, but I tried to keep every human conversation brief and ambiguous so no one could guess my homeless status. Then up to this small hill beside Grandville Island Marina and tennis courts, which offered a superb city and water view. I would lay down on the park bench until I was bored out of my box and then head to Subway, as lunch was always the worst meal of the day and never a reason to go back at noon. I knew my choices from Subway's menu never upset my gut.

To say I was bored stupid is a massive understatement. I knew, though, that I needed this time to recover from my psych-ward ordeal and regain my strength on all levels before reclaiming any sort of semi-normal life. Back in the shelter, I would lie down on my bed for the remaining 90 minutes before being relegated back to the streets at 2 p.m. Now, how do I kill another three hours?

My usual route, especially when it was raining—which it does a lot in Vancouver in the fall and spring—was to go to the central library and onto their computers, since my laptop was long gone. I'd send everyone I was still speaking to (really only my mum and very occasionally my kids) an email update. My short mailing list was not, as you might think, because I had burnt all my bridges; rather, it because of my pride, as I was no longer living the dream with a beautiful family, all the toys I ever wanted and a home in Whistler's privileged millionaire's row. I had lost everything I'd worked so hard for so long to achieve. I was in a homeless shelter with next to no earthly belongings, living off C$10 a day, and it felt like my only real friend left was my beautiful dog, Cheyenne. I felt like a loser, and I simply could not face getting in touch with my old friends.

How would I even describe my situation to anyone? It was something even I could not come to grips with, so how the fuck would anyone else comprehend it and not brand me a failure? So I decided to do what I had learnt to do in my embattled months in Yaletown when my world collapsed around me: isolate and become semi-recluse, with the only reason to walk out the front door or talk to anyone being my dog, Chi. It was like my mental state had entered my own DeLorean time machine and somehow returned to that of my childhood, when I was terribly shy, especially with girls.

I would hit the Tim Horton's on Robson just beside the central library to pick up my daily treat, a vanilla latte and a honey-glazed donut. Sometimes I splurged on ten Timbits, as for the first time in ages, I didn't have to feel guilty—there was no way I was going to bike race that season, or maybe ever again. I then headed to the library and spent hours in front of their Internet terminals.

After I had written another daily update to my mum—these were often *War and Peace*-like size-wise—explaining my current state and all my hopes, dreams and fears for the future, I would go onto YouTube and/ or Vivo, turn myself into a VJ (video DJ) and simply watch and listen to my beloved music. Somehow, it made me feel almost human and sane, and most importantly, put me in my happy place where the tears would be averted except when I put a song on that reminded me of my long-gone glory days. Thank God for sunglasses is all I can say. I still to this day use them whenever possible to hide my sad and all-too-frequently teary eyes.

There were many times when the memories the songs conjured up, combined with the lyrics that with my current life experiences made so much more sense, literally brought the song to life in almost a different dimension, similar to what a good 3D movie coupled with a great story, acting and action can do. Songs that I knew every single lyrical line to all of a sudden came to life and now meant something to me. I had finally figured out that, as with most things in this life, Aristotle's saying perfectly applies: "the whole is greater than the sum of its parts." The combination of notes, instruments, lyrics and voice all of a sudden join together in a masterpiece we call a song. It somehow magically comes alive as it perfectly narrates my very thoughts and feelings of a specific life experience I had lived through—the ups, downs, loves and hates that this life can throw at you, which a particular song so beautifully encapsulates.

If you ask me, great song and storybook writers, along with funny comedians, are the world's purest and truest geniuses. We all need escape from our paycheque-to-paycheque life. I had even started listening to genres I'd never really explored before, especially rap, dance/trance and even country.

The latter in particular had always been a no-go area, but now I understood most if not all the sad subjects they were trying to express. I could relate to the new modern pop-country stuff, like Shania Twain, Faith Hill, Lady Antebellum, Taylor Swift and Carrie Underwood. Most of all, though, I started listening to the older classic country stars like Johnny Cash and, more recently, John Denver, as I could relate to their struggles with women, drugs, rehab/relapse and losing everything you hold near and dear.

I got Johnny Cash's autobiography *Walk the Line* and read it just like I had read MJ's *Moonwalker* the first time I was in the shelter (and for that reason, I can't recall any of it—except the line that the difference between Michael and other greats like Bruce Springsteen and U2 was that his songwriting inspiration came from the heavens as opposed to the street). The absolutely brilliant and Oscar-winning movie made from Cash's book quickly became one of my all-time favorites. I had almost lived the modern, normal (non-famous) equivalent of his story.

My other alternative was a quick visit to the library and then a visit to Vancouver's main shopping precincts, like Robson, Granville and even the gay area on Davie Street, as I was determined to face and hopefully overcome my dumb-ass yet terrible reality-based flashbacks from my childhood that led to my lifelong discomfort around male homosexuals. When it was raining, I would go into the Pacific shopping mall, watch their TV and look at all the cool stuff, like clothes and electronics, that I used to spend a small fortune on and now couldn't afford any of. I became the ultimate window-shopper. This evolution was hard to explain and even harder to actually do. My aim was to take my mind off my present circumstances living in a godforsaken yet good-Samaritan homeless shelter. I craved to return to a normal life, complete with all the trimmings that normal people take for granted.

Tuesday was my special day, as the local movie theatre had cheap admission. You either got a discount ticket in Tinseltown or a large popcorn for free in Scotiabank. I would treat myself to a matinee or early evening flick to further help me escape my less-than-desirable existence. All of this was in service of one thing: surviving another three-plus hours until dinner at 5 p.m. and the rooms reopening at 5:30 p.m. I simply could not stay in there and deal with the never-ending drama and extremely juicy gossip.

The Yukon fueled my eternal desire to escape my reality and find my inner peace, or at least a happy place where I could recharge that thing that had been my nickname: Quiet Strength. I never really got the meaning of the name; the words seemed like a contradiction to me in my "good life" years when the world truly was my oyster. It wasn't until the hard times came that I got a crystal-clear understanding of what my friends meant by it, and thereafter I put everything I had into its pursuit.

I had finally learned first-hand it is the quiet ones, the sleepers, the humble yet quietly confident people you had to be worried about. I not only aspired to be but genuinely believed I was one of them. Don't believe the hype; the arrogant, loudmouth bastards in this world are really the ones who are lacking self-esteem and confidence. They are very insecure omegas behind a brilliant disguise of money, toys, power and lies.

It was somehow comparable to my taste in cars: going for the sleeper hot hatch like my black Ford Fiesta XR2 and my favourite, my very cool Renault, Clio Williams edition, that with its acceleration and handling could blow off in-your-face pimp rides and even put exotics like Porsches, BMWs and Jags in their place. This is obviously back when I could actually afford to own and drive a sick automobile instead of my current hurting scene where I constantly struggled to find enough green for my next meal.

Retail therapy used to be my happy place. I would go out and buy a new car, snowmobile, skis, board swag, electronics or my favourite name-brand sports clothing, watch, etc. Now that option was gone. My new bliss was relaxing in the heat, safety and pure relaxation of one of the shelter's two male baths, which somehow I had failed to locate in my first tour of duty in my psycho days. I would spend sometimes two hours just letting my fears, demons and past melt away in my poor man's steam room. I would enter something bordering on a meditative state with an extra-long soak while listening to my tunes or the best radio vibe. I would stretch out in there and relieve all the tension that riddled my body from years of heavy-duty sporting abuse and my newfound stress and depression, which I did not know back then can actually cause physical as well as mental and emotional pain.

Not only did these baths relax me and keep me sane in an insane reality but I also found them to be one of the best weapons for keep my Crohn's-and IBS-stricken gut in check. I knew deep down I could never deal with narcotic gut syndrome again, with its extreme constipation and drug withdrawal. I had committed so much of my nothing life to researching it to finally explain what had happened to me and cost me everything. It really should have killed me.

After a long soak, I would go back to my room hoping my roommate had gone out. There, I would chill with my dog until my evening shot on the Yukon's computers kicked in, either just before or after 9 p.m. snack time, which ranged from sweet leftovers donated by the local Starbucks to fruit, crackers and sandwiches. It was all just another distraction to take your mind off the truly surreal drama while pretending to watch the mind-numbingly boring TV programs they always seemed to choose.

After witnessing yet another silly fight over what to watch next from the loud ones jockeying for a position at the pinnacle of the Yukon's personality hierarchy, I would take Chi downstairs. I had to wait until all the snacks were gone, as otherwise, with her one-track food mind, she would start a scrum eating someone else's treat and fuck up her gut with non-canine-friendly human food. Two out of three visits to the Yukon had given her pretty severe urinary-tract infections. Before you knew it, it was time for her last walk of the day to end. I gave myself a pat on the back for surviving another day in my homeless world and taking another step on my comeback road to recovery and maybe even re-entering the real world at some point.

Living this kind of life was a huge contradiction. On the one hand, I was genuinely grateful to have a roof over my head and food in my belly for no financial outlay. I tried to repay in the only way I knew how: volunteering to wipe down the tables, help out in the dish pit, break up boxes or pick up butts from the front steps and garden. On the other hand, I felt that I was in a completely foreign earth-based form of what I imagine the real hell to be like, where everything is consumed in a dire struggle and fight just to get by day to day. All I knew is that by the grace of God, I was in a better place this time around. As MJ sang in "Scream," his only duet with his sister Janet, "I've got to get stronger, then I won't give up the fight" and "You tell me I'm wrong then you better prove you're right." I knew I had to access my inner Quiet Strength.

I know that many contestants on *American Idol*, *The Voice*, *X-Factor* and *So You Think You Can Dance* claim that music is their life and has been their saviour. But trust me, there are very few people who can claim that this medium, along with a lifelong love of dance (a direct human extension of the music, as it is a way express music through movement), a love of sports, my blessed dog, my mother, my two beautiful daughters and a few other key people really did save my life. Music has always been but especially now, for the new me, is much more than a tapestry of noises; rather, it is like a religion, a spirit and soul, an integral part of me, almost as important as breathing. It is as close to a happy place as you can ever attain in this barbaric money-and power-driven world that is slowly but surely killing us all.

I must admit, the second go-round in the shelter was like a whole new awakening for me. I was on the other side of the tracks, as my old dear used to say. The first time, I wasn't all there. I believed it was a temporary test of my willpower before I went on to bigger and better things.

One shocking memory serves as a milestone for my recovery. I was doing my usual afternoon routine, sitting in front of the library's computer. But instead of going to my happy place, I challenged myself to sit there without the armour music offered my fragile mental state by blocking out the very real threats that often, with just one word, opened the doors to another PTSD flashback. I decided to test my paranoia, and after about 10 minutes of silence, I realized that I wasn't this rock star with everyone watching my every move. I was no different from anyone else. I was just another person, and no one could give a fuck what I was, where I had been and what the future held in store for me. I was alone, pure and simple.

It was truly a watershed moment in my recovery and existence on this planet. Reality hit hard, and shock, disbelief, pure grief and inherent depression were now my greatest foes rather than the scourge of drugs numbing all my painful past and present. Armed with the power of knowledge, I was determined to stay on my road to recovery. I finally saw addiction for what it was: the fiercest, most vicious and most brutal opponent I had ever faced. I will tell anyone that beating my 12-year prescription-drug addiction that started because of my Crohn's disease—especially in a homeless shelter rampant with every drug known to man—was easily the hardest and longest road I have journeyed down.

Please listen to me, kids, adults, anyone on any kind of drug: be careful with them, be they street drugs like crack, coke, E, acid, meth or mushrooms; weed and alcohol; or the seemingly more innocent and legal drugs that really are synthesized versions of their ghetto counterparts. Learn from my mistakes. I wish I'd had the benefit of reading this so I wouldn't have lost everything I worked my hardest throughout my life to build, just to see it all taken away from me, not because I loved the artificial high but because it seemed a necessary medical solution to my autoimmune disease. At the end of the day, my inevitable dependence really is no different from addiction, and who really cares whether it was blind faith in my doctors or going to Vancouver Eastside to get my desired hit/IV line? The results are the same. Both involve the disease called addiction, and apart from possibly man's abuse of the world's finite resources, I believe it poses the biggest threat to our existence.

At this point, I was absolutely and totally focused on one thing: beating the addiction that I believe claimed some of the world's biggest and brightest stars, including Elvis, Amy Winehouse, Whitney and Prince. The list is almost endless, but of course the most important name on it to me is my own personal hero, MJ. It was as if I was going to avenge his meaningless death, along with my own personal "bad" history, and show all my haters—just like Johnny Cash and the list of totally unknown soldiers who beat the seemingly impossible and overpowering disease of addiction.

The only thing I knew how to do was take one day at a time, just as I had every training and competition day with sports. I put every ounce of my being into beating my new enemy—the most powerful I'd ever had to face. I had the help of some amazing people, to whom I will be eternally grateful; but when all is said and done, no one can do it for you. To make it back from the darkness drugs bring to your world, you have to do it for yourself. Ultimately, the fight is yours and yours alone. It is a very long and lonely road, but believe me, there is light at the end of the tunnel. Although I am still on "The Climb" that Miley Cyrus sang about, and I still face an uphill grind and accept that sometimes I will lose, ultimately I truly believe this cloud must have a silver lining. Someone, somewhere, is looking out for me and is not ready to welcome me through the pearly gates just yet.

That was my existence for my four-month second stay in the Yukon while Sharon went to bat for me trying to find my own escape from the rock, as I called my journey back to the light. After a few possible avenues didn't come to fruition—and left me in a worse place, as they built up my hopes just to have them dashed, kind of like getting rejected by a girl you like but on an entirely different level—I even in complete desperation wrote a "let's get back together" letter to Carol. We both know it was just a "please help me get out of this fucking place" letter, so of course it came to nothing, something I regret to this day.

Word finally came down that a possible move to the residences in the North Shore shelter might be in the cards, as the Lookout Society, which was Sharon's principal employer, had big-time influence over there. This was a much better solution for me than trying to get into the upstairs residency a few privileged souls from the Yukon managed, like my good friend Chris, the recovering gambler. I just had way too many triggers in this place, and complex PTSD was starting to take over my life and become my new health adversary.

The North Shore residency fit my need to get out of the Yukon and into affordable temporary housing. It offered the potential of cheap yet secure housing for up to two years, time enough for me to overcome my demons and get back to a real life. In a strange twist of fate, I had actually been earmarked for a place there during my first stay in the Yukon, and it came up just as I was pink-slipped to the five months in the Richmond psych ward.

Thankfully, the longer I stayed in the Yukon, the stronger I became physically and, more importantly, mentally. Although there were still insane thoughts and very loud voices in my head, the big difference was that my sane brain could recognize them for what they were: the lingering aftereffects of my psychosis. My grey matter treated them almost like email providers like Hotmail and Gmail do with spam, banishing them to my own internal junk-mail folder.

The weather was very slowly starting to switch into the sunshine mode I loved so much about Vancouver over Aberdeen. You actually can count on a pretty decent summer from around May through to September.

THE HOOD

Although I have no explanation for it, as much as I was in denial about getting older, going through that hell had given me an excuse for the grey hairs and ever-deepening crow's feet. The hard-hitting lyrics of my hero's song "Man in the Mirror" seemed to sum up my very existence in this new life.

Although I came to Canada originally for the winters, I was beginning to prefer the heat of summer. Sure, I still loved the snow of Whistler, but I hated the corresponding rain of Vancouver. Just like the weather, my prospects were starting to seem brighter, but things were moving way too slow for my liking. I was desperate to get the fuck out of that place; I had already spent way too much time there and was sick to my teeth of the head games.

My life was beginning to resemble a *Groundhog Day*-esque slow-motion replay of itself, with the same shit over and over. I felt like I was quite literally getting nowhere very slowly on the ultimate hamster wheel. I knew that I had no choice but to grind it out and try everything to overcome my weaknesses and learn patience, something I'd never been able to gain in my full-on fast life. My personality was *I want it all now*. This time, I knew I was powerless and had to put my faith in Sharon to find me a place.

Eventually, after what seemed like an eternity, word came of an available room in the North Shore residency, thank God. Sharon was fighting with everything she had to make sure it was mine, because these places were so hot, driven by the most basic of economic theories of very small supply and ridiculously high demand. All I could do was pray— something that I was getting really good at. When you have no power, you become resigned to looking to a higher power for divine intervention. I remembered from Johnny Cash's autobiography his struggle to get and stay clean and how he turned to religion as his rock. If it worked for him and so many other recovering addicts, maybe it would work for me. Nothing ventured, nothing gained.

I had started to spend some of my afternoons looking into this thing called Christianity that I had a love–hate relationship with. My love was the thought that maybe there was a higher power, fate, karma-like deal so that if what goes around comes around, there was indeed some hope for me. Surely after hitting the depths of depravity, my time was going to come around again. I had paid my dues and then some. My hatred came from all the wars, cults, Sunday morning open displays of wealth and power, and mostly, the pure divide that we humans had twisted religion into.

I read an article about Obama in a *Reader's Digest* in the locked ward in which he often quoted lines from the Bible. That seemed so relevant even today. Hey, anything was worth a try. Maybe God was the reason I was still alive, or at least He might keep me alive. I found a church that was open during the day called the First Mission on Burrard Street, and it did what I genuinely feel all churches should do: gave back by offering free meals for the homeless at 5 p.m. every day as well as temporary beds in the winter. That was very cool in my eyes and just what the Bible tells us to do for our fellow human beings.

I must admit to some apprehension in going back to the house of God, as with my disastrous dark past, I felt like one of His forgotten souls. I tried to convince myself of the critical point that He might have stood by and let me get Crohn's, narcotic gut, severe drug addiction and drug-induced psychosis. He may have allowed me to be evicted and badly beaten and robbed on the streets. But He came through in the clutch by saving me from a definite death.

In *The Pursuit of Happiness*, a story so close to my own tale, Will Smith explains God's work so aptly. The story goes something like this:

> There is a drowning man in the ocean. A cruise ship goes past and offers to save him, but in reply the man says, "Don't worry, God will save me."
>
> After three more boats do the same with the same result because of his undying faith that somehow God will save him, he eventually succumbs to the waves and drowns.
>
> On his staircase to heaven, he is met at the gates by God himself. So the man queries God with, "Why on Earth did you not save me, as my faith was so strong and unwavering?"
>
> To which God replies, "I sent four ships to save you that you refused. I gave you the vessels to save yourself. So you only have yourself to blame."

It was such a powerful story that I kept it in my back pocket throughout my worst times, especially in the shelter, where you always had the born-again Christian God Squad that brought every conversation back to the same kind of advice: "Don't worry, son, God will save you."

I would politely smile, think of that story and walk away muttering under my breath, "Yeah, right, maybe. But sometimes in this life, with or without God, you have to be the catalyst for change and ultimately save yourself with God's help."

I spent many chill afternoons in the church actually reading probably the most important book of all time, something I had never done before. To explain its impact on me is incredibly difficult. Suffice to say it was mind-blowing, almost overpowering, as its uncanny scriptures seemed to explain so many things I had never known. I had thought it was an out-of-date document that caused more of today's problems, like wars, than it ever solved. I realized for the first time that regardless of whether it was fact or fiction, its underlying messages were so pivotal to our very existence as human beings and this home we all call Earth that if people stopped misinterpreting, it could in fact be the missing piece of the puzzle to not only explain our journey as a species but provide the very answers we all seek to begin anew as a people.

Fundamentally, to me, it provided the reasons I was seeking to stay strong throughout my painful comeback, riddled with all too many frustrations. I even started attending Sunday service in St. Andrew's church opposite, because the service's timing was more conducive to my schedule and commitments at the shelter. This was quite harrowing for me, as it was in this very church, when I was insane, that I'd booked an appointment with the minister to reveal my belief that my hero, Michael Jackson, was actually an angel sent down by God himself to save the world and every one of its inhabitants, and as with Jesus before him, the evil within us all had contrived to kill him. All we had to do was listen to the messages in his uplifting lyrics to find a road map to follow to a better world.

The minister couldn't contain his opposing views of Michael being an accused pedophile and even laughed in my face, which I found so annoying and strange. I stormed out. Was it not, after all, the church that had a history of being one of the biggest culprits of child abuse ever?

Although I knew the minister would remember the incident, I had to face my fears of flashback city. I attended many of his fairly insightful Sunday services over four months with the aim of trying to find a better way to live in this second chance at life God had so graciously granted me.

Like Sharon said, this time, it couldn't be about money or power. By going so hard at everything I did, my mere human shell of a body had to bend, buckle and break. This time was all about non-materialistic and intangible things, like the quest for true love. Right at the top of my list was being as good a person as I could be—giving back to the world that damn near killed me and then brought me back from the brink of death. Other goals were finding a job I actually wanted to get up for, even if it meant taking a sizable pay cut. I had learnt the hardest way possible that personal enjoyment and fulfillment are way more important than dumb shit like disposable income and toys.

I wanted to travel the world and see all its rich cultures, history, geography, topography, languages and people. One thing I could never understand is how our language barriers get in the way of communication, especially the old-school face-to-face kind, something I am sure is absolutely critical to our survival and, with the ever-growing progression of technology, becoming a lost art. Why don't we teach our kids and ourselves the best, most universally accepted form of sign language? As a species, we aren't the best listeners, and so a non-verbal type of communication is a much more comprehensive way of getting your message across. Not only could we speak to everyone, even the deaf, but when both languages are used in conjunction, we would improve our retention of information even with those who speak the same language.

I have always been gifted with an out-of-the-box, lateral-thought-based intelligence that has both its pros, like terrific idea generation, and its cons, like ADHD, poor attention to things I am not good at or find dull, and weakness at detail-orientated tasks, putting my out-there ideas into practice and listening. I was convinced my insanity had actually increased this trait, as it was as if I was doing a full-scale business and marketing plan with its intrinsic mission statement and SWOT analysis (strengths, weakness, opportunities and threats) on not only myself but more generally on life, the universe and everything. It was like I was working again as a business and marketing consultant as I had decades earlier. I needed to create work for myself to stop getting so bored and vulnerable to relapse.

I also needed work to overcome my increasingly disturbing complex PTSD, which in many ways resembled another form of psychosis. My only defence was something that Celia had taught me through the best therapy I had ever found: cognitive behavioral therapy. It involves moving forward with your life, and every time you experience triggers for flashbacks, remain in that moment and don't let your brain drift back into memories. In effect, it meant not focusing on my very painful past but rather doing everything to stay in the present, as that is all I can affect.

Looking back, especially at everything my family had to deal with because of me, a few dumb incurable diseases and a mental breakdown, I got so good at acting normal, no one really saw me as another human being with a story. It really does hurt when you think people are laughing at you, a mind trick of complex PTSD.

Finally, my time came to move out of the Yukon, hopefully forever. I truly was starting to doubt it would ever really happen. Emotional doesn't even come close to explaining where my head was at, as on the one hand I was so gigantically amped to move out but I was also so scared of the future without Sharon beside me. I had to learn to stand on my own two feet with next to nothing and start all over again. I had to tell myself that contrary to my character and previous existence, this time around I had to learn to walk before I ran. I simply could not afford another trip and fall, as it would probably mean death this time.

My guardian angel Sharon and good friend Chris helped me move all of my remaining earthly belongings out of my Yaletown mini-storage and ship it over in the driving rain to the tiny but godsent new pad for free. Finally I could come "home," close the door and shut out the world to recharge instead of living with a roommate who was dealing with his own personal issues that were part of the territory in the hood and having a living room filled with more than 70 people, most of whom would sell their grandmother for a profit—sorry, more likely for a fix. I even had a TV and sole possession and power over its controller. At last, I could watch what I liked when I liked. Basically, I was going to regain most of the things that everyone, including myself, had always taken for granted. It was the best thing that had happened to me in so long, although I knew it was fraught with potential snakes. I had actually restarted my lifelong game of snakes and ladders, and this could be the first ladder in my journey back to life.

After many trips back and forth from the Yukon and storage, I found myself all alone, sleeping on the floor in my new home, in my sleeping bag, cuddled into my dog, Cheyenne, and crying my eyes out. It was hard to know which tears were the happy relieved ones and which were the not-so-positive sad ones, filled with memories of what I had endured. My overall concern was, is this really going to be my savior? Like it or not, I was still in a homeless shelter surrounded by all my demons, skeletons, ghosts, fears and temptations. I eventually convinced myself that none of that should matter. I was indeed a very lucky guy, and I needed to enjoy this moment for what it really was: an answer to my prayers. It was a giant stepping stone back to what most call a normal life. I must admit, the second go-round in the shelter was like an awakening for me. I just wish I could remember more of it, as I know there are so many funny stories from my time there.

I visited my long-time psychiatrist, Ron Remick. This was a hard thing for me to do, as when I was in my crazy years, I felt he wasn't doing as much as he could to help me overcome my disease of addiction. I would write basically attacking him and warning him that if he didn't do more, I would take it to his "highest" superiors, and failing that, I would take my plight to the media. That was back in my asshole addict period. I had also sent quite a few totally off-the-wall emails asking him to save me from my inevitable death.

I also did that with my previous employers, like Whistler Blackcomb and, worse still, Ecolab. I wanted to come back to my high-paying territory manager position, but in line with my doctor's advice, this time without the 24/7 on-call pager deal. When they refused, I hired an employment lawyer and successfully sued them for C$30,000, but in the longer term, I had forever lost a decent reference or a job opportunity in the industry I worked so hard and long in.

On our first meeting in over two years, Ron spelt it out in the most basic terms. I didn't want hear it, but I kind of knew deep down that there was no magic pill to keep me clean, deal with my intense complex PTSD and cure my terrible depression. Worst of all, he confirmed that I had hit my brain so hard with all the drugs that not only had I most likely taken many years off my life expectancy but also the lasting effect of the drugs had left me with a condition very similar to post-concussion syndrome.

Finally, I had an explanation for my brain not being as sharp as it used to be. With every thought, decision and verbal communication, it was as if someone had hit the slow-motion and pause button on my brain. Just like a computer, it would freeze until I closed the other windows to give it enough juice to let me focus on the immediate task in hand. This was most prevalent when I would get goaded into a slagging or ragging match, as my brain was simply too slow to come up with the much-needed witty reply.

Actually, thinking about it, the worst is when I am speaking to a girl I fancy. All of a sudden, a combination of nerves because of my shyness coupled with my severely damaged brain meant a big-time loss of my swag, mojo and game. All I could do was rely on my politeness, chivalry and decent physique, as my brain had somehow been damaged, possibly past the point of repair.

At AA meetings, they hammered into us not to date because friendship could become a fix/need just like a drug, and if you broke up, it was a proven temptation to relapse because of your neediness. Instead, we were advised to stay as far as possible away from the sex, love and romance gig for at least a couple of years so we could prove to ourselves that we had indeed come clean through willpower and no longer need a fix, be it chemical, emotional or whatever, to numb or at least ease the pain. We needed to be able to make our journey to a life without any external chemical intervention to get through the hardest times.

This is something I took to heart. I was determined not to be yet another victim of relapse. If you look at the figures, less than 4 percent of addicts (even less if you consider addiction, mental illness and homelessness) successfully beat addiction in the long term. Come hell or high water, I was on a mission to prove to myself and the world that I was indeed a champion not only of a sport but this time of life itself.

The prescribed two-year celibacy resolution actually has turned into six years for me, fuelled by my willpower to beat my new adversary, which is addiction, and the still very clear painful memories of how my 23-year romance with Carol had turned into the nightmare that was my new life. I knew I wasn't strong enough to venture onto that minefield ever again.

CHAPTER 14

NOT AFRAID

Well after yet another move, God I was beginning to wonder how many more as I had moved so many times in such a short period of time after walking out on Carol so many years earlier. I just appealed to myself that this time it was for best and not to a hell like all my moves since my traumatic eviction had sent me, and I had two whole years to get my shit together. But trying to stay positive when there was all my crap all over the floor it was hard to start all over again, like how many times I have to do this before I find my paradise. I decided that instead of me getting all the stress from the mess, I would just do a little a time, and spent the next few days spending a couple of hours a day going to through all my stuff. One big bonus was I had finally got my pimped out wardrobe back including my passion for clothes, especially cool: t's, tops, hoodies, hats and most important of all my sick kicks, a stable for dancers must have the most unique exclusive and coolest. Problem was the residency rooms were so tiny, like smaller than the smallest room in our Whistler mansion and yes going from a 2700 ft2 house in Whistler to a 400ft2 studio not only hurt that thing we call pride, but also something had to give as I didn't have the storage to fit it all in. Screw it, like always I would figure out something if I just left it alone for a while and leave my sub conscious to figure it out. I don't think there had ever been a time that I was so mixed up emotional-wise, on the one hand I was truly filled with sadness as was this is what my life had been reduced to as all my worldly belongings could now fit into this tiny Spartan box. But on the other, for the first time in so long, I had got a place all to myself where I could close the world out by simply shutting my front door. I decided I needed to concentrate on the later and start doing the glass is half full rather than empty.

Like it or not, I had to accept that what my drug infested psychosis told me that somehow someone would have pity on my plight and give me my dream Whistler &/ or Yaletown life back, wasn't going to happen Andrew: not now, not ever so time to man up and get on with it you idiot-yes negative voices have become another insecurity that comes as part of my Complex PTSD package that I do everything to hide from the world. It was a very different perspective/ outlook on life, the harsh reality that basically slapped me in my face bigtime one morning when I woke up. Still I decided I should, no must try to be proud of myself for the fact I was still alive and yes I needed to try with everything I was to completely forget my glory years by trying to erase the memory and just accepted my new reality for what it was, a new beginning and a massive step in the right direction compared to where I had spent my time since my eviction. Just as the Eagles proclaimed "Get over it" or the football coach: "So now what". Problem was and still is: Complex PTSD does exactly the opposite and dredges up the past continually for some reason usually wins to which I am sometimes absolutely powerless – being a bit of a control freak it is something I hate more than words!

Armed with that thought and a few hours spent sorting out my basic living essentially I decided to go out and check out my new HOOD. My new home was very basic but again I made that a positive by the simple realism like: Andrew what could you realistically expect to get for C$325 in Vancouver with the most inflated real estate market in the whole of Canada. Why that is the case I will never know as there are so many avenues for them to build more in the surrounding forests to better match supply and demand. Match in fact was a website I had decided to join as I felt that some of the criteria I had used to not date as really how could you chat a woman when you are: in between jobs, had no car to go to their place to pick them up in but critically had to go back to their place as I still lived albeit upstairs in a homeless shelter. Be honest women, how many of you would have given this loser even a second glance if you knew the truth, none right as quite honestly I would have been exactly the same with you ladies if I knew the same about you. Even watching Will Smiths Hitch or Mel Gibson's What Women Want movies would save my lonely world until I fulfilled the most basic checklist of today's somewhat erroneous dating criteria, namely:

- Are you clean not only from personal hygiene point of view but also free from drugs
- What you are wearing?
- What job do you do (and therefore how much are you worth) car you drive etc.
- Where do you live?
- Personality, chemistry and humor? Again my sense of humor was always different because it is a simple fact there is a huge gulf between European and American sense of humors, why I will never know which means I was never going to win a girl over here because of my weird sense of humor especially now with my drug damaged brain.

And yes in that order when really in my ideal world the order would be turned on its head but to be honest after my ordeal, all I cared about was the non-materialistic ones like how you looked and did we have a spark to get my juices flowing.

So rather timidly I opened my front door to my new life and decided to go for a walk with Chi around to the local shopping mall at Capilano. I went down the elevator to the shelter part of the building and introduced myself to the front desk staff who seemed cool and walked Cheyenne around to the mall about 10 minutes away. Well put simply, it was just another mall full of memories how my life used to be as we used to hit this mall with my family in my good old days and now it was just another trigger for my emotional pain as I couldn't afford any the cool toys it offered. But again armed with my new positive take on life, I tried to turn reverse the negative into a positive as at least it was new surroundings as I had seen enough of downtown Vancouver shopping to last a lifetime. The biggest bonus there was a Starbucks to give me the excuse to daily leave my homeless shelter to visit the normal people for a couple of hours and therefore be treated like one myself as no-one there knew my bad rap past and that I had to return to my homeless surroundings which labels anyone in there with a red flag target placed squarely on your back. It also offered me the opportunity to email my folks on my precious I-pod Touch as I still didn't have enough green to buy a new net book or laptop. Emailing from a Touch is tricky at best but you have to cut your cloth deal and make do but yes my new goal was to try to save up enough to buy a new computer. On my way back I checked out the Extra Food's Superstore that I had visited yesterday to stock up on the absolute start my life all over again essentials that my folks had offered me through Sharon C\$500 to get me back on my feet & agreed to pay my C\$325 rent which was a huge but very welcome surprise. Nothing really jumped out at me apart from some real nice and rich North Shore yummy mummy's as Vancouver's North Shore is not just an international mecca for my new favorite sport, mountain biking, but also is millionaires row because of its simply stunning views of the more than spectacular Pacific ocean, snow-capped mountains and cityscape that made it Hollywood North a primetime tourist hot spot as well as a very addictive place to live if you were like me and loved outdoor sports.

Back to my new home, I tried everything to duck any conversation with its inhabitants and went back upstairs to my new pad and figured out the basics like where to plug the TV into and called Shaw cable to make their connection for my very own TV, a normal pleasure that I hadn't had since Yaletown as both Rogers and Telus were still chasing me for unpaid balances from watching Pay Per View movies and my Ultimate Fighting Championships obsession. After another few hours of unpacking there was a knock on my door and I was met by this tall lanky dude called Mark who was more than a bit geeky and creepy but guessed he was a veteran of the place and lived just around the hallway from me. Just for the record creepy is another word that I hate as when I was in VGH, I overheard the nurses outside my morning shower call someone creepy and my fucked up Complex PTSD and especially easily its worst symptom; hyper vigilance and the resultant trust no-one that tricks you to believing that as you scan literally everyone's conversation and somehow it decides all of them pertain to you. This is something I hate more than anything because my logical side of my brain that tells you that it is just a trick of your mind, but my new mental disease counters and over-powers any logical brain wave and replaces it with what it wants you to believe. It's just like a form of psychosis: extreme anxiety, insomnia, depression and at its worst, very real bad panic attacks that makes you so tired at the end of every day. It is often confused with Autism (is something your born with) as these two mental diseases are so similar as displayed in The Good doctor TV show, Beautiful Mind & Extremely Close Incredibly Loud, all very fine flicks.

Back in my new home, I looked out the window to see my new view of the Oasis car wash opposite just to remind me of how much I had fallen as all the over-priced German cars went in to get sparkly again to announce them as the yard stick of your success on this planet. Rather than hiding the real fact that I wish I realized before I did waste a small fortune on some very fine rides mainly just to prove my new millionaires rich bastard status. Just as just as Johnny Cash proclaimed decades ago, cars are the biggest waste of money and natural resources this planet has ever seen fueled just like prescription medications by yet another gigantic political lobby from both the manufacturers and their suppliers right down to the oil lobbyists. Again I tried to find the positive but this time I couldn't find one so I did what I always do when life gets too hard to bear, find some mellow music and go to my happy place as it somehow melts my thoughts away in a piping hot bath followed by a cup of tea and curl up in bed with my beloved pal Chi.

Despite the huge mess, it didn't take me very long to get into a kind of daily routine, thankfully this time was self-imposed as probably the biggest plus of my move was I didn't have to leave the apartment apart from walking Chi and could get up or crash at any time I liked. On top of this the Shaw cable guy had hooked up TV and I was finally in complete control what I watched and was eager for the World Cup of Football. Or for the reason I still don't understand, in North America it is called soccer as compared to the mega popular American Football which really has got fuck all to do with any balls at feet, but like rugby was predominately a hand on ball game! In truth I was never the biggest fan of the world's most popular "beautiful" game as I had only gone to one football game in my life which was a total bore, a scoreless tie between Aberdeen and Hibernian in the pouring rain at Pitodree where I bought the worst grease ridden meat pie to overcome the boredom. Yes I actually prefer American Football now as it more like my favorite game Rugby.

It didn't take me very long to realize that the residency contained above homeless shelters only really differed from the downstairs was you were on a much longer time line (two years) & you could make your own schedule and most importantly you could shut the world out by closing your front door. But very crucially in terms of clientele, there was absolutely no difference as it was in effect an outlet for the lucky inhabitants of shelters to transition to. Nowhere was this more evident than my supposed neighbor directly across the hall Brett, a French Canadian guy who was indeed an addict of my favorite poison, namely liquid morphine and was more than willing to continually offer it to me as Mark who proved the biggest juicy gossip merchant (he should have been a women) So almost as soon as I had shared my dark secret with him, namely my more than a decade of prescription painkillers, within days of me admitting my addiction to that dumb ass, it spread like wildfire to seemingly everyone in the joint, now maybe you understand my trust no-one armor. On my floor there was another disability guy called Richard who was a huge pothead but seemed trust worthy and this Japanese guy that had a cute girlfriend but I just could tell there was something sketch about and it didn't take Mark long to inform my suspicions were correct and was a huge junkie himself and was affiliated to one of the biggest Asian triad drug gangs in the city. There was also a real quiet guy in the next room who was always super polite and respectful to both me and Chi, and opposite him this 50 something lady named Sarah who was kind enough to come over and welcome me to my new HOOD with the book of one of my favorite films: Marley and Me as it sums up the magical bond between humans and canines so well along but the last 30 minutes get me every time as I always cry remembering my beautiful Golden retriever Vharie from my childhood and worse still, the realization that somewhere in the not too distant future, I was going to have to face that extreme trauma again with Cheyenne's passing, quite how I simply have no idea as that will hurt more than anything I have been subjected to so far as she is the only friend that never pointed the finger, judged or dropped me through my very worst times (see even writing it brings on the tears, take 5 time)

After being there a few weeks I had finally managed to condense my life into an even smaller package of belonging by donating almost half of my remaining wardrobe to charity as I was determined to give back to the organization that had saved my soul. In truth I wish I never gave so much away as especially I decided to get rid of some real cool winter gear as it was coming into summer and I had no idea how long I was going to stay in my new home. I was living off a mattress on a cold floor and living with a bunch of ex-cons, criminals, mental illness and addictions running rampant but so be it, it was still a God send compared to the Yukon. Sharon came over from time to time but after about a month informed me she could no longer be my rock of a social worker in my new digs but tried in vain to show me how to cook food, another one of my biggest weaknesses.

It was also around that time I found out firsthand how close to the edge I still really was. It came one night when completely accidently I had ran out of my must have Zopiclone sleeping pills and in a desperate attempt to get some sleep that night, I popped two Cesamet pain pills which really are just a man-made version of marijuana as I knew it mellowed me out and in my teenage years sent me to sleep. After popping that couple which had the numbing effect but not the switch off totally, I popped another 4 as it was now 4am in the morning and I needed some shut eye. Well no joke, within an hour my mind was tripping, but this was not a good trip. No more than just a buzz, it had somehow opened the pathway back to the ever present world of hurt that is psychosis/ schizophrenia in my mind that I had such literally insane memories of. As such, my brain was both numb and racing at the same time and all I could think of was being pink slipped certified all over again, more than scary. Although I wanted to hide in the hope that the symptoms would subside over time, I couldn't because I had to somehow cure my insomnia so I decided to go to the mall and get my repeat prescription from the walk in clinic there. Well as soon as I left my pad the intense psychosis kicked in but this time my whole being couldn't handle it as just like before my brain was tricking me that everyone and everything was looking at me and it wasn't going to be long before I was back in the Looney bin, something I simply could not face. The impact on my brain was so profound that when I reached the clinic, I literally could not string a cohesive sentence together and trust my luck they were lined out the door with patients. I knew I could not handle the hour wait time and promptly left the mall and sat outside trying in vain to collect myself and hide the war between sane and insane that was the present state of my brain.

Thankfully I made it back to my digs and Mark came around and didn't take him long to figure out what was going on. So to my absolute amazement he went around and got a prescription of my sleeping pills for himself and gave me what I so desperately needed to sleep. It was not only a huge setback for my brain as it genuinely felt after the psychosis subsided nearly a week later, it felt I had been concussed from the numerous times I had endured that same fate in my various sporting activities. My brain was bruised beyond belief and all I could do was try everything to rest it while it recuperated but also the biggest scare ever as I had no idea it was so easy for me to re-open that drug induced crazy file in my filing cabinet drawer in my brain back to psycho-ville. But now I knew exactly what Dr. Remick had been explaining the post-concussion syndrome effect drugs could emulate on my grey matter and warned me to be extremely careful of any mind altering drugs whether it was prescription or street style. To this day, that means no matter how sore I get on any level, I can't take painkillers to ease the physical pain & my Crohn's makes it impossible to take Ibuprofen so I am left with my very high pain threshold with some really cool ways of dealing with physical pain but none come close to the medicinal solutions. Believe me it really sucks when I am sore as everyone just looks past my pain & in their consummate knowledge think I am just wanting to "chase the dragon" again even though that view is so far from the truth as I am 110% committed to not screw up this merciful second chance at life.

Thankfully after about a week, the psychosis symptoms had abetted somewhat but my brain was both still real sore and "crazy" slow (now you know why I hate the crazy new word so much because it is yet another huge trigger to put me right back in my psyche ward) as it honestly felt like I had taken a full power round house kick to my head. All I did was focus all my remaining brain cells on the task ahead: making this room into my new home and although I have never been a Mr. Clean freak, rather a pretty tidy person that can put up with some mess but yes I hate living in a tip like some men. What a relief to get finished and yes I won't lie, it had restored a modicum of pride in myself as for once I was moving forward rather than my more usual going nowhere fast: 1 steps up 2 steps back (just like the powerful lyrics in the same name Springsteen classic). I was, however, still broke beyond belief as despite my folks thankfully agreeing to pony up the C$325 accommodation portion of my new pad, I now had to buy all my own groceries with still only being on CPP disability of C$600/ month. I just kept telling myself better being skint but having my own space and privacy as I always have been a very private and guarded person, but even more so now as my past is something I desperately wanted to hide from everyone. I managed to get by as I always do and still managed my daily treat of a Starbucks Skinny Supremo Vanilla Latte and went online to escape reality for a while. I put myself on a super strict budget as I was absolutely determined to save up enough to buy a laptop. So the South African Football World Cup came and went, in fairness it wasn't the most exciting tournament I have ever seen but was a good waste of time, something I was beginning to be an expert at even though I fucking hated it.

As the weather started to turn into summer, I decided to venture further afield and explored my new hood more as I was still very fragile and yes unapologetically timid as I knew deep downside I was still very weak on all levels but especially mentally. I found this totally chill tiny park beside this marina with a spectacular view of the city over the water and latterly a dog friendly park at the back of the adjacent Auto Mall where I used to frequent deciding on what car was going to be my next flight of fancy, yeah right!. I would walk around there about 2pm every day and just chill in awe of the view and occasionally spot a sea lion basking in the harbor bay, a super laid back piece of nature tucked away in the heart of suburbia. It also offered me the opportunity of meeting some "normal" people as it always amazes me how a dog can initiate conversations that would never otherwise arise without our canine friends. Why then do we have all these stupid rules like no dogs or up to between 20-50lbs breeds when they are usually the ones that have the small man's mentality and not allowed on public transport, have to be on leashes (how would you like to be ushered around like that, and not allowed to bark as it's their form of communicating) etc. I had also become intimately aware of just how much Cheyenne was helping me with my increasingly difficult struggle with my Complex PTSD which seemed similar yet different from my psychosis.

The crew at the front desk were really helpful and hooked me up with a religious based organization across the road from the shelter that not only offered to help me with counselling and even had a mini food bank. There aren't words to describe how small I felt when I eventually put my pride aside and accepted their offer to go shopping in there as everything was in this free mini market just to get me back on my feet. It was such a demoralizing experience I vowed I would never go back because of my fiercely independent character but knew the counselling might help my worst enemy, the war that was my head. They hooked me up with this free counsellor who was very welcoming and professional and although she was no Celia, I was still incredibly thankful for her help as she reintroduced this mind trick called Cognitive Behavioral Therapy to help me cope with my horrendous memories which were triggered in my all-encompassing shell shock flashbacks.

After a couple of months I heard from Carol that she too was wanting to move on from what was our 25 year romance so we scheduled a meeting at her stupid expensive lawyer who really was the biggest bitch of all time that had literally wiped me clean and put me on the streets and all the rest. Despite being hugely anxious and nervous of having such a meeting on their turf, I agreed as I knew that at some point I had to face my fears and only then could I truly make a new life for myself. The only downside about being in the North Shore was without any car, it was quite the trek on public transit including buses and sea ferry to get downtown which was a pain but seeing I had spent the last few years of my life walking the downtown core, I only really went there once a fortnight, especially on Welfare Wednesday when I received my government payment to treat myself with some small reward for staying clean just like the reward method I had used decades earlier to quit smoking so I knew it worked for me. I had thought long and hard about what I wanted the meeting to include so I got dressed smartly and took a big breath and entered the palatial offices with a stunning view of Vancouver skyline. It has always amazed me why society holds these individuals in such a high regard seeing they are some of the biggest vultures that let's face it mainly prey on our hardships and conflicts and do it in an oh so under hand way that we have no choice but pay their exorbitant fees as they like their professional counterparts in the medical field intentionally continue to use the bygone language Latin and a set of rules that is impossible for the average man and women to comprehend if we don't use them when we try to defend ourselves, good luck with that or utilize the next to useless free Peoples attorney straight in school law students.

The meeting was a simple: how do we divide up the remaining assets from our love partnership and yes like always the divorce system is so biased towards to the female (no I'm not being male chauvinist here because in fairness I do appreciate there are many other avenues in this life males have the upper hand) that I knew I was going to have to bite my lip and more than compromise big-time if I was going to get what I wanted from this meeting on enemy territory. The biggest thing I wanted was one or two of my more than a dozen top end bikes that she had collected from my Yaletown apartment right after she fucking evicted me (how the fuck can you sell someone's possession that I paid for? A fact I had only just learnt when we had moved to the North Shore and I was still livid about and had sold them without telling me to help fund her ludicrous C$110,000 lawyer's fees to bury me in various garage sales. So yes when all was said and done, I got what I wanted and after the meeting she gave me back one of my road bikes back, my endurance training Specialized S-Works Roubaix ride as she had sold my favorite pimped out super light-weight race weapon that was my Trek 5.2 Madone steed which for some reason was the best climbing bike I had ever had (and in reality that was my weakest link in my cycling exploits with my body type) and promised to bring down the last remaining Scott Spark mountain bike on her next visit. As much as I wanted to challenge her sole custody, visit protocol of less than a few hours not even once a month drove me nuts but I knew I would be wasting my time with my medical history and having no means of either going up to Whistler to see them or most importantly pay child support which I genuinely felt bad about and will always applaud Carol for not chasing me for as I obviously had no way of paying. In fairness, her tactics were a major part of the reason I couldn't work so yes she decided to bite the hand that helped fed them for so many years. That is the primary reason I never chased our/ my investments in pensions, savings etc & we had many worth a great deal of green.

Of course the tires were flat so I walked over to the local Specialized dealer: Simon's Bikes in the heart of downtown and borrowed their floor pump and took my beloved top of the range white Italian stallion Sidi road shoes that had treated me so fine for so many grueling kilometers without a single hitch and threw my leg over my baby and immediately entered my Heaven on Earth. It was one of those pure magic moments that you will treasure all your life as it was yet another momentous occasion on my 'road" to recovery. In a strange twist of fate, my favorite rapper Eminem had also decided to get clean at the same time and it was as if we were going through exactly the same hardship and struggle at the same time as I listened to both his Relapse and his new album so appropriately titled for both of us: Recovery. He just had an uncanny way of expressing through his powerful lyrics almost every thought I had run and re-run over and over again. In particular his iconic "Not Afraid" song became my new anthem that I played over and over again as although deep down I was frankly terrified of so many things, especially relapsing, I had learnt to put on this tough persona needed to hide my let's face it more than colorful past and very real and justifiable demons that the normal world would be so judgmental of, and not in a good way.

Well it didn't matter a jot that I had lost every ounce of cardio fitness and was sweating profusely and could hardly breathe on roads that I thought nothing of previously, but who cares, I was the King of my World that day. I remember grinning from ear to ear on entering Vancouver's jewel in the crown Stanley park and rode it like a kid that had just taken off his stabilizing wheels off and had learnt to balance on a bike and discovered the absolute freedom it offered. I stopped at my special spot and watched the float planes take off as flight which was always my kid's fascination and was in sheer contentment that even the tourists around me seemed to be put in a good mood by my infectious smile. Then I set off to head back to my North Shore home and up a rather steep hill before I hit Lions Gate Bridge. Well again it mattered not a jot that everything in my body was screaming stop to give me a break from the physical pain, it only made me push even harder as good old Lance would say in the same position "Pain is temporary, Glory is forever" (a saying I use more than most in my new life) and I was on top of the world riding over the Lions Gate bridge that was so nearly became my ultimate resting place when a few years earlier I had stopped and genuinely contemplated ending it all by becoming yet another jumper. Although I really should have gone right back as my legs and lungs were on fire, I just had to stay on it for a while longer as I was in pure ecstasy, but this time it was from a natural high of adrenalin, testosterone and endorphins. A thought came over me that for maybe the first time I was actually starting to believe that maybe this time around, THIS IS IT, and instead of becoming a corpse like my lifelong pal Michael, against all odds, I could actually complete my comeback this time.

For some bizarre reason, this time I could actually cope with returning to the shelter as I was so pumped up after my ride as this was something I had dreamed of so many times over my ridiculous few years but never really knew whether I would ever get to enjoy the danger, pure pain, excitement, breath taking (excuse the pun) scenery and the wind in your hair that your entirely self-propelled speed that is riding a bike does for me and my very inner soul. And in a strange twist of fate, I actually managed to have a real sleep that night, so totally content in the knowledge that I was indeed back and more determined than ever to make this one stick and prove all my judgmental haters who without even knowing both sides of the story so damned me because today I was again a champion in my own eyes. I had finally reached a point that you pretty much couldn't give a fuck what anyone said about me because like it or not, I had been called every derogatory name under the sun and instead of letting it get to me and in effect let the naysayers win, I was going to try to rise above it all not because I was now a better person, instead that I had finally found a place where I had indeed found a modicum of the inner peace, security and self-belief that I had craved so much for so long. I knew like everyone I am only human and therefore far from perfect and don't know everything, but just like humanity has to learn from our History, I had to do the micro version of that and indeed learn once and for all from my experiences both good and bad and sculpt an entirely new life for myself and my soul mate Cheyenne. I just kept telling myself that I had survived things that would have broken most men or women, and although it had also broken me, just like exercise breaks down muscle tissues and then the body rebuilds them even stronger than before. Most crucially, the shit that I had been through was not going to define me as a man, instead give me an inner strength and resilience that I could only dream of before I was dragged through the gutter.

After meeting all the residents in various gatherings the staff organized for us, it didn't take me very long to realize that if I indeed wanted to regain a "normal" life if such a thing existed as I was seriously beginning to wonder, that I needed to surround myself with normal people and escape the shelter life completely. It wasn't that some think that I believed I was better in anyway than them, just the basic facts that these places are hotbeds of serious alcohol and drug addiction, mental illness, physical fights and people that were trying so desperately to survive their lives in the shadows, they would do anything and everything to get what they needed at any chosen time, usually their hit of choice. This was proved more than ever when after months of scrapping by I finally had saved enough I could finally go and buy myself a new laptop from the local Future Shop. I was so happy I could scream but my joyous state was short lived as one day out walking my baby I am pretty sure I had locked the door as it was an absolute must in there, but a new resident who was well known for being a huge thief and I was to be his first victim. He somehow had picked my front door lock and helped himself to my brand new laptop and more critically my escape from reality it brings. To say I was crushed is simply nowhere near strong enough and it was that incident that pushed me over the brink. How I never went over to teach this leech a lesson I will never know (well I really it was solely fight=eviction to the Hood) but I knew I couldn't as that would just lead me back to a place I was trying everything to keep at arm's length i.e. a return to the down and out streets of Vancouver.

After that I was set on moving out but to where. Whistler was the only place I knew in my new adopted country of Canada and although there was an enormous case for moving back to "hometown" of Aberdeen, I was determined not to run away from my fears instead confront them head on. I went up to the local Library that was a decent climb on my bike and hit the free internet there and got all the accommodation adverts in the online Whistler Piquet, Question and good old Andrewslist and decided that the only way I was going to prove my return to health was to go back to the place that both made me and broke me. The most important reason was ultimately nothing to do with my procrastinators but a chance to reconnect with my adorable kids that I missed more than words can ever express. It had obviously been real hard for them to understand how once their father had gone from King of the Hill in ritzy glitzy Whistler to become a drug addicted dead beat Dad in the gutter of Vancouver that has to be seen to be believed. As the terrific The Beat CTV police reality show demonstrated so clearly that Vancouver rather than the equally brutal streets of its American counterpart squalors like Detroit, Chicago, New Orleans etc was indeed North America's biggest drug capital. Don't get me started on that one, unbelievable is the only word that comes close to describing the anarchy and mayhem there where even the cops stay in their cars and turn a blind eye on most of the crime and drugs that goes down there.

It was coming around time for Whistler biggest summer festival, a massive tribute to my new favorite sport mountain biking and when I lived up there I didn't miss a single competition to either enter or watch myself.

So again I saved up the best I could and caught the early Greyhound and headed back to my old stomping grounds with more than a bit of trepidation at who I would meet there and how they would or wouldn't accept me. I had pre-booked a bed in the youth hostel as I simply could no longer afford the overpriced hotel accommodation and although I knew it wasn't ideal as it is situated 10 kilometers from the hub of the resort town, it was the best I could do for now so just suck it up Andrew. The irony of my situation was not lost on me, how the hell could I go from one of its most financially comfortable residents of this millionaires paradise that was really the international Mecca for the rich and famous to hardly being able to afford to eat after I paid my lodging and bus fees, yes it bit me harder than even I expected and unbeknown to my 3 roommates, I cried myself to sleep every night and countless other times during my visit, just as well for my intimate knowledge of washroom locations that my Crohn's dilemma had taught me to hide my tears in and my last pair of Oakley shades to shield my tell-tale bloodshot eyes from the world I used to be part of.

Well just as expected, some of my old friends would not even look at me now and other more empathetic friends spoke small talk in an almost show of compassion as like it or not, the whole town seemed to know my rags to riches and back to rags tale all too well. I just told myself over and over again the best strategy was to just ignore them as they were the ignorant and arrogant judgmental bastards that I had learned to do so much and as if they thought like that, they weren't real friends anyways so weren't worth getting all screwed up about. Like everything it was easier said than done and yes deep down inside it really hurt worse than any physical pain could, but I was determined not to show it and I put on the Andrew courageous face even though my guts were turning themselves inside out at the thought, easily the hardest act I have ever had to put on. And while I loved every minute of the competitions, I was quite literally aching inside. Going to my old neighborhood of Spruce Grove with most of the same fellow residents whilst seeing my kids from their rental house just around the corner was one of the most emotional things I had ever faced in my life. Walking around my previous millionaires HOOD (again how could you use that word when there was so much opulence) to standing outside my old mansion I did everything to hold back the tears I had bottled up seemingly for years, at least close to losing my first dog Vharie when I was 15, a life that was now lost. I pictured my yellow Ski-do Summit snowmobile sitting in the deck of my white and gold Ford F150 Lariat truck and Carol's top of the range Toyota Sienna Limited parked in the driveway. Also all the kids meeting up for another Epic Riders and Rippers mountain bike progression session clinics at the nearby Baseball field where we walk Cheyenne every day. I had started Epic again in the desperate attempt for me to create work for myself to improve my mental state and gave me back a portion of my slain self-esteem. As even though I somehow knew it wasn't going to turn a profit as long as it broke even which it didn't even come close to but yes I again hark back to that invincibility and verging on cockiness that the drugs offered you. On the one hand I was proud of myself getting through my last few years of easily the worst struggle known to this man but on the other wishing, no pure sadness that I had no way of turning back the time (Cher) &/

or gaining the benefit of hindsight as I would have done things oh so differently if only I had known. All I could think of was Carol breaking down in tears almost a decade before when the doctor gave her diagnosis of my Crohn's disease that only now could I understand WHY! But even Carol could not have foreseen just how monumental the impact of my GI disease was going to have on all our lives forever.

After trailing around for hours visiting different accommodation ads, I was still without a definitive yes and I was left with what seemed the most promising last one that not only they allowed dogs but was something close to my C$800 a month limit that I knew my ski or snowboard instructors pay would almost cover. I was met by this real mellow Ozzie guy Stewart and we shot the shit for a while until this French Canadian guy Brian came home as it was his name that was on the lease and the guy I absolutely had to convince I was indeed the ideal tenant. Thankfully again all my sporting competitions gave me a non-choke confidence that I knew I could and would come through in the clutch no matter how much pressure was on me, and trust me this was big time pressure almost akin to getting a girls phone number or to get to home base but on a whole different stratosphere. I am still dumbfounded why the former is so hard as if it was true that everyone was looking for either NSA or love and women do indeed have as big a sex drive as men, why in these liberated days is it still up to the male to make the first move to talk to, dance with, shag, as much as rejection is tough, it's when the girl says some attitude statement "with you, ha-ha in your dreams old man" hurts. Well after about an hour we were thankfully shaking hands and organizing a move in date – PHEW! There was still couple of things to do, first check out the out of the jewel in the crown of the Crankworx festival, the Slopestyle Freestyle Expression Session on the grand finale, a must see on Saturday night. Again the mixture of emotions and memories more than overpowered me but I was there and no-one was going to make me run and hide, no matter the more than obvious in your face dirty looks and talking behind my back. Second was going to be the hardest of them all, go back to my kids place and thank them for their undying love and say goodbye for the last time which broke my heart as although I promised myself I would not cry, I cried harder than ever embracing my youngest daughter Iona on her deck and heading back to my hostel. I must admit I was so incredibly emotional I couldn't even fathom out what emotion was going on in my head, there are sometimes so many hit you all at once and all you want to do is fall to your knees and go back to that embryonic position that brought us all into this world in the first place. Again it took everything within me and more to keep a semi form of composure not to break down but yes I cried so hard that night once I got into my bed that I was only thankful that luckily my other roommates were still out getting drunk so no-one heard the sound of and felt the bitter sting of my tears.

I lucked out the next day as my new German roommate was also returning to Vancouver and offered me a ride if I chipped in for the gas so that was a no brainer. We talked and laughed all the back as again although I was dreading going back to the shelter as the contrast of Whistler to homeless land was more than stark but for the first time I knew for a fact my time there was finally coming to an end forever. I spent my last few weeks in there mainly riding my bike progressing further and further as my cardio started to improve. It seemed way harder this time around but because of my prescription pain killer addiction, it finally dawned on me that these drugs could have had a secondary function in that really I unknowingly had been possibly cheating myself with all my so called glories of riding to Whistler, doing the 200km lung association ride &&& basically every mile in training and therefore racing (even though to my knowledge I never used when I was racing) were as a result really a fraud just as these Olympic world class athletes that choose doping to gain an unfair competitive advantage aka my hero to zero Lance Armstrong. The only way I could prove to myself it was me rather than the drugs that had achieved such conquests was to do them all over again but this time clean and that's exactly what I was going to do. After trying this for many rides both totally clean & others with a variety of painkillers I have used in past & to my disbelief, although they might reduce muscle soreness (which to be honest seemed to be worse than when I take nothing) they turn you into a zombie like status with nothing in the tank & no second wind so yes I found it was actually easier to ride clean than with any painkiller, happy pills etc.

I will never forget early on in my time in the North Shore how much what was in effect an everyday ride from my drug infested years in Yaletown out the super scenic coast but hell of an undulating road to the ferry terminal at Horseshoe Bay that I had used and abused for so many of my training rides. Well this time I was so unfit but did my usual run before you can walk deal, I very nearly stopped to catch the bus back the first time ever I tried it since my demise as I was literally exhausted. But I just kept telling myself I had honestly never quit at anything in this life and a dumb road ride I used to be able to do in my sleep so I wasn't about to quit now regardless of the painful cramping in my disease ravaged legs. As always I made it but only just & was completely bagged. Again talk about a fish out of water, the looks I would get leaving the impoverished souls in the shelter when I was all kitted out in my spandex and pimp daddy road bike when they would love to get their hands on my trusty steed as it would keep them in their chosen drug state for weeks.

I informed the staff to their absolute amazement that I was leaving my highly sought after room in the shelter to return to one of the most expensive places on this Earth. I was dreading yet another move as only 4 months prior I had moved into the shelter. This time the move was going to be 110% on my shoulders and I packed up my gear as Sharon was dead against it and yes it didn't take me very long to realize why. After finding out my only real friend in there creepy Mark was a "converted" drug dealer and now made his money selling everything and anything on his E-bay company. So I did another dumb ass Andrew moves and entrusted him to sell what I had left of top of the range bike parts & vintage 45s & Albums, both worth a decent worth and send the proceeds of their sale to my new home in Whistler. Yes I hear you, how could I be that fucking stupid I will never be able to answer, suffice to say that although I was too slowly regaining my physical strength, my emotional and especially my mental state was so totally removed from where they were prior to all the shit hitting the fan that looking back all the damage from my drug addiction and their induced psychosis I now had the equivalent brain of a young child, including all the innocence and maybe even bordering on naivety that I somehow believed this ex-con was going to come through for me, yes I know dumb & dumber right! The day finally arrived and the removal van pulled up and packaged up my tiny world in the back of their truck and it coincided with a visit from Carol and my kids so they very graciously offered me a run in their car to welcome me back to my old home. In the space of a decade I was returning to the place that drew me to Canada in the first place, but this time it was completely foreign to me as unlike the successful business and family man I was previously, I more resembled that of all the youngsters who became Whistler transient community that had little to nothing but the promise of a good time to attract them to this temporary home (another Carrie Underwood anthem I have sung more times than I care to mention) No matter, this was going to be a time that I was going to make the most of, especially to regain my kids trust, affection and friendship that I had been without for the majority of my time in Vancouver. My time had come and by God I was going to make the very most of it whether my haters liked it or not.

CHAPTER 15

BACK TO THE FUTURE

E ver heard the song from Evita, "Another Suitcase in Another Hall"? Well, this was me. How many times did I have to move to find some inner peace and tranquility to still my racing mind? I suddenly realized how much stuff I had, and there was no way it was all going to fit in the tiny back room in my new home. I had no choice but to buckle down and start fresh all over again.

These moves were beginning to get demoralizing, but I just kept telling myself, *A few hours a day, and I'm going to have it whipped into shape in no time.* After all, how could I be unhappy? I was back in my old playground. I had finally escaped the nightmare flashbacks that Vancouver constantly held for me. Problem was, there were just as many memories of my good life and flashbacks of my gradual decline littered in every corner here in Whistler also. All I kept saying to myself was that regardless of everything, I was going to stay as positive as practically possible.

Our house was at the end of this cul-de-sac, and it was like night and day compared to my various homeless shelters. It was, indeed, what I desperately wanted: a place of quiet, peace and tranquil serenity. I have watched too many episodes of the amazing reality show *Intervention*, so I know most addicts end up in rehab facilities that are exactly like my new home—a wilderness retreat. It's very similar, as if by coincidence, to soldiers returning home from conflict with PTSD. They are also usually sent to a place surrounded by Mother Nature's delights, which is Whistler to a T.

With the soldiers, they also found that the best medicine to overcome their petrifying flashbacks was a dog, which comes as absolutely no surprise to me, as I am convinced dogs are man's best friend and the best medicine for a huge variety of our human twentieth-century illnesses. It only lasted one season, but a series that explains this better than I ever could is *Dogs of War* on A&E.

After a few trips up to the village, I started actually feeling like I had indeed come full circle and was finally home. Despite the animosity directed towards me by many of its residents, I was in a place where the in-your-face temptation of relapsing to drugs in Vancouver that had made me lose everything in the first place was next to nonexistent. Although, like most places, Whistler has a very real (though well-hidden) underground hard-core drug scene, on the surface, it is only the natural drugs of adrenalin, testosterone and endorphins that rule most people's lives up here.

My biggest worry was not what the local idiots were saying not-so-subtly behind my back, as I had faced that and then some in my stays in homeless shelters, being called every derogatory term known to man. Instead, it was the very real need to finally return to the workforce. I still hoped to get my ski instructor position back with Whistler Blackcomb. Although I could not remember precise details of my complaint, there was a very faint memory of ugly emails, telephone calls and threats at the end of my last employment with them. Some of my previous bosses and friends were still working there, so I called up and emailed what I thought were the most amenable and amicable among them, particularly a friend called Martin. We had spent some time together at Ski Esprit Pod, a multi-day program that I loved working.

As I had hoped, he was very professional yet welcoming and friendly. I could tell straight away he knew the basics of what had happened to me, and thank the Lord, he wasn't one of those who put the usual stereotypical slur on drug addiction. He assured me he would do his best to talk to another friendly mentor, Bruce, who I had done my Canadian Association of Ski Instructors Level 2 course with. He had since been promoted to Snow School director. (Otto was slowly but surely getting the cold shoulder he deserved, because put simply, that guy was a jerk of the first order).

Because of Bruce's European connections, he got my sense of humour and knew that when all was said and done, even during my drug-infested years, I had an enviably impressive record with the Snow School where it really matters at the end of the day: the satisfaction of the paying customers. As with everything I do, I honestly gave it my all to go above and beyond each and every day I was working, and I told my students that I didn't expect a tip. For some reason, I was never comfortable accepting the North American way of rewarding excellent service, instead saying something along the lines of, "If you did enjoy my style of instructing, please could you tell my bosses by filling out a customer survey form in guest relations rather than giving me a tip." Although I never won any of their Ice recognition awards because I couldn't brown-nose, the comments probably saved my job and my ass this time around.

I remember being so worried when I was finally called for a meeting, which in reality was an interview with Martin and Bruce. Without this job, I was up shit's creek, as it was my instructing job that I had based my move on. Thankfully, it couldn't have gone any better. When asked about all my negative remarks, I replied simply, "I'm so sorry. All I can tell you is that the prescription drugs turned me into a monster. I don't fully know myself even now, but I assure you that wasn't the real me. I learnt the hardest way possible what powerful mind-altering drugs can do to anyone, and I am no longer that person. I am 110 percent clean and ready to go back to coaching, the passion that brought me to Whistler so many years ago."

This was a statement I could genuinely back up, as it was approaching my one-year anniversary of a drug-free existence, with the only exception being the following:

1. Happy pills called Elavil, because as much as I hated to admit it and did everything to hide it, I was still brutally depressed. I am still, but really, who wouldn't if they followed my rocky road, as my latest and greatest shrink advised me?

2. Sleeping pills called Zopiclone, as just like any kind of pain is somehow amplified at night, all the flashbacks from my complex PTSD, especially my street beating, hit me as soon as I turned out my light and had none of the distractions the day offered.

3. A painkiller called Cesamet, which is really a man-made version of marijuana. Because of my rough experience with the product,

I have learnt to be very careful with them. If I take too many, it will induce my psychosis like it did that one time in the North Shore shelter.

Thank God, Martin and Bruce accepted my sincere and genuinely heartfelt apology, and the conversation soon turned into the more normal one of which pod (group of instructors) I wanted to join. Ski Esprit was my pick. I loved that program for the simple fact that in four or five days, you could rebuild a student's technique and confidence through a well-designed progression, rather than the almost emergency-room clinics that were one-day privates. Although I had lost all my hard-earned seniority as an instructor because of my seasons away, if I proved my worth, I had a much better chance of working, as I really needed the coin to pay my rent.

I came out of that meeting simply over the moon. My favorite employer was willing to give me something that I believe everyone deserves but so many in this world wouldn't grant me: forgiveness and a second chance. I was determined to repay their faith in me. I was literally glowing, and I went straight home, put on my bike stuff and rode like the wind in the pure ecstasy of the miracle that I was soon going to regain a semi-normal life in a job I knew I could do no matter how nervous I was. Truth be told, I was scared stupid. My biggest worry was that maybe I was only a good coach because of the artificial high the drugs gave me to get through each and every workday. I reassured myself that I did this job before any Crohn's disease and the delusional and fake courage of painkillers, so I could do it again. I had to learn to cope with life without any drugs except the natural ones.

After another week or so of unpacking, sorting out my overpriced room, and cursing all the time about how much I hated moving and how often I had gone through the ordeal over the past few years, I started to find my feet in the place I emigrated to Canada in the first place for. To say I simply love Whistler still falls short of my true feelings, as it has everything an outdoor sports enthusiast like me needs. My place was only a 30-minute walk from the village (as this time I had to get around without a vehicle) or a five-minute rather steep and hazardous hiking trail down to the closest bus stop.

After scoping it out on foot, I was determined I was going to clean my last remaining mountain bike, the cross-country racing weapon that was my fully pimped Scott Spark. Although it was a terrific bike, it really was too racy for Whistler's super-technical mountain bike trails, but my ex had either sold or was lying about selling all my other bikes, including my favourite steed, my Santa Cruz Nomad, again tricked out to the max. Regardless, after where I had been, I was in my utopia, and with my decent cardio from riding the roads of North Vancouver, all I had to do was relearn my off-road skills.

I started out with the tourist-orientated Lost Lake trails that were a ton of fun for a cardio rip but really below my previous skill set. I didn't care; I was so focused on not injuring myself prior to the ski season that I just started competing with myself by timing my routes, as although I no longer had the considerable benefit of my superb Garmin Edge heart-rate monitor, I did what I had learnt to do: make the most of what I had left. I found an app for my iPod touch that did a similar function but without the heart-rate monitor.

Like everything in my life, it wasn't long before I realized that, as Bruce Springsteen sang, "with every wish comes a curse." Although I had come home, home was not the same as it was when I was a multi-millionaire. Simple tasks like grocery shopping, a chore I had always hated, were now a nightmare. At the local supermarket, called IGA, I would invariably bump into so-called friends who either talked politely but with an air of suspicion or flat-out shunned me because of my drug-infested past. They had squarely placed themselves in Carol's corner, which hurt so bad. I never ever let it show, but as we all know, keeping a brave face drains your core energy source.

Much more crucially, it became very clear that I was an outsider in my new home, as my housemates Stewart and Brian had already done a full winter together and were tight. I was different from them on so many levels, but especially maturity and humour. Although I tried my best to fit in, I just could not be what I wasn't—and anyway, why should I change who I am to suit other people? That's something I had never done before and wasn't about to now. I could handle Stewart; I think without Brian's influence, I would have got along with him. But Brian was a fucking douche of the first order. He strutted about the place like he owned it. He was just another arrogant motherfucker who thought he was better me. He was so damn immature for his almost 30 years, and we really had nothing in common. To be honest, I just wanted to take him outside and fucking break the asshole, but I knew I couldn't, as I would be out on my ass.

My only saving grace was that he was planning to save up his carpentry wages and head to South America with his Aussie girlfriend for almost a month. Phew! After a few dull house parties that I hated, because obviously my non-alcoholic stance didn't go down too well, they headed off finally and gave me chance to bond with Stewart. Although we were never going to be bosom buddies, we got on much better when Brian wasn't around. It made me sick how much he had his head up Brian's ass.

I started getting into a daily routine whereby I would hang out at home in the morning or sleep most of it, as my sleep cycle was all over the place for some reason. Then I would either go out for a major bike ride, be it road or mountain, or head up to town and grab a coffee at either Starbucks or Blenz with Cheyenne and my laptop, which I picked up just before I left Vancouver. This time around, unlike my previous must-have latest-and-greatest model, I was making do with the most-value-for-money cheaper version.

I would time it so I left the house just before Brian came home from his carpentry work, reducing the time we were forced to be together. Sometimes in my local and loyal Blenz, I would get to speaking with someone; other times, I would be in my quiet persona mode, which usually went hand in hand with some mental or emotional trauma flashback from some external or internal source. The change that came over Cheyenne especially was so marked that I was beginning to think this was the best move ever for both of us, despite the obvious split at our new digs.

It didn't take long for the weather to start to change to fall, along with the cold rain and the white gold appearing on the hills and the massive influx of transient workers that really make Whistler tick over the primetime winter season. I stayed on my bike for as long as possible and started to alternate between the gym and biking, depending on what the unpredictable weather threw at us.

The gym was a particularly hard thing for me to restart, as my new body was not used to the strength training that had been so much part of my life when I resided up here previously. Not boasting, but yes, I was a huge gym rat back in the day. My Swedish mate Glen and I were the biggest, baddest, strongest locals, topping out at 225 pounds before finding all that show muscle was practically useless when riding a bike, especially up a hill. I had then fallen back to my more natural ideal weight of around 180 pounds. Glen could beat me at chest, back and traps, but I could outdo him at core, arms and legs. Every gym session was an enormous testosterone-fed competition of gargantuan proportions.

Little did I know then that Glen's claim of a serious protein powder diet also included juicing up on steroids, which he admitted to me in a very brief meeting again in the IGA. Unfortunately, Glen had gone through a similarly harsh divorce in my time away, and he had turned into a recluse and given up the gym. He was unwilling to go back, as it brought back memories of the demons he was plagued by. He was like a ghost of his former self, both physically and mentally, as was I, if I'm being completely honest. Someone once told me divorce is second only to bereavement in terms of grief, and I knew that all too well—especially after over two faithful decades and two kids.

I knew that it wouldn't be long before the Norse God of snow, Ulr, would pour its shroud of white over everything and the hills would open up. It was always a bittersweet time, as although I truly loved skiing and snowboarding, I got really bored looking at white for almost half a year. And I can't quite explain it, but as I got older, everything in me started to prefer the summer, which is Whistler's best-kept secret. I think a lot of it had to do with the broken and injured pieces of my body preferring the heat to the cold, as they seemed to hurt more when the thermometer started to plunge. No matter, it was still going to be a complete contrast to my recent winters spent in homeless shelters and locked psych wards. I had gone from the shadows of poverty, drug addiction and mental illness to the overboard opulence of ritzy glitzy Whistler.

I decided that as fiercely independent as I had always been, it was the best decision I had ever made to swallow my pride and knock on the Lookout door that was Sharon's base. Especially considering all the animosity that was my new reality in Whistler, I knew deep down in my soul that if I was going to remain clean, I needed help. The main pressure was returning to work in the Snow School, as I was no longer one of the big bosses with a multi-million-dollar lifestyle but a nobody ski instructor renting a room in a house of losers. The way people I used to be friends or just casual acquaintances with were now ostracizing me with dirty looks and back-stabbing comments was easily more painful than any of my physical ailments. Physical pain pales in comparison to mental and emotional pain. For me, words hurt way more than any physical abuse.

To get help up here, I would have to go back to the place that was the catalyst of my downfall: Whistler's medical and ER centre, where Carol still worked. I knew I was a very polarizing topic: some people hated me and blamed me for everything, while the more sympathetic souls believed I was at my core a nice guy. The latter group knew it was the drugs that changed me, not some personality defect, and were therefore willing to grant me the forgiveness that I sought more than anything else.

Thankfully, my first time back there, I was greeted by this French Canadian receptionist who had always been so kind to me and was genuinely pleased to see me. She gave me a much-needed hug and said something along the lines of, "Regardless of what others might say or do against you, there are many like myself who are so proud of what you have done and survived." It was a morale booster I desperately needed and brought tears to my eyes.

Upstairs, I returned to the doctor's office where I had been given the news that was going to change my life forever: my Crohn's disease diagnosis. It was harrowing and then some, as I fought the tears back from behind my shades. Eventually, I got hooked up with the mental health team, which included my psychiatrist, Ron Remick, with whom I have had a love-hate relationship, and a very pleasant social worker called Nancy. I dreaded every single visit, as I knew I would have to open up about my past, fears, flashbacks and demons, which always caused my gut to tie itself in knots. My first meeting with Dr. Remick was more than awkward, but just as I knew in my heart, he told me he understood why going back as an instructor filled me with so much fear. There was no magic pill that would overcome my worsening symptoms of complex PTSD, depression and the almost overpowering temptation to relapse on drugs.

After a few visits, I decided that, fuck it, I had to face all of my fears. I dug really deep and rode out to the local recreation centre, which I had frequented to rehab my tib/fib injury and was my life five to six nights a week when I was gym beefcake. As always with me, despite promising myself not to go crazy in my first few visits, I could still remember my weights for most of my exercises, so I tried to take 25 percent off and go with that. I didn't factor in that I hadn't lifted a weight in years, and I paid dearly for my stupidity. I could barely walk Chi for close to a week after my first few times, as I was so sore from the onslaught of delayed muscle soreness. Another warning: don't ever overtrain your calves. Pure agony, and all because a young guy was on the calf-raise machine and, with my competitiveness, I just had to beat him.

Although I was given the cold shoulder and even mocked by most of my previous fellow gym rats, I bumped into an old friend, Simon, who somehow understood and was a very welcome friend indeed. Before I knew it, just like always, I started piling on so much muscle that even my housemates were convinced I was on some bodybuilding juice. It was simply my sprinter body type.

As much I really had outgrown the gym and didn't enjoy my time in there, I knew the benefits—increased energy, improved mental outlook and self-confidence/self-esteem—far outweighed any negative thoughts. I still don't really understand it, but being strong, fit and cut improves my mental outlook and reduces depression. It also gives me a feeling of invincibility which I so needed as an armour to deflect all the reasons I should just run away and hide, or worse still, curl up and die somewhere.

A day that will stay with me until I die happened just prior to the start of the ski season. My housemate Brian invited me to earn some cash-in-hand money in an odd job his boss had offered him to clean out and fix a water leak in someone's basement. I agreed, as on the one hand, I really needed the money, but possibly more importantly, if I had refused, it would not have reinforced all my haters' attacks that I had indeed turned into a lazy, spoiled, bloodsucking leech on society. In fact, I had to prove this to myself way more than anyone else, so I agreed. Of course, it had to be just around the corner from my multi-million-dollar home in Spruce Grove in the subsidized employee housing complex. I knew there were more than few haters going, "Serves you right, asshole."

Well, if this is what people do for a career, I have to take my hat off to them. Crouching down all day on my knees getting sprayed by freezing cold water from my dick housemate, mixing cement and repairing the leak was one of the hardest and worst days of work I had ever experienced.

Suffice to say that after decades where I spent money like water, as all that seemed to happen was after years I would keeping adding zeros to my net worth in a Midas-type existence, that day I learnt the real meaning of money. It was easily the hardest C$100 I have ever earned.

There was always a lull before the storm in Whistler in the fall months when people transitioned from their diverse summertime pursuits to the winter ones. It always amused me that even before the hills opened, as soon as there was a dusting of snow, the Whistler rookies (usually Aussies because of their abundance of testosterone) would end up blowing themselves up on handmade jumps that littered backyards everywhere.

Before the season kicked off in earnest, Whistler staged the biggest snow sale in Canada, where demo gear and the previous season's equipment was sold off for a song. Only thing is, when you're flat broke, it doesn't matter how good a deal it is. I couldn't afford any of it, which really hurt, as I used to spend a small fortune, most of the time on wants rather than needs—a differentiation that only now was I beginning to grasp. Eventually, American Thanksgiving and opening day on Blackcomb rolled around, so my housemates kindly invited me up for a session on the hill. After not being on the snow for so many years, I sucked ass, and they ended up dropping me on the first run as I rag-dolled down Cafe Cliffs' powder.

In a weird way, I was pleased. I needed to concentrate on my technique, as my skiing had never been as good as my snowboard skills. I had only ever had one ski lesson, so I had some seriously bad ingrained habits to resolve. I was dealing with a combination of being so damn rusty from being off the snow for God knows how long and 15 seasons dedicated solely to riding my board, which moves sideways as opposed to straight downhill and therefore utilizes slightly different techniques and biomechanics. But just as with everything I do, the only way to improve was good old practice-makes-perfect. I made a commitment to hit the hill six days and the gym four nights a week. I knew if I got strong and got the mileage in, I would be able to overcome most of the shortcomings in my technique, to a point where I would at least have broken down some of the very real fears I had about returning to work.

It wasn't long before my first day of training came around, and although I wasn't the worst skier, I knew I still had some way to go before I got back to the level I had after returning from my freestyle snowboard crash. In fairness, it wasn't my technique so much as my personality I was worried about the most. The concept of once bitten, twice shy had enveloped me, especially with women, even though in truth I had always been incredibly shy when it came to the game. My shyness now, though, was on a whole different planet.

Actually, truth be told, only now have I figured out that I have no problem speaking to women I do not fancy, as there is no fear of rejection. I was never going to chase their ass anyways, so why be shy, right? The problem was that the majority of Ski Esprit clients were women, as their men would go and chuck themselves down or off almost anything and therefore needed to lose their partners. They dumped their ladies into a Snow School program to avoid being restricted or slowed down by them.

It's funny, but snow sports really highlighted a big difference between the sexes for me, namely, if a guy can make it down a slope no matter how my times he falls or sketches out, he can claim it for his testosterone-fed ego; whereas a girl has to be able to make it down with style before she can claim to own it. The other thing that snow sports does is level life's playing field, as you could not rely on money or power to succeed. Most of it comes down to natural talent.

My first day back coaching came around way too soon for my liking. I was petrified, although I had done everything in my power to prepare myself. I put together a week-long coaching plan and inputted it into my iPod touch so if I did panic, at least I had something to fall back on. I got all suited up and made the 30-to 40-minute trek up to my locker. All I could think of was that it was so much easier when I had the big fancy house in Spruce Grove and a vehicle to drive me to work, as ski gear gets pretty heavy after a while. God, sometimes you really have to fake it to make it. I got changed, went to the meet-and-greet zone and hung out like a spare prick with absolutely no clue what the fuck I was doing. Still, I did everything possible to not let it show.

The worst thing about the whole Snow School deal was that despite being with the mountain for years, I was now back on the bottom of the totem pole with zero seniority, which I thought was kind of rough but fuck it, I had a job finally that might just be the stepping stone I desperately needed on my road to a full recovery, if that even existed anymore with my severely traumatized brain. I was now relegated to the novice level 2 and 3, which I really didn't enjoy, as I was a much better coach than an instructor and enjoyed the intermediate and advanced classes. As with my studies or anything I do, if I am having fun, it's reflected tenfold in my work. That was one of the main reasons I went back to the Esprit multiday program. For one thing, they don't accept total beginners. I knew that from teaching beginners during my time as snowboard manager that it actually started to reduce my passion for the sport I had grown to love. I really wanted to avoid the same thing happening with skiing.

I also appreciated the fact that the classes took place over a week, so you got to formulate a planned progression beginning with the most fundamental basics. I learnt over the years that realistically, you can only focus on one or very rarely two issues in a single day. As someone once told me, it takes over a thousand times trying to overcome a bad habit.

After a little organized chaos, I finally got my group. They were level 2, which meant they could only just ski on easy green trails using the most basic ski technique called the snow plough (it's now called the wedge, as the so-called pros in CSIA had to switch things up to merit their positions somehow), or pizza if you were teaching kids, as that is the shape your skis and feet were angled at. No more of the level 5 or 6s I used to teach back in the day. Though it was a bitter pill to swallow, I just kept telling myself that regardless of everything—people, snow quality, pouring rain, whatever—this was still a fuck of a lot better than where I had come from, so give yourself a kick up the derriere and make the most of this fantastic opportunity.

It then dawned on me for the first time that your perspective on life is really molded by your own experiences throughout your life. If I was still living the dream, I would have had a real problem getting the lowest-ability group, but when you have been where I had over the last few years, you gain a certain humility and learn not to take anything for granted, even the things most others just accept as normal life. I had to focus on how lucky I was to not only to be alive but working in one of the world's premier winter sports resorts, and for that I had to be eternally gratefully, end of story.

We boarded the gondola, and it was like the spotlight was on me. I know people think, in this country anyways, that a ski or snowboard instructor isn't exactly a prestigious jobs, more like bumming than a real career, but if you haven't ever done it, trust me, it is way more of a challenge than you might think. The hardest part for me was not the coaching but all the small talk you have to do in the gondola, chair lifts and cafés when you aren't on the snow. Despite the façade I try to keep up, I'm actually a very quiet guy.

Easily one of the two hardest classes I'd ever had was with this black girl from Nigeria who was a total snow virgin. Not only had she never done any kind of sports, she had never even seen snow before, and the rain was coming down sideways. I tried everything in my book of coaching, and despite the fact that I wasn't the best beginner instructor, I never ever quit. I earned every cent of my pay that day. All I really wanted to say to her was try another sport and not to quit her day job, as learning to ski from a biomechanical perspective was not for her.

The other lesson that stood out was this typical nouveau riche girl from LA who eventually turned up over an hour late for her C$750-day private lesson to tell me she didn't have any equipment, so she was going to the shop to buy it now. After two hours in this top-of-the-line retail store, she emerged all kitted out in tight-fitting designer-branded Bogner, Descente and Spyder swag to show off her trim figure. We were finally set to hit slopes, but as we went up the Wizard chair from the base, all of sudden she explained that she hated skiing, but her bigwig sugar daddy loved it, so she had to grin and bear it. After every run, we had to hit the café so she could name-drop all the celebrities and superstars she knew. I played along, trying to look impressed, but inside I was screaming, *I don't give a flying fuck who you know; you're still a spoilt whiny bitch.*

What become abundantly clear that day was that something had happened to me that irrecoverably changed the very person I was. I still can't explain it, but I had gone from this straight-out cocky, loud and brash individual to a very quiet, reserved, guarded, quietly self-confident but, most crucially, super-humble person. *Confidence* is a word we all use almost flippantly, and it is no coincidence its first three letters are *con*! I truly believe it is one of the most misunderstood words in the English language. Like the old saying goes, it is not the loud, arrogant, I-am-somehow-higher-up-the-social-hierarchy-than-you types you have to be careful of; it's the quiet killers or sleepers. They are the confident ones, as they did not have to hide all their insecurities, demons, hopes and fears behind bravado and materialistic prizes that they believe make them better than other people.

THE HOOD

We are all the same regardless of race, colour, creed, where we live or what car we drive. One of my favourite songs of all time is John Lennon's incomparable anthem "Imagine." Its lyrics illustrate this better than a mere mortal like me ever can.

Back to that first day on the job: I was like the swan metaphor I'd heard years prior, where the swan swims along so gracefully on the water but its legs are paddling like crazy underneath where no one can see. That was the feat I was trying to replicate, and I actually think I pulled it off, even though I was sweating and shaking like crazy. I could go into way more detail, but suffice to say, it was one of the hardest working days of my life, as my group really didn't want to ski but rather do a couple of runs and hit the café. I called people like this the cappuccino cruiser set, and it was my worst-case scenario. I went home completely bagged from trying everything to make conversation, as I knew this would be a very long and slow week. Fuck it—I had finally done something that gave my life meaning.

Although it was one of the hardest work weeks of my life, it was also one of the most enlightening, as I had finally found a temporary cure for my complex PTSD: namely, work. Every time a trigger came up, I just had to ignore the flashback as best I could, as I couldn't let it show in any way or form to my clients. However slowly, I made it through the week, and then more and more weeks. As I proved myself, I slowly but surely started to creep up the ladder, as my boss realized I shone when I had higher-level groups. I started getting the level 3s and even 4s, which finally were more about coaching than instructing.

I had somehow stumbled on this unreal method of coaching that relied more on the individual learning themselves through some well-designed exercises rather than the more traditional method of telling them the proper method utilized by most other instructors. I guess it's because I have always been predominately a cognitive type of learner as opposed to the more common seers and doers. To learn something, I had to understand why it was the best way to do it, so I designed this guided discovery method whereby I would get the clients to learn by practicing the two extremes of doing something, which relied more on feel rather than complicated instructions. It had worked before, and so it would work again now. I got some real encouraging comments coming back from my lessons, which again reinforced my growing belief in myself. I am indeed someone who has to work rather than being a work hater like some of the residents of the homeless shelters.

I was working most weeks. The rare weeks I was not needed because of my low seniority, I would go up and practice my ski technique. Before even I expected, I started to reach my old technical ski ability. Even more critically, I got into a groove with the clients and started to open up a bit. I even started thinking seriously about dating again. With all these women around me, I was able to relearn how to speak to them, and not all of my clients were taken.

In particular, there was this girl from Glasgow called Lynne who was a pure sweetheart. Unfortunately, she *was* taken, but there was definitely a connection. Then came this Australian girl who was dating a former instructor from the Snow School. We got on so well she invited me to spend New Year's in a club called Tommy Africa's. Despite feeling like I was old enough to be most of their clientele's father, I danced myself stupid and got so drunk I for the first time ever fell over hard on my way home, walking the icy paths with my sick dancing kicks that offered no grip.

In a crazy twist of fate, the DJ stuck on "Billie Jean," and I busted out all my MJ moves on the dance floor. A killer night indeed, which as always, turned into deservedly the worst two-day hangover from hell. Once again, I was reminded of alcohol's effect on my gut.

Of all the women I noticed, none compared to this Australian, very well-to-do middle-aged women who was big on the international equestrian scene. She was obviously not only very rich but also very athletic and dead cute—just my type. Only problem was, I had my eye on this Czech girl instructor called Nadia and couldn't make my mind up who I wanted first. I was in a totally bizarre situation, as I had never been available when I had what the locals somewhat derogatorily refer to as the *pro ho syndrome*, where girls are attracted to you if you rock as a jock.

Then, just when I was on the cusp of getting somewhere in this life, just when I got my head above water, I crashed and burned big time. It's as if my haters' voodoo doll reappeared and pinned me down.

I had not gone to enough training mornings purely because I still really wasn't sleeping well. A 5:30 wake-up was needed to get my shit together prior to a 6:45 meeting time, and I have never been a morning person. My boss told me I had to attend this particular training session just as I was on my last legs of working five weeks straight over Christmas and New Year's. You had to, as they were the busy weeks. Whistler was like a ghost town come mid-January. So I made it to the meeting, but I was still really half asleep.

We got sent into different groups, and I chose my favourite coach, Brian. I related to his coaching style better than anyone else. We were working on probably my weakest technique: cranking carved turns on the groomers. It was also no coincidence that Nadia was in our group, as I was going to somehow time it right to be on the same chair as her.

Before I got anywhere close to that, on the very first time down an easy blue run called Cruiser of all things, my life took another turn for the worse. Whilst trying everything I could to mirror the exercise, and while doing one of my best carved turns ever, pretty much totally balanced on the one downhill ski, I did everything to hold my speed in my carved thin line on the run. All of a sudden, I looked up and realized I was heading straight off the run into a tree section, so I had no choice but to lay it down. The thing I was focusing everything on was trying to take my snowboard technique of turning with my hips out of my skiing, which is a big no-no. After 15-plus years on a board, it was easier said than done. Brian had me sitting lower and back more than I liked to get rid of my hip-induced turns.

With the benefit of that bloody hindsight deal, I was in the ideal position to blow my knee. And that's exactly what happened when I had no choice but to fall before I hit a tree at full speed ahead. I felt something pop pretty sorely in my knee, but being a trouper, I just sucked it up, especially in front of Nadia. It wasn't until we got further down on this slightly steeper run called Zig Zag that whatever had happened earlier to my left knee got dramatically worse, although I did everything in my power to ignore it. I almost crashed on every right turn, as my left knee buckled every time until it fully gave way. I had no choice but to give in to avoid any more damage and headed down the nearest easy green that took me to the chairlift and ski patrol.

I headed back to the Rendezvous restaurant and went immediately to the washroom, where I popped my knee back into place. My higher-than-usual pain threshold came in real handy there. I knew deep down inside that it was not going to be good, as although I had never torn my

ACL, from others' descriptions of it, I was pretty sure the same thing had now happened to me, which the ski patrol also reinforced. Problem was, my group was on their second to last day, and my hot Australian girl was waiting there in the café.

To my amazement, my boss told me I had to go and talk to the group, even though I was in a lot of pain, until a replacement instructor was found. Talk about putting a brave face on. I talked to them and apologized for my indiscretion.

Put simply, I was fucked again. So I enjoyed a full-scale greasy-ass breakfast with all the trimmings and then very stupidly skied out, because my dumb-ass male pride would have it no other way. On my way down, I was super cautious. On coming across a group of kids, I decided to stay as far away from them as possible, which led me over this drop-off and again dislocated my knee. The base could not come soon enough.

Once there, this completely off-the-wall idea entered my brain. I had been eyeing this crazy cool pair of goggles, so in a desperate attempt to cheer myself up, I bought them with what little money I had left before going to the ER. *Fuck, not again. Why me? What the fuck to I have to do for God to forgive my sins?* rang in my head as I hobbled through the village on my own to the ER. Of course, it had to be on my dicky left leg that had the crushed tib/fib from seasons before, which I knew wasn't good.

After a few hours in the ER and more pain meds, which almost scared me more than the injury, on my way home I bumped into Norm, who pleaded with me to show up for the end-of-week festivities. That was the last thing in the world I wanted to do, but I capitulated because I wanted to say goodbye to the girl who had hit on me all week. *Intense* is the word that springs to mind. We both knew that the adult fun we were going to have from there on in was now no longer possible. Why does bad luck always spoil my plans?

The worst-case scenario came true. I was out for what looked like the whole season, which just as luck goes, happened to be the second best ever for snowfall. Just to add insult to injury, my trustworthy social-and-mental-health worker decided it was time to go solo and left me with the crushing news that she was leaving in a few weeks. I can't quite explain it, but I absolutely hate telling my story. Opening up to anyone is hard when you have complex PTSD, because you have this automatic distrust of everyone. After going through the homeless shelters especially, you had no choice but to be like that; experience had showed me without any doubt that when you trust someone, you get burnt nine times out of 10 … no, more like 99 times out of 100.

To say I was having a torrid time isn't strong enough. Watching all these skiers with grins from ear to ear, covered in powder, getting off the hill talking about the most epic snow day ever eats at you after a while, especially if you're as passionate about snow sports as I am. My mood went from bad to worse; I just couldn't fathom how my lifelong curse of bad luck had got me again after everything I had done, the chances I had taken and the fears and very real demons that I had faced full frontal. Now I was fucked all over again through something that wasn't really my fault. By trying to do everything within my power to be a better skier and a better coach, I had followed the advice of the trainers, which was absolutely 110 percent the reason for my injury. I had been skiing and riding hard on slopes all over the world for almost 30 years and had never even come close to injuring my knee.

Yes, I was pissed bigtime. All I could do was hold on mentally whilst trying everything within my power to get back up there. I hit the gym six days a week and had four very painful visits per week at Whistler Physiotherapy, the place I had gone for over 10 months to come back from my crushed lower leg injury years before.

I was relieved to hear that, because Stewart was over Whistler and was heading back to Australia to get a real job and a real life, as we all like to say in Whistler, and the dumb-ass teenage kids in the basement suite were also moving on, Brian had decided to throw in the towel and move to another pad so that he didn't have to take on a humungous rental agreement with his girlfriend. Our time together was over, thank God! I had already decided I was moving on the day after our hometown hockey team, the Canucks, lost their thrilling game 7 Stanley Cup Finals run to the Boston Bruins and the stupid riots went off in downtown Vancouver.

I knew I had to leave Whistler, as much as it killed me to leave my kids, especially Iona. For reasons I still don't fully understand, my relationship with my oldest daughter was now strained. I put it down to the teenage rebellious years; I had certainly experienced them myself to the fullest. Just like me, she had to learn about life the only way you can: by making her own mistakes. I can never understand these so-called helicopter parents like my ex who put doorstops and plugs on electrical outlets. I have learnt the hard way that you can only fully comprehend anything if you have lived it, breathed it, felt it, cried it and bled it.

CHAPTER 16

DÉJÀ VU

Could I stay in Whistler, become a lifer and basically jump on the hamster's wheel, running to stand still but having fun doing it? Or should I escape the cocoon of a resort town in an attempt to start all over again with practically nothing to regain a normal life? As far as I could see, it was an absolute no-brainer; but as Sharon said, this time, it couldn't be about the money, rather personal growth and happiness. She also warned me that it wouldn't be plain sailing. The occasional curveball would knock my teeth out, and I would end up on my ass. Truer words have never been spoken.

I decided that I should either run away from all my demons, fears and flashbacks and return to my homeland of Scotland or Ireland, or face all my demons, fears and flashbacks and return to Vancouver, with the hope of getting a real career that, for the first time in a very long time, challenged my brain rather than my body. I had to admit that I was starting to feel all the heavy-duty use—no, abuse—my sporting addiction had subjected it to.

I am no different from anyone. The easy way out was definitely appealing: a move back to the auld country. We all possess a fight, flight or freeze reaction in times of crisis. That's exactly what I wanted to do, as quite honestly, I was starting to believe my folks' insistence that my education would actually mean something there, while every Tom, Dick and Harry has a degree here in North America. The grass-is-greener images through rose-coloured spectacles started bombarding my brain, but my only problem was that I had my best friend, Chi, to take care of. After checking with the local vet, I found out that she'd need a bunch of super-spendy shots, most importantly her rabies shot, which would need to ferment for six months. So as appealing as running away was, it wasn't a practical option.

In many ways, although I was distraught at yet another door-closing deal, it was a blessing. It had never been in my nature to run away from anything. Rather, I would grow a pair and stand up and fight like a man. My only option was to return to Vancouver and find a decent job. I searched through my namesake Andrewslist, and the only place I could find was C\$1,200 a month, which would seriously drain what little money I had left. With everyone's advice that I indeed had an impressive résumé, and although it scared living shit out of me, I made the move. I had already faced all my worst triggers and haters in Whistler, so I told myself I could do it again in a place that harboured my worst memories.

All the what-ifs started seeping into my brain, stripping me down to a place where I felt almost naked to the world. It was a case of *suck it up*. Although I knew I wasn't fully recovered from the deepest scars from my decade of prescription-drug dependency, I knew the key piece of the puzzle was finding a job so that I could at least break even financially. Being without a job manifests all my self-doubt and convinces me that I am indeed useless.

Let's face it, even in today's modern world, it is still the man who is seen as the main bacon-getter. It also provides immeasurable self-esteem and confidence by giving your life some purpose. At its very core, sacrifice equals reward. No different, I guess, than the way we train our pets. I cannot do what others in the Yukon did by dating in a homeless shelter, because the old-school values my parents instilled within me over and over again state that there's no point coming to the table if you're not bringing something to it.

After tidying the house and packing up seemingly for weeks, it was time to move the 125 kilometres back to Vancouver. Thankfully, my good friend Simon had a van and offered to help me move for free. I will never forget the last night I spent with my youngest daughter, Iona. Our goodbye that night was just too much. You know when you tell yourself you're going to be brave and not cry, and despite every single piece of emotional armour you bring to the situation, it still isn't enough to stop the tears from flowing? That was me that night, bawling like a little baby because I knew our precious time together was going to be seriously curtailed. I had no car, and Carol was far from honouring her court agreement for my visitation rights by bringing her down to me once a month. Although I thought long and hard about going back to the legal system to challenge this injustice, I knew I simply wasn't strong enough or rich enough to pursue that avenue quite yet.

I had moved so many times since originally leaving Whistler when we sold the big house and my dream life way back then. Was this the final move to find the happiness, friendship and love I so desperately yearned for? I had learnt that material things only offer a temporary solution for grief and sadness.

After a quick dog walk to check out my new hood, I settled down to cry myself to sleep with the *Why me?* and *Am I strong enough?* questions beating up my brain all over again. I am not quite sure why, when I decided to take this place, I had not figured out that my new address was just around the corner from one of my worst triggers: St. Paul's hospital in downtown Vancouver. It was there I had spent way too much of my life battling Crohn's disease, initially having gross tests like colonoscopies and endoscopies. I was convinced that it was as a result of my bowel resection in my three-and-a-half weeks at St. Paul's laced with a morphine pump that I started my dependency on prescription painkillers, as I could press for medication anytime.

Quite honestly, recovering from that surgery had my pain threshold on a whole different level than anything else I had ever been through, as unlike other body parts, you can't stop your intestines with a sling, cast or whatever. Add to that another two weeks of sheer hell trying in vain to get weaned off all the prescription meds, especially the most addictive painkillers that were putting an unbearable stranglehold on my life. Worse still is that this is the place I would come night after night on my 30-minute trek from my new home in Yaletown to get my fix of IV painkillers, which directly resulted in my lowest of the low: my detention in their locked psych ward.

As if my new home's location wasn't bad enough, I had unintentionally landed in gay central, giving me another chance to look my lifelong demons in the eye. Rumours of my brother being gay that somehow meant I was too; being called a gay Gordon because of my parents' choice to send me to a private all-boys school; my male form teacher abusing me in my formative early teens; my best friend Colin coming out in my bed on holiday; my Fine Fare colleague abusing me—as much as I wished I could lock those memories in a filing cabinet drawer, throw away the key and move on, I just couldn't. My brain still wasn't ready to forgive or forget. This was really going to test my resolve, composure and morals more than I can describe in words. I just kept telling myself that despite all of those painful experiences, plus my lack of comprehension of their choice, I would support that choice if they supported mine to be straight and didn't cross the line. It did, however, put a new twist on riding my road bike with shaved legs (which I never really understood why I was doing apart from fitting in) and spandex.

It unfortunately didn't take long for me to figure out why roadies shave their legs, as after just over a month living downtown, I went out for my usual ride of 10 or 12 circuits around Stanley Park, approximately 80 kilometres per lap. The park was the jewel in Vancouver's crown and recently, deservedly, was voted the best green space in any city worldwide. I had already bought advance tickets for the latest installment of the *Transformers* trilogy for that night at the 6 p.m. show, so I rewarded my effort by treating myself to Starbucks in my old Yaletown outlet.

On the short trek back to my pad, I was stopped at a traffic light when all of a sudden a couple of tight roadie chicks lined up behind me. The testosterone kicked in, and I decided to show off my sprinting prowess and kicked hard on my pedals. Before I knew what was going on, I was lying on the ground, gushing from my extensive road rash and a particularly sore right shoulder and left elbow. There aren't words! How do you explain these accidents logically to yourself? It was yet another one of those speed bumps that seemingly creeps up and sucker punches me every time I try to make a decisive move to come back. I am also pretty sure I lost consciousness, as I couldn't think straight.

The girls I was trying to impress told me to sit tight and also got a photo of the driver at fault's number plate and contact details. But for some reason, I didn't get their names as witnesses, and I ignored their pleas to sit a while longer to get all my senses back and then head straight to the nearest hospital, namely St. Paul's, to get checked over. No; Andrew did one of his dumb-ass hero moves and stupidly raced back home, hit the shower and did the gruesome task of cleaning the entire road rash out of too many places on my body.

In all honesty, if it was any other hospital, I'm sure I would have followed their advice, but going to St. Paul's was almost as hard as going back to Richmond's psych ward. Even passing it triggers so many insane flashbacks. Finally, in my bloody shower, painstakingly cleaning out my severe road rash, I realized the main reason roadies shave their legs: hair would only have complicated this brutal cleaning.

I got dressed just in time to make the movie. Problem was, less than 15 minutes into the sick flick, I started to shake uncontrollably—so badly that I couldn't even hold my popcorn. In typical Andrew fashion, I soldiered on with the movie, then gritted my teeth for another 10 sleepless nights until I threw in the towel in and went to St. Paul's in the wee hours of the morning just to find out there was nothing to be seen on the X-rays. I knew myself there was more damage than what the X-rays were showing.

Imagine the worst nightmare you have ever had, and then you wake up and find it wasn't a nightmare after all, rather your living reality. That's what going to St. Paul's was like for me. It is still just as harrowing as every time I relive a flashback from my complex PTSD. Worse still, after being fast-tracked, I was met by a male nurse who, almost unbelievably, opened a file in my hated homophobia drawer that I had forgotten existed. All of a sudden, I was faced with this gut-wrenching video flashback of the same nurse befriending me many times but on one night, crossing the line by running his hands up my legs inside my ER robe and caressing my genitals while I was so out of this world tripping out on my chosen cocktail, sufentanil and morphine, I couldn't even try to stop him.

As any recovering addict will tell you, it is exactly this type of literal and metaphoric fall that opens up the devil inside. Your head begs you to reach for a way to numb all the physical, mental and emotional pain by ingesting any chemical that transports you from the ultimate doom and gloom to a cloud-nine happy place where nothing really matters. I was now back downtown in the city with the largest black market for pills of any and every description, readily available for ridiculously low prices. Despite my efforts, the job-hunting was not going as planned, and the pressure was starting to mount all over again. Without a job, I was heading straight back to my homeless hood and life on the streets.

I knew I was living on borrowed time and had to find something like yesterday. Although I did eventually find a mind-numbingly boring temporary labour job putting up and tearing down exhibitions, which literally hurt like a bitch with all my ailments, the hours were erratic and, put simply, were not enough to pay my extortionate rent.

My only solution was to get back in touch with my guardian angel social worker, Sharon, from the Yukon shelter to help me, as I really was alone on so many levels. In typical Sharon style, she gave me the blunt truth that I already knew but was too scared to admit: if I couldn't find a job within two months, all my money would be gone, and I would again be on the streets. So why exhaust my remaining next-to-nothing savings on a flogged horse? Everywhere I had applied, I faced the dreaded Catch-22, namely:

1. Despite my impressive education and work experience, I had been away from the commercial world for too long to regain a middle-to higher-level managerial and/or representative position.

2. I was seriously overqualified for a lower-level position. In my absolute desperation, I had even applied to Starbucks, Walmart and McDonald's, places less than a decade ago I would have pissed myself laughing at if you'd ever suggested it. But nothing, absolutely nothing from anywhere.

I was sending out résumés like crazy, but not a fucking dicky bird. God, what had I become? Always in the back of my mind was something so intensely terrifyingly that even my new stronger character could not face the thought of it: returning to the Yukon homeless shelter for the third time. All my brain could think of was that I would rather be dead than go back there. I knew I could visit my fears, but living in them was a completely different proposition.

I decided I was going to prove to myself that I was now strong and brave enough to face anything my past had to scare me by riding my bike over to Richmond Hospital and revisiting the psych ward, which was easily the source of my worst memories. There are simply no words to express just how insanely traumatic and humbling my prison for five months really was. To be honest, the homeless shelter wasn't that far removed from a locked psych ward, as most people there really should be locked up in either a ward or a prison cell. Instead, they were semi-functioning mentally ill addicts of booze or drugs.

After a major battle in my head, I decided to ride out there, not only to thank all the nurses and doctors who literally saved my life but also to somehow expel those demons by gaining a real-life visualization of my flashbacks. I walked around the gardens, where I distinctly remember I would sing and dance whilst avoiding every crack on the stone walkway (why I did this, I still have no clue), whilst this war raged in my head as to whether I was indeed strong enough to actually enter the hospital. As truly frightened as I was, I knew if I went home now without doing what I had come for, I would beat myself up so bad. Really, I had no choice but to grit my teeth and face it.

Just as I remembered, inside the doors was the Starbucks where I used to beg money for my daily java fix. Then onto the elevator, which I genuinely believed, every time I entered it, was like a magic carpet whisking me out of my hell into a TV-game-show-like frenzy, where I would be surrounded by media as I accepted the premiership of Canada and start my new and improved life as a well-deserved real-life superstar. No lie, that was 110 percent genuinely what I believed in my psychotic state.

Finally, I came face to face with the locked doors of the psych ward I had spent hours trying in vain to escape. I was about to re-enter the site of my worst nightmares. To my amazement, it was exactly as I recalled it. I passed the staff Sharpie notice board where, for some strange reason, I would draw a compass-like mural each and every day; I was convinced they put the wrong date on it to further confuse me. Then I walked past the fitness equipment I had tried to use, but my ridiculously short attention span back then would never allow me to stay on the cycling machine for very long. Even the table football (soccer) game was there, where I would put spaces on the counting beads to represent life milestones. Right after that was the nurse's station with the sign-out book that I used to autograph, as I believed my fans wanted me to do. For the sake of their privacy I am not going to mention any names, but yes, to my surprise, the same nurses who helped me were working that day.

We shared a quick hello and "thanks for everything." I could see their pure delight that I indeed had not only survived but looked fit and no longer was the 87-pound shell of a man I had been. I just wish I had a photograph of my very unhealthy skinny state back then so I could show the world just how close we all are to becoming that feeble and frail.

Past the nurses' station and on the left was the double room that was my first resting place, where I would write verbal riddles to myself that no sane person could ever have a chance of interpreting. It was also the place to which way too many security guards were called. I refused to go to bed, so I was manhandled into one of the solitary cells in the back that no one except actual badly behaved residents would ever see. Quite honestly, if the real world did see, someone would do something to humanize them.

Then I moved on to the eating area. I would get up early and come here to pinch my favourite cereal. It's also where the arts therapy took place. Past that was the site of my favourite therapy: the large electronic keyboard where we would do our music therapy. Every weekday late morning, we would do something different in the way of therapy. In the kitchen, we might learn to make succulent and sweet desserts.

Next came the only place where I felt I could touch the outside world, and as a result, it was my favourite place in there: the TV room. Here is where I watched pretty much every Winter Olympic sport possible. Thank God it was on then, as although I wish I was not so sick so I could have gone and seen the action in real life, it was still a godsend to pass the time in there. When it wasn't on, I would watch Much Music (Canada's version of MTV) to get my much-needed music-therapy escapism and *So You Think You Can Dance* with Joy (her name to this day is still a trigger for my flashbacks), an older lady who loved ballroom dancing. We compared notes on the contestants, and in truth, we were more often than not spot-on with our critiques. It was here that I would write the telephone number of the ward and change the channel to BBC World in the insane belief that my folks could somehow see my plight when they too tuned in to their favorite channel.

Finally, a quick right turn brought me to my single room, where I would watch all the planes taking off and landing, and tell myself one of those planes would eventually come to take me away—or bring someone who loved me to help me survive my incarceration. No one ever came, which is probably the most hurtful ... shit, here come the tears again. Break time.

Then on to the showers and bath, especially the latter. I can't explain, but this was my happy place, a sanctuary from all the madness that was my life. The hot water had healing powers, almost like ctrl-alt-delete button for me to reset my crazy life. To this day, when life gets too much for me, I will run a hot bath and sing to myself—or, more often, switch off all noise and light to reach the most underrated sound: silence. It's my cheap version of the all-new isolation chambers, I guess (but I was first on that idea). I enter this almost spiritual unreal meditative world that I can't explain but somehow works for me to this day. I even shaved my legs in there with Bic razors. All I can say is, never try it, as I bled all over the towels. Looking back on it, why they would ever entrust this suicidal zombie with a razor is beyond me.

Actually, the most memorable thing about this was that every so often, we would get this black nurse on the ward, and my brain had decided she was a spy for President Obama. He had heard my story and was grooming me for a high-powered position in his new term. Yes we can!

Finally, on to the laundry, where my sick orange and purple Puma kicks disappeared, and I would waste time trying to find a beat and dance to the noises of the washer and drier just like my hero MJ had done so many years before. Then the corridor that completed my circle of life, where I would sing and dance with reckless abandon, invariably to Michael's awe-inspiring music, past all the staff and meeting rooms.

When all is said and done, without music, I just end up making it myself. I tried to learn the harmonica for its sound and portability, but like most things, it's way harder than it looks. Why didn't I listen at my private piano lessons when the instructor tried to teach how to read music? I literally live and breathe music, but I can't play an instrument apart from maybe drums.

My visit time was over, and I had seen enough to maybe, hopefully, close that chapter of my life. I said all my goodbyes and gave my highest appreciation to the staff, and I left feeling really proud of myself. Although the visit did not offer me the closure I had wished so hard for, it did somehow comfort me that my insane memories of the place were indeed rooted in truths rather some mystical world that was entirely a creation of my imagination.

It also reinforced the fact that I was now not only physically but, much more importantly, mentally and emotionally stronger than I had ever been in my decade of demise. Despite all the still-open mental and emotional scars, I assured myself that if I could do that—visit my darkest demons and somehow make peace with them—maybe a return to the Yukon could be some kind of watershed for me. Reliving my fears would turn each fear on its head to become an inner strength that no one could ever buy or teach.

My past had somehow molded me into a very different person than what I was when the world was my oyster. Still, going back to the Yukon struck the fear of God right into my very core and soul. I knew that it could possibly open the neuro pathways that led me to the other side of sanity and, possibly worse still, make me relapse in an attempt to numb my memories. If there was any other option, I would have taken it, but there wasn't. So, reluctantly, I finally caved and called Sharon to accept her offer of a shared room upstairs in the Yukon.

Oh, dear Lord, not again, is all my brain could think about. Was I indeed strong enough to go to the place that nearly killed me the first time around? No lie: my last night in Barclay Street was yet another case of déjà vu. By 3 a.m., I had finally finished packing up all my shit and tidying the apartment, and I again found myself sitting on the floor with all my meds debating whether anything, yes even suicide, was better than returning to that hell.

Here's something I will never comprehend: Just as I tipped all my pills into my hand, Cheyenne, seeming to know what was going on, came over, licked my face and lay in my lap. When I say to people that this dog has been to hell and back with me, saved my life too many times to mention here and become the best friend I have ever had, I mean it beyond words. She is my heart and soul, my pride and joy. To me, she is the most beautiful and smartest living thing on this planet.

I love that dog more than I have ever loved anything before, even my first dog, Vharie. I tell no lie: you could offer me all the money, fame, fortune, power, literally anything in the world for her, and I would never give up on her love and friendship, which are so deep and strong that she has truly taught me to be a better man. Genuinely, nothing, but nothing, is more important than true love, as only love lasts forever. Put simply: she is my everything.

I got next to no sleep that night—as really, how could anyone sleep if they were in my position? The next morning, Sharon arrived as planned, and yes, I made another move, and another chapter in my "another suitcase" life, to quote *Evita*, was about to begin. Dread is simply not a strong enough word to describe my emotions, but I knew I had to do everything in my power not to show it, as I knew firsthand that this was just like in the animal kingdom. Everyone in the Yukon had to be perceived and treated as an adversary. If my fellow residents sensed any fear, they would rip me apart like vultures do in the desert with no oasis in sight.

After countless trips to the mini-storage to say to goodbye to all my precious belongings, I was left with my Dakine roller bag with a couple of days' clothing and toiletries. Then I was back in Sharon's truck to go back to the Yukon homeless shelter, a place I had already devoted too much of my life to. Yet it had become my temporary home again. My only saving grace was that Chris, the reformed gambling addict and total pothead I had befriended the first time around, was still in the upstairs residency, so at least I had him and Sharon in my corner.

That said, I knew this was a fight for survival, quite literally, and I had to win it all by myself. From a 2,700-foot million-dollar mansion in ritzy glitzy Whistler to a tiny shared room in a homeless shelter—you don't fall from grace quite like I did. I knew I had to grow a pair, man up all over again and survive in any way possible.

CHAPTER 17

INVINCIBLE

S o here we are, back in the Yukon for the third fucking time. I must admit, I am truly scrapping for words here to try and describe my feelings. Sometimes when things are so deep, they creep into your very core, your bones, your skin, your heart and soul, literally every part of your being. They are so intense that words simply can't mirror the most basic feelings that fight, flight or freeze represent. I genuinely doubted whether I could get through another stay in the Yukon.

I could not make up my mind whether the fact that I was as close as I can get these days to being sane would make a difference; as my various psychiatrists explained, once you have opened the crazy doors (or the neuropathic highways), you can never fully close them again. Literally every minute of my time in there, I had to deal with the real fucked-up flashbacks my complex PTSD kept throwing in my face. I just kept assuring myself that I was no longer a rookie at this, and although I was maybe not quite a seasoned vet, I had always been blessed with more than most in the street-smarts department. With that and my previous homeless experiences, I was in a much better place to deal with this hell, for hopefully the last time. Problem is, as soon as you enter this place, you become immediately aware of three factors:

1. **The bad news:** Every day, there's a review a meeting where the staff tries to get rid of you. As with every business, turnover is how they make their money. Let's just say some staff are more sympathetic

than others (mostly the ones who have gone through similar shit as opposed to college kids who just didn't get the plot). My first day, my brain somehow forgot that you had to shower and spend your day in clothes that resembled what prisoners in jail wear because of the potential bedbug infestation from the street crew. It was a demoralising way to start. My welcome meeting was with this twentysomething kid obviously fresh out of college. When I told him of my Crohn's disease, his lovely comment was, "You're obviously an asshole then." It made me want to fucking kill the little bastard right there and then. Every review is an opportunity to be tossed back on the haunting and very dangerous streets of Vancouver—a dread that sat like a monkey on my back each and every day.

2. **The good news:** If you were able to find a place that didn't require you to have a job and would accept your government cheques, you were one of the very few who beat what I call the homeless/poverty trap. It was the ultimate Catch-22: you can't get a job because you live in a fucking homeless shelter with no real address, no real work clothes and as many holes in your résumé as in your shoes because of your present predicament: namely broke and at the bottom of the food chain. With no permanent address except a homeless shelter, good luck getting any kind of job. And with no job, no landlords in their right mind will offer you an apartment, especially in a city with a real estate market so inflated with hype generated by the real estate industry—never mind that it is now rated the second most expensive city in the world to live in.

3. **The reality:** You do everything possible to survive until you either get kicked back out on the streets or, marginally better, do like so many of your homeless homies and shelter hop, going from one to another until you use up your stay; that's two or three months at a time if you're lucky. Maybe you manage to score a residency in the heavily subsidized, three-year-wait-time BC Housing or the all-too-few rooms upstairs in the homeless shelter, where you could live for up to two years, as with my time in the North Shore residency and my mate Chris's in the Yukon. As a final option, you got punted out into one of the horrible government-acquired

bankrupt hotels which had been turned into very grotty homeless residencies.

Needless to say, none of these options is very attractive. I tried not to focus on them, instead remembering the old adage that it's not the destination but the journey which is of importance. I resolved to get through each and every day using my new knowledge of the ghetto life and the insane psychology that you needed to practice every second in there, since as soon as you let your guard down, you will be screwed over even by those you considered friendly. That was one of their key weapons to fuck with you: befriending you until they got what they wanted.

This is one of the reasons that, to this day, I have serious trust issues. I trust no one, as like it or not, I have been dumped by everyone, including all of my family at one stage or another. And yes, extreme distrust is yet another lovely symptom of complex PTSD.

I know this sounds somewhat cheesy, but I finally found a use for my too many wasted hours of watching reality TV, especially *Survivor* and *Intervention*. It always amazed me that it was very rarely the strongest physical players who won that game but rather the shrewdest. Don't get me wrong; my still somewhat athletic build came in handy, as I know it made people, especially guys, think twice before they fucked with me. But this knowledge combined with a few old sayings I never really understood until now were the pillars of my new life, namely:

1. Fly under the radar.
2. Keep your friends close but your enemies closer.
3. What doesn't kill you makes you stronger.
4. What goes around comes around.

Those seemed to help the winners of these types of shows more than anything else. So I extrapolated that knowledge to what I truly feel is the ultimate game of survival.

I knew I had to formulate a game plan. It was simple: I had to return to the world of psychological warfare, where you have to treat everyone as a potential enemy. The more I knew about the participants, the better my chances for survival. After being in this hell of drug addiction and my painful slide down seemingly every known snake known to man for over a decade, I was pretty much an oracle on my own SWOT analysis of the man I was and had now transformed into. I had psychoanalyzed myself over and over to find the reason for ending up in this precarious position in the first place. Very simply, my extremely high risk-taking traits and use of painkillers were the main reason I ended up in this mess of a life, plus more than a few very strange decisions by some of my medical professionals, one of which I still think about suing for her complete lack of professionalism and common sense.

So now what? It was simple: I had to treat my first few days just like special ops reconnaissance behind enemy lines, as the consequences of defeat were pretty similar and this place could become my resting place for real. Instead of armies, I had to deal with urban gang members who wouldn't think twice about blowing my knees out with a baseball bat or smashing my face with a poor man's blade (broken bottle) or a knuckle-duster, no lie. In my opinion, as the place hadn't changed but only the people on both sides of the workers' desk, I reckoned the only logical thing to concern myself with was learning as much as possible about my new shelter homies. To be honest, my first few weeks in there were damn hard, as I literally had to face every single day one of the way-too-many demons that whispered negative messages in my head with ruthless abandon.

Thankfully, just a few blocks away was this park where I could escape and listen to my iPod Touch or, more usually, the radio in my phone. I only very vaguely remembered this park from walking Chi in it before. There were these kid and adult swings I would sometimes go on, even when it was raining. Every time I was in the Yukon, it seemed to be rainy season in Vancouver, and that made life infinitely harder, as I simply could not hang out indoors. Even the depressing drizzle or flat-out Pacific storm was better than the constant and ever-changing drama of the homeless shelter.

Have you ever tried to swing yourself on a swing? If not, try it sometime. Then and only then will you truly understand what my physics teacher Bongo Bain introduced me to decades earlier as the very real theory of momentum and inertia. Without using the ground to push off, I would challenge myself to get the swing to move by simply swinging my legs. If you try it yourself, you will find it takes so much more effort to get going than if you use the ground to push off or get a push from someone. But after a certain number of times, it gets increasingly easier, on an almost learning-type bell-shaped curve.

I like to compare the push from someone to wealth/cold hard cash, the metaphoric push from family and friends. Inertia is exactly the reason so very few people truly escape the vicious cycle of poverty and homelessness. Now throw in mental diseases and addiction, and it becomes impossible to use the ground either, because your "issues" further weaken your willpower on all levels. Now maybe you'll understand what it is like to live with nothing.

It's kind of like floating as compared to treading water. When you have all the creature comforts provided by money and power, you can do the former by just relaxing, as compared to the frenetic panic nothingness brings. Those of us who struggle fight every day to keep our head above water. It takes literally everything we have to keep up the frantic paddling instead of giving up and drowning.

Thankfully, it wasn't long before I got moved into a room by myself, which I must say was a total savior. Believe me, it's a gigantic relief not to have to make polite BS small talk with another street rat like yourself when the only thing you have in common is the daily struggle to survive life with next to nothing. I knew Sharon must have been behind it, as always.

To be honest, my complex PTSD had turned me into a huge loner, as it's hard to make friends when your brain has been rewired not to trust anyone. On top of this, the 12-step program in AA/NA warns against dating too soon, as most become too dependent on the new partner. When it ends, your desperation just marches you back to the new and easiest way to get over grief, by numbing it with your sweetest friend.

It became very apparent early on that this time was going to be different than any of my previous stays in Vancouver's homeless world, as despite the never-ending war with my complex PTSD and Crohn's, I was actually sane this time. It was both a blessing and a curse. There was no more vagueness about my situation, with the voices in my head convincing my brain that this wasn't really my reality, rather some kind of messed-up nightmare that I just had to survive until I awoke in my pimp-daddy sleigh bed with Carol beside me in my extravagant Whistler lifestyle. Now I had to deal with the brutal reality and survive every day on my own. It wasn't long before

I got a good handle on the mental politics of the place. It was like there were three groups, almost gangs, fighting for supremacy:

1. First was the gangster-wannabe crew. I guess they were actually as close to modern-day gangsters as you can get, as most of them were connected to the very real and dangerous Vancouver drug gangs. These were mostly young males doing the full-on in-your-face cocky testosterone-fueled aggression bit, trying everything in the book to dominate, intimidate and bully anyone they could. There were a couple of leaders of the gang: Dan. this late-teen kid who was really messed up after a kicking on the street and now was popping antipsychotic pills like they were going out of fashion while listening to hip hop on one of two free computers; Andrew, Dan's wingman, a much more menacing hard nut on an eternal search for dope to mellow out his high-strung personality; and Don, a drug dealer who used humour and a quirky personality to get him through, as it was obvious he wasn't one to be feared physically.

2. Next was the intellectuals crew, a much quieter conglomeration of people who were either not cool enough or simply did not want anything to do with the dope gangster crew. This was generally an older bunch, but they were just as imposing and actually more threatening, as what they lacked in physical prowess, they more than made up for in intelligence and pure life experience.

3. Finally, there were the independents, the people who kept to themselves in an attempt to get through this ordeal the best way they could. They had their own game plan on how they were going to escape this hell.

Then there was me and Cheyenne. I guess if I had to put myself anywhere, I was mainly an independent, but I had my foot firmly planted in both of the other tribes. This was because of my chosen dual strategies of survival: fly under the radar (with the intelligents) and keep my enemies closer (with the gangstas).

Unfortunately, although I tried so many ways to reduce my heightening stress, it was starting to take its toll on both my mental (complex PTSD) and physical (Crohn's) state. Before I had even gotten my feet wet, excruciating gut pain required me to go back on the very drugs that had almost a decade earlier put me on my path of self-destruction. And just like before, the opioids played very frightening tricks with my mind. In less than a month, the vicious cycle of narcotic gut syndrome reduced me to a walking wreck. I couldn't sleep or eat, as almost everything I ingested I ended up throwing up.

My last night at the Yukon before going to hospital summed up my struggle perfectly. After another greasy dinner, I was doubled over in pain, throwing my guts up. Then, just as I tried to go to sleep, Cheyenne was stricken with the worst case of diarrhea I had ever seen. Within no time, my fellow residents were quite rightly bitching about the disgusting smell. I went downstairs to get a mop, but in line with my mad bad luck, I got the gayest of all the staff. He had sussed out that I thought he was a big pussy, and in his warped mind, he got his payback by only offering me these dumb napkins to pick the mess up with. Again, I had hit rock bottom.

The next day, I did the only thing I knew would help: I knocked on Sharon's Lookout Society door. She took one look at me and immediately knew what to do. She drove me to the nearest hospital: Vancouver General, the place I went when I smashed my leg (really the first major downer on my very swift fall from grace) and later my all-night escapade when they refused me any painkillers the first time I was at the Yukon.

For reasons I've never figured out, I was put in a ward with very contagious lung diseases, and everyone was walking about with masks on their face. Before I could say boo, I was rushed into another lovely cleanse with this rocket juice that had a disgusting taste. It was called Go Lightly, which, trust me, you don't go lightly on that shit. It did a number on my gut in prep for my next-day colonoscopy. I hated that so much, as a camera or enema in my ass is not my idea of fun.

Although the doctor assured me he would knock me out like my new GI guy in St. Paul's always did, he never took into account my high resistance to any drug, and I was very uncomfortably awake throughout the gross procedure. Well, I was pissed. After being left on this bed in a corridor after my procedure, lying in my own excrement waiting for someone to help me get back to my room, I gave up and literally jumped off the fucking thing—exposing my crown jewels in the process—just to get to a washroom where I could clean the filth off myself.

THE HOOD

Thankfully, things started improving when I hooked up with their psychiatrist, who listened to my condensed version of my story. After the usual shock, she got it and, half-jokingly but half-seriously, advised me I should really consider moving away from all my triggers in Vancouver and really all of British Columbia and start again somewhere like Calgary, Alberta or back in Europe. It was there and then that my nitrous-filled brain decided to play one of its PTSD renditions. In the shower, washing myself, I overheard the nurses call what I believed me to be a creep, and now every time I hear that word, it immediately transports me back to that time.

How can I explain complex PTSD? Take the absolute worst, lowest of the low, shockingly scared you have ever been. For example, a female friend explained that her panic attacks are way more prevalent every time she rides in an elevator, because back in her childhood, she was raped in one. If you take all my troubles, extending as far back as I can remember—for example but not limited to being uncomfortable around gay men—you can start to understand why I am an admitted homophobe … or is it part of my complex PTSD because of all of my sexual assaults? That is one question I don't think I will ever find an answer to.

So come on, be big enough to confess: what's your biggest insecurity and/or skeleton in the closet? We all have them. Ask yourself what triggers your memories and pushes your buttons the most? What immediately starts to replay the terrible video associated with that fear or trauma in your head that makes you anxious even now? Even superheroes like Superman have their kryptonite. The following are some of my triggers:

1. When I hear a siren or watch an emergency services vehicle fly past me on the road, I get stiff with fear, as I remember being in the back of all of them through my many suicide attempts, scrapes with the law and, worst of all, trips back to the homeless shelter or locked psych ward.

2. Every GMC or Chevy puts me back in the psyche ward awaiting delivery of my brand-new and completely free (because of sponsorship, I believed) top-of-the-range Camero SS complete with a *Starsky and Hutch* red-and-white paint scheme.

3. Every time I escape to my happy meditative place of a hot bath with music, I remember lying in my yuppie Yaletown apartment

writing to everyone I knew a subtle suicide email, followed by my best attempt to kill myself through pills and drowning. Sometimes it puts me back in the Yukon shelter escaping my horrible reality in the lockable upstairs bathroom, trying to figure out how the fuck am I going to get out of this gutter of my new life. Worst of all, it transports me back to the Richmond psych ward where I started my bath meditative state and decided one time I was getting out soon, so I shaved my legs with the cheapest Bic razor, which left blood everywhere. I thought I was preparing for my next bike race season, which couldn't be further from the truth. When you're psychotic, your brain makes up bizarre shit.

I could go on and on. There are so many traumatic experiences contained in the darkest corridors of my drug-ravaged and disease-driven mind that I have absolutely no defence against when the drawer of the biological filing cabinet is opened by random triggers everywhere, regardless of which of the five senses are the trigger point. The worst part is that the more I try to escape it or fight it, the worse the intensity of the attack.

It's almost a mirror image of my personality, whereby I gain strength from all the smears and innuendos from my haters. It is called, in medical terms, hyper-vigilance. You are always on guard for the next physical, mental, emotional or even spiritual attack, mainly from being places where you had no hope left and truly did have to watch everything, not just your back.

Again, take your biggest fear and try to relive it every day of the week, and then you might understand why I am the way I am. Forget about the weak link or lack-of-willpower label people like to paste on mental health issues. These are very real diseases. For some fucked-up reason, diseases of the mind are not classified along with all the other medical diseases like cancer, MS or heart disease, although they are just as real and need medical intervention to overcome. They carry a very bad rap, and everyone mocks, condemns or fears them thanks to the *Psycho*-type stereotypes from Hollywood's many flicks that portray and mimic mental illnesses.

It's like the name TSN sports reporter Michael Landsberg, who came out and admitted he too was troubled with depression, gave his crusade against all the dumb-ass "dude, get over it" responses: Depression—a Sickness, Not a Weakness. Enough said!

I have completely researched complex PTSD on a ridiculous number of websites, and I have developed a few cool strategies, like those highlighted in Celia Laval's sensational letter to me. The company and feeling of security my darling dog Chi brings helps a lot, and I take her with me pretty much everywhere I go. Another major shield is my music, which not only completely extinguishes one of the worst triggers, noises, but can also help me with the mood swings that comes as a result of the disease.

The best defence of all is having a home where you can close and sometimes slam the door to the outside world to regroup, refocus and re-center yourself after all of the demons, critics, haters and events drive you to the very basic human instincts of fight, flight or freeze. This obviously is impossible when you live in a homeless shelter with 80 other residents who all are on edge in some way or another. But believe me, being on guard every time you open your front door is so draining, especially mentally, as you try everything to hide your very real disease from everyone so successfully, they erroneously judge you as some kind of standoffish, arrogant, rude, probably faggot or maybe drama drag queen, because the only female you have in your life is your loyal adorable canine friend Chi.

Somehow, by magic, we have gone full circle in this story of my very real life—not the "based on a true story" theatrics of Hollywood and BC's Hollywood North, just the truth and nothing but the truth, so help me God. After surviving what I had already been through, I decided in my insane days in the Richmond psych ward that from this point on, I was going to do everything in my power not to lie. I figured out that when I did, I usually had to tell more lies to back it up, and at the end of the day, it was just another unwanted stressor to play havoc on my Crohn's affliction. This time around, honesty was my best policy.

After a couple of weeks in Vancouver General, I celebrated my 45th birthday alone. The very next day, MJ's doctor, Conrad Murray, was sentenced to the maximum five-year imprisonment for helping my hero kill himself. No one will ever know if it was a mistake or a well-scripted suicide, but I like to believe Michael would never intentionally kill himself, given his real love for his kids and his chance to finally show them the artistry that made him not only the King of Pop but simply the best entertainer of all time.

There will never ever be another Michael Jackson, and we have only ourselves to blame, as the deadly sins of greed and jealousy joined forces. False accusations drained the very existence out him by bending his biggest passion, namely kids, against him in an immaculately planned web of exaggerations and flat-out lies. Unfortunately, he was not the first and disturbingly won't be the last celebrity who paid the ultimate price for talent, success, fame and fortune.

I was thrown out of the hospital and back to the Yukon within a day of my rebellious airing of the news that pointedly put the blame for MJ's death where it belonged: with the overzealous doctors who medicate us all with Band-Aid solutions like the overuse of pills, potions and lotions instead of trying to get to root cause of our problem with lifestyle changes, physical touch therapies and natural solutions. I left with a list of medications longer than my arm. Most worryingly, I was back on my chosen poison: the hydromorphone "just to get through."

Worse still, when I returned to the Yukon, I had lost my right to the single room. Somewhat ironically, this gay hairdresser, Steve (who I got on really well with, actually), got precedence because of his HIV disease. I was moved back to a shared room with this guy called Dan. It wasn't long before I realized he was one of the most hated people in there. He had this "I know everything about everything, especially women" male-chauvinistic attitude that made you want to just slap him. Because of this, he would spend almost every possible minute hiding in the room, and that meant I never got peace to just to chill with my canine soulmate, Chi.

As if that wasn't enough, he was the dirtiest—not sex-wise but personal-hygiene-wise. Because of his paranoid nature, he would not wash, as he was convinced his increasingly grotesque flesh sores were being caused by the shelter's choice of laundry detergent rather than because he didn't clean himself. Although he was a bit of a knob, I knew I was far from perfect too. Once I got through all his BS macho walls, he was actually a decent bloke who I shared more than a few joints with. His real personality shown through then, and it was a hell of a lot more pleasant than the one he liked to portray to the world. It's funny: only the new, much more forgiving me, armed with a solid grip on human psychology, would give him the chance to redeem himself. I simply had no patience for people like that in my glory days.

I could write a whole book on my last five months in the Yukon. Maybe I'll save that for the sequel. Instead, I'll offer some highlights and lowlights of my final stay in there. The guy I was most worried about was Dan, not from a physical threat, as I knew I could take him, but just his overconfident and judgmental demeanor pressed all my buttons. Instead of starting a war with him, I loosely befriended him using both our passions: music and dance.

Everything was fine until he said he would buy my HTC Desire smartphone and then tried to royally fuck me over on the deal. I told him he didn't want to pull that shit on me or I would either kick his ass or phone the cops. He decided that the former was his best strategy, and despite all my friends begging me not to go outside with him, there are times in there when, if you were male and cowered away from a fight, it sent a message to the rest of the thugs that you were full of bull. The hounds would feast on you because you were a walk-all-over wuss. As in most cases, calling his bluff worked.

I wasn't some born-yesterday fool. I knew his aggression was fueled by the typical UFC night on the TV, where the angry drunks and druggies decided they were Georges "Rush" St-Pierre and wanted to fight the nearest person regardless of whether you were friend or foe. It's funny, but on another occasion, the same thing happened. On comes Pride and UFC, and a fight breaks out between a couple of low-lifes. Out of a deep sleep, my angel, Cheyenne, rose to get between me and the altercation, brandishing her fangs as she had done during my beat-down on the streets. I would die for that dog, and I know she would do the same for me.

Dan had already pulled this shit a few nights before when he tried to call me out of my room in his attempt to get under my skin by shouting my newly acquired nickname: "Where are you, Irish?" I never gave him the satisfaction and carried on watching one of my all-time fave flicks, *Top Gun*, in my room. So yeah, the long and short of it was, he backed down. We shook on it and smoked a blunt together.

Yes, I said it: a blunt. *Oh my God, he's now doing street drugs!* I kind of thought like that too, but I needed to escape my reality somehow. I remembered the buzz from my Cesamet painkillers from my drug-infested years, which were in fact basically a man-made version of cannabis but with a much lamer high. Quite honestly, I challenge anyone to live in a homeless shelter for any length of time without using something to escape the intense pressure hell brings with it. Regardless, I reckoned that it was the least of the sins that were readily available in there, and fuck it: if my oldest daughter, Michelle could do it, why the fuck couldn't I? I didn't have the alcohol alternative, as a bender causes me two days of blood and intense pain from my Crohn's backlash.

In truth, compared to most, I hardly touched the stuff. I made a rule to use it no more than three days a week and never during the day, only at night, to ensure I didn't get addicted on yet another drug.

Sorry but I'm going to rant again: *Why the fuck is chronic still illegal in so many countries?* I think they still see it as a street drug, with all the obvious disdain that goes with that. But if the government sold the stuff, it could not only dramatically increase revenues but also take it out of the hands of street dealers, removing the risk of the slippery slope to harder drugs offered by the dealers. Most importantly, I would take a stoner over an angry drunk every time—an opinion shared by many in the medical field.

I remember one time in particular when Chris offered a night out of the shelter. We hooked up with this kid Stilo who I met working the Levy Show job. He drove us up the Cypress Mountain road, and with a spectacular cityscape and a glorious sunset, we got truly baked out of our minds. I had trouble walking up the stairs of the shelter on my dreaded return to hell.

It was not easy to juggle grass and the hydromorphone I needed for my renewed gut pain, not to mention the 30-plus other daily pills the team at Vancouver General had prescribed for me for all of my health woes. I knew that was completely ridiculous, but I had more important things to worry about, like protecting my dog and my back. To this day, I look over my shoulder way more than I need to, as you simply have to when you're homeless.

It was this grand-finale stay in the Yukon that accelerated my complex PTSD to the level it is today. It is very noticeable even in Cheyenne's actions, as she hates to be left alone, especially outside. When I have a java break at the way too many coffee shops, I tie her up outside, and the only way around her panic attack (highlighted by barking her head off) is to find a place where I can drink my coffee with her on a patio.

I had to figure out how the hell I could realistically get the fuck out of the place by either finding a job to give me the money to afford and the reference required to gain accommodation and/or finding a new pad I could use as a base to find a job and regain a semi-normal life. It was the almost impossible puzzle that afflicts everyone in homeless hell. Days, weeks and then months started passing by within the ever-changing environment of the Yukon, as residents (or as I saw them, threats) came and went. The dynamics of the challenge was constantly in a state of flux, and to survive, you had to keep an extremely close eye on everything.

Sharon wrongly thought I had started to find my groove in that place. It's true that I was becoming more and more comfortable leading the shelter life, as to my amazement, the longer I stayed there, the more people started befriending me. That was always part of the plan, but I never expected it to work as well as it did. In truth, though, behind my external composure and self-confidence, my survival routine involved a very delicate balancing act.

To kick off every day, I would set my alarm clock for 7 a.m.—30 minutes before our official breakfast wake-up call—so I could get one of the two washrooms that had a decent bath/shower combination. That way, I would beat the morning rush, as I hated using the communal showers. It would also give me enough time to wake up and don my mental armour so I was ready for breakfast—probably the worst time of day, as pretty much everyone would be there. It was at mealtimes, especially breakfast, that people would try everything in their power to get under your skin by doing things like intentionally walking right in front of you or talking extra loud about subjects they hoped would get a response from you. I was too much of a veteran to fall for that trick, even though sometimes it was so hard to bite my tongue. I was still a fiery, feisty Gael and a wearer of heart on my sleeve.

Then, regardless of the weather (which was usually pissing outside), I would walk Cheyenne around the sea wall past my old Yaletown yuppie pad to my trusty local Blenz. While sipping my C$3 pot of tea, I would read the paper and try to waste time until about 11:30 a.m., when I would either head back to the shelter for lunch or, more usually, get a C$3 sub from the local Subway, as lunch was always the worst meal of the day in the shelter.

On non-rainy days, I would fill up my newly acquired Starbucks thermos mug with tea from breakfast, and I would walk Cheyenne the opposite way to a park beside Grandville Island, up the small hill, and hang on a park bench that offered a stellar view of False Creek. Then I would hit the Subway.

Rooms opened upstairs from 12:30 to 2 p.m., so I would chill in my room, usually listening to my iPod Touch or the radio on my phone for the 90 minutes or grab a quick shower if I had slept like crap, which was all too often the case, and didn't have one in the morning. Then, way too quickly, it was time to vacate the rooms again and find a way to waste another three hours until the rooms opened for the night at 5:30 p.m.

The afternoon was slightly easier, as I could leave Cheyenne in the room. I would more often than not head to the central library, where I would write *War and Peace*-style emails to my mum, who it felt like, apart from my kids and dog, was pretty much the only true friend I had left in the world. That was at the beginning of my stay there; the longer I lived there, the more acquaintances I seemed to develop. My closest friend was this guy called Darren who was, to be honest, a bit flakey, but I liked him because he was almost too pure, innocent and naive for his own good. Apart from Chris upstairs, he was the only person I actually felt I could trust, as he never betrayed me.

It amazed me, but even over my years of experience in homeless shelters, I still fell into the trust traps that people would play, like the one where they would so skillfully try to get you to lend them a small amount of money, which they would repay. They would then borrow more, again repaying, until they had your trust. At that point, they would borrow a larger amount just to fuck off to wherever, and you were left with the bitter sting of the *WTF Andrew, don't you ever learn?*

Afternoons were usually spent chatting with Darren, hanging out in the library watching music videos, or walking the main streets of Vancouver looking at all the cool swag I wouldn't even blink before buying back in my heyday. However depressing it was to face, there really wasn't anything else to do, because with my Sharon-imposed budget of C$10 a day (try it sometime), after my tea and sub in the morning, the rest was often spent on Tim Horton's coffee and donuts, a Canadian tradition, apart from no double-double (the popular double shot of expresso and cream); mine was a skinny French vanilla. To this day, I don't really like coffee that much, but it helped keep me regular with all the pills I was popping.

I had figured out the meal schedule, and on the days I couldn't eat what was offered, either because of my fussy taste in everything or because of my Crohn's, I would save the remainder of my money and buy myself dinner out, quite often at the new cheap Indian takeout or the nearby Wendy's, still my favourite fast-food burger joint. The Baconator was pure culinary paradise on a budget.

After dinner, I got into this weird habit that started off as a refuge from a bad day but developed into an almost-nightly ritual of having a long, slow soak in one of the two baths. Back then, I used the excuse that it would help my gut behave, but now I realize it was so much more than that. In truth, it was the only place I could be truly alone, safe and sound, naked on all levels with my thoughts, feelings and demons behind a locked door and armed with music as my main therapy to avoid another bout of craziness that life in a shelter could inflict on even the best minds on this planet. It is a habit I have continued to this day, as it is my form of meditation when exercise is not available.

To cap off my dreaded day in hell, I would book a spot at one of the two desktop computers around suppertime, grab my snack and go online or watch some TV if anything decent was on—which, in reality, meant pretending to watching TV while actually watching the much more compelling drama unfold in the shelter. Finally, I would pop my nighttime meds either just before or at lights out at 11 p.m. before crashing curled up with my baby, Chi, on the incredibly uncomfortable single bed, which was still way better than a park bench.

Although I met many incredibly colourful characters every time I ended up in homeless land, very few came close to my buddy Robert, aka Sticks. He was more than a rampant alcoholic but an absolute gem. A better, more genuine, honest and caring man you will never have the pleasure in meeting. Actually, I nearly missed him, as like me, he spent as little time in the shelter as possible. The only time you could find him there was for breakfast, when he was too hungover to really talk, and then from dinner onwards, when he was so drunk he could only string a few sentences together. More often he just put a few words together, like "Come on, Andrew, let me take you to my office," which meant, jokingly, a street fight. Like me, he'd had way too many of those, but we were too good friends to ever go there.

I swear, if he didn't drink so much, he could have been a stand-up comedian. Despite the ravages the booze was inflicting on his brain, he was one of the sharpest, wittiest and funniest people I have ever met.

By the time I got to know Sticks, I had also become good friends with an older lady called Martha who, to my eventual detriment, also turned out to be lifelong alcoholic. She hung out in the corner with the intelligents crew. Our first meeting was because of Cheyenne, as she was an animal lover and had two of the cutest Pomeranians herself. I had just come back from my horrific stay in Vancouver General, during which Darren was looking after Chi. He had tried to use that connection to hit on her to satisfy his older-woman mother-type-figure fetish, which as usual got him nowhere.

I was in a foul mood having to re-enter hell after being in the almost-normal setting of a hospital. Yes, even being in hospital was better than the homeless winter months of rain, so street people often pretend to have a mental illness to get indoors. How people can be so deceptive, I will never know.

Martha and I started to spark up a friendship because she too stuck out like a sore thumb in the shelter, as she too had obviously come from a place of wealth. She had worked in California tending to all of the original Lassies, which Cheyenne is the spitting image of. Those films and shows were in fact the main reason I got a sable-coloured Scottish Rough Collie myself, I guess to fulfill a childhood fantasy. Only problem was, Martha's group of friends included this total bitch Karen, who obviously hated me as much as I did her, and this loser Lenny, who spent every waking minute playing online fantasy games on his laptop, with Karen as his lapdog apprentice trying everything to get into his pants.

We just tried to be polite around the others as our very real friendship blossomed. She would feed me information not only about her life and her knowledge of animals, but more importantly, about each resident, daily events and, generally, the whole homeless scene. We were a modern-day Bonnie and Clyde, if you like.

THE HOOD

Having a partner in crime was invaluable and cemented our position of strength. Between Martha and Darren, I had a couple of genuine honest friends who had my back and vice versa. Sticks had also become friends with Martha and used her as a sounding board like myself. He had revealed some of his past with her. It is almost wrong to condense it to a few sentences, as like many people in there, this guy's life story could have a blockbuster Hollywood movie made about it. But that is the reason he drank so much, as like a great many addicts, it's a mind-numbing exercise. Sometimes if you're really lucky, a 40-ounce bottle of Bacardi will help you forget the past.

Like Darren, Sticks had an abusive upbringing, followed by various police incidents over drug deals. After firing a shotgun at the cops, he spent most of his youth behind bars. Since then, he had been living on the streets—for well over two decades. How, I will never ever comprehend. Like the out-of-area backcountry where we used to carve up in Whistler, there is no ski patrol on the streets, no umpires, refs or judges, to save your sorry ass if you got into the losing side of a vicious street brawl.

I had already got that plot, as years early, me and my gentle giant mate Drew got what I now know is called baiting, whereby walking home one night, these two guys started staring us down while walking past us on the sidewalk. Before I knew WTF was going on, the one closest to Drew threw a shoulder charge, to which he obviously took offense. Before I could react, the guy's friend, who I had already put flat on his back, whistled and eight more of his posse came around the corner. Despite my martial arts and street-fighting background, and as much as I liked to think I was as hard as my icon Bruce Lee, even I knew this was a lost cause. I did what I do best: survived in my embryonic position while they kicked the living shit out of me before throwing me through a hairdresser's salon window. I now know just how thick those mothers are.

Back to the Yukon, where things were going from bad to worse: I was now back on the hydromorphone, a lot of my friends had left or were about to leave, and Sharon was no longer speaking to me. I later found out that it was because when I stupidly ran out of painkillers, I poached one off my mate from my first stay here, Chris. He then, I hope innocently, told Sharon. She believed, like a lot of people, that I was back chasing my dragon (relapsing). I simply wasn't. I was keeping a close eye on my usage. I have always said: If I screw up once, it's a lesson learnt, but if I do the same thing again, I only have myself to blame. And with drug addiction being the main cause of my fall from grace and almost death, however tempting it was, there was no way I was ever going to make that mistake ever again.

I also knew that without Sharon's help, I was already past my sell-by date in the Yukon, and I was at the top of their hit list to be sent back on the streets, a place I simply could never ever go back to. It was situation critical, and I desperately needed an evacuation plan ASAP. Maybe someone was trying to tell me, indirectly, that Canada and I just didn't mix well, and a return to my homeland with whatever support network I still had there was my best option. I was going nowhere fast where I was, because of that homeless inertia trap that seemingly no one ever made it out of.

I must also give a shout-out to another true friend in there, a former Canadian bodybuilding champion named Reid, who was a nice down-to-earth guy when he wasn't tripping on his drug of choice. He was obviously dealing with a bad addiction, which I later found out was crack cocaine. When he was with it, we would go over to Starbucks and shoot the shit, and unlike most of the made-up stories people would lie through their teeth about in there, he showed me photographs of himself in his prime with Arnold Schwarzenegger and other bodybuilding legends. He was as cut and buff as any of them. Before he shared these pictures, it was hard to believe he was once this brick shithouse, because he was now this poor hunched-over wreck of a man.

Just a heads-up to all those testosterone-fed gym rats, as he admitted himself: it is very easy to over-train your favourite show muscles—the ones we can see in the mirror. When you get older and stop training, you end up like the Hunchback of Notre Dame. Much respect to Reid, as he helped me train in my room with nothing except my own body weight and gravity.

Unfortunately, after Reid was sent back to the streets (although he tried to get back into the Yukon almost every other day), his obviously worsening drug addiction and resultant physical but especially mental health was impossible to ignore. He was found not long afterwards face down dead in the hood after taking too much of a bad batch of cocaine. RIP my good friend Reid. Even to this day, every time I hear that name, I look up to the heavens and remember my true friend. Maybe now you can understand why, as much as I try everything to move on, when you combine all the tragedy, crisis and trauma stuck in my head, my complex PTSD simply won't let me let go.

My friend Darren was soon evicted and then Sticks right afterwards. Martha moved out on January 2. I was getting more than my fair share of reviews, all starting with the more than obvious innuendo that I'd had more than my fair share of time (over three months) and the powers that be had me in their sights for expulsion. After speaking at length with my folks—well, my mum, really—I started to formulate an elaborate plan that involved leaving Canada for good and starting a new life back in my homeland. There were only three downsides:

1. What on earth was I going to do with my soulmate, Cheyenne?
2. Was I strong enough to leave my kids in a place that was halfway around the world?
3. Was I willing to give up Whistler, Vancouver and Canada, all places I had grown to truly love and where I had spent over half of my adult life?

You know—those questions that you have no answer to until you actually make them a reality.

With much help from Martha's veterinarian experience, we figured out the Cheyenne problem. It was quite complicated, but because I'd gotten all her injections up to date in Whistler, she now met the really tough criteria to be transported back to the UK. The other two from the list above, who knows—but sometimes, you just have to follow your gut. Whatever happened, I knew I would not be going back to a life on the streets there. That was better than the nothing I perceived I had in a Vancouver homeless shelter.

To be totally honest, even if I didn't make my plan stick, it gave me some breathing room in the Yukon, as for once they could believe that I had an "out" and wasn't just sitting there for free with my thumb up my ass. I also informed Sharon, who I knew would be amped, as I remember her saying way back when, "Why the fuck don't you just run for your life? It just ain't happening, for whatever reason, and despite your valiant attempts, here in Canada." The more I thought about it, apart from leaving my kids, the more it made so much sense. My inner perfectionist and control freak started beating me up for not thinking of this sooner myself before I even ended back up in hell all over again. This was a side of me I wished I could lose, as it just added constant stress and pressure. At times like this, it was really the last thing I met watching the daredevil kids throw down at the bottom of the Whistler bike park. I would watch green with envy, as I used to do all that stuff, although maybe not to the level of these riders, especially in airborne stunts (both on the dirt and snow). That was an area in which God only blessed me with what I like to call Friday skills: do any of us work that hard on the last day before the weekend? No. We go into cruise control. Well, maybe God is the same when he is creating us.

Of course, even if I did have the skills, not only could I not even afford a day-lift pass but my witch of an ex had sold both my pimped-out Santa Cruz Nomad free-ride bike, which I used to race on for the easier, more pedalling race courses, and my downhill steed, my Giant Glory, for the super-sketchy, burly, gnarly courses. I actually saw a teenage kid riding around with my Glory. All I could do was shake my head in an attempt to shake off the pain of losing so much, all because I had unintentionally fallen into the scourge that is drug addiction because of my Crohn's disease.

I had a new friend Roger that I had reconnected when I first moved back to Vancouver, and we hung out every so often. So after I bumped into him on one of my daily walks on Robson Street looking at all the stuff I couldn't afford, we went for a coffee. Because it was cheap Tuesday, I told him I was going to see a flick at the Tinseltown movie theatre, and he was welcome to join me if he had nothing else to do. Well, to my absolute amazement, when we got to the cashier booth, he turned around and expected me to pay for him. Come again? I could hardly afford to pay for myself and had never offered to pony up for him.

After a huge argument, as I was so sick of these leeches expecting me to help them when I was in a worse position than they were financially, I walked out of the mall. He followed me, calling me out for everything. I can tell you, after four months in the shelter, I was right on the edge of losing it on anyone. A few weeks earlier, I'd kicked this guy's Audi RS4 for pulling out in front of me coming out of this underground car park lot, and when he got out of his car, I begged him to hit me with his best shot. He backed down, as he could see how much pent-up anger I had. I literally wasn't scared of anyone or anything, even of dying, which made me even more dangerous.

A few weeks earlier, this guy Mike in the Yukon, who liked to think of himself as a UFC street fighter, asked me to arm wrestle with him when *UFC Unleashed* was on the TV. I said, "Let's do peanuts instead." When I picked him up, he decided to punch me in my gut—which I hardly felt, as my core is the area I train the most for, not only for that reason but because I believe that a strong core gives you so much balance. It helps in every sport, more than any other muscle group.

Two things immediately popped into my brain: all my stupid fights and my martial arts training. How was I going to tell Mike and anyone else in the shelter that I was the wrong person to fuck with? Thankfully, at the very last minute, instead of grabbing his head and nailing it with my knee, I chose the lesser of two evils and redirected the blow to his balls. That swiftly ended the confrontation. My favourite Kiesha was behind the desk that night and saw the whole thing, so instead of pulling me aside, she called Mike into the office, as he was indeed the instigator.

Back to outside the movie theatre. Roger decided to hit me with a more-than-pathetic right, was so much on the brink by that stage that I blocked his punch with my elbow, which supposedly broke his hand, and threw a couple of straight left jabs. As much as I tried to control it, because of my dire living and financial situation, my bad temper was back with a vengeance, as I would normally never hit someone that easily.

While walking the 30 minutes back to the Yukon, I tried everything to calm down and access my logical brain rather than the emotional side that was running riot inside my being. I just knew deep down I had fucked up majorly, and this stupid fight would come back around—which it did. It didn't take long for the boys in blue to arrive and take me around to the police HQ, which somewhat ironically was a stone's throw from the homeless shelter. I knew I needed to stay calm and humble and not react to their in-your-face, get-under-his-skin tactics. Thankfully, it worked. After about an hour of questioning, they got the picture and even shared the fact that this was not something new for Roger, as he had done this kind of thing many times before.

They eventually released me with a warning and a pending assault charge that would require going to court. I couldn't believe it; if they sided with him and I got convicted, it would ruin my escape-to-Scotland plans, as I would have to remain in Canada to pay my penance. *Fuck, Andrew, when are you going to learn? You're too old for this shit.* The voices beat me up in my head all night long.

As if I needed more crap to deal with, all of a sudden my darling Cheyenne started acting really weird. It wasn't long before I figured out what was up with her. After what we had already endured together, you won't get a closer, tighter and better bond between animal and human anywhere. I can't say for sure, but just like the first time we were in the Yukon, as soon as my health started to take a nosedive, as if by magic, so did Cheyenne's.

It all started with some blood in her urine. Like last time, I guessed she had somehow contracted a urinary tract infection because of all the human food leftovers people treated her with. As if that wasn't bad enough, she also had real bad garbage gut, but I also started to notice this growing mass by her hind hips. I can't tell you how worried I was. You could take away everything I am as a man, literally take everything from me (which is pretty much what happened), but I would never let anyone take the best friend I've ever had away from me. I would die for that dog, and I know she would die for me. She was really much more than a dog to me. It's crazy, but every time there was any physical confrontation, she would position herself between me and the trouble. She was the one loyal friend who stuck by me through the best and, most crucially, worst that life threw at me.

With Martha's pet expertise, it was obvious to ask her for a diagnosis. She confirmed my worst fear, namely cancer. She also said there was a very good chance that it was a non-malignant fat growth—a lymphoma, I think is the vet terminology. With the last of my savings, I followed Martha's advice and took her to the SPCA to run the necessary tests to uncover the cause. I cried harder than I think I ever had over that Christmas as I faced my worst demon of all: being left in this struggle all by myself. After waiting what seemed like an eternity, the best Christmas present ever came down the pipes with benign results on the tests. Phew!

Even with such amazing news, it was difficult to stay positive over that special family time alone with my dog in a homeless shelter. I couldn't even afford to buy anyone any presents. It was literally impossible to put any kind of positive spin on things. This was highlighted perfectly when

THE HOOD

I awoke on Christmas morning and, instead of being treated to priceless family excitement, I stepped in the shit that was all over the washroom right outside of our bedroom door. No words can express my pure disbelief. I hope I never have to endure such a disgusting experience again.

As much as I battled with myself to look to the future rather than grieve over my past, how could you not compare your circumstances, having previously had all the trimmings and precious family interaction that is at the heart of the Christmas message? I couldn't remember a worse, more gut-wrenching and lowest-of-all low time, which in my world, leads me to isolation, depression and the temptations of suicide. I had already tried everything in my power to escape the scourge of homelessness, and years later, I was right back in the same gutter.

But I was not going to give in to hiding and crying in my room. Instead, I got dressed and wandered down for snack time at 9 p.m. To my amazement, the staff had come up with this exceptional buffet of snacks, and we spent a lovely time together. Apart from a drunk asshole trying everything to feed Cheyenne, we made the best out of an awful Christmas. Then, after a few swigs of Sticks's smuggled 40-ounce bottle of Bacardi, I went around to the local Starbucks with Martha and Sticks. We literally pissed ourselves as I showed Sticks the Victoria Secret fashion show, with him salivating all over the floor.

However hard Christmas was in that joint, I was determined to spend New Year's in more Scottish style. In an attempt to have some spending money both now and when I stepped off the plane in sunny Tenerife, I decided to sell one of my two remaining bikes on my somewhat dodgy namesake website Andrewslist. As I thought, I got shady enquiries from all over the world, but after my previous very costly experience, I wasn't going to make another Internet mistake. Instead, I turned the tables to my advantage by accepting one of these sketchy offers and putting the cheque in the bank, even though I was sure it was bogus. I was all of a sudden minted, and anyone who says money can't buy you happiness is only partly right. Believe me, having no money for as long as I did can make one very unhappy.

For a short time, I could handle the homeless life a smidgen better. When Hogmany (Scottish for New Year's Eve) came along, I could afford a few beers, so I went out and did what I hadn't been able to do in seemingly forever: bought myself a dozen Coors Banquets and opened a few with my remaining acquaintances in the Yukon, including Darren. The staff turned a blind eye on letting him into the TV room and my alcohol consumption just this once.

After half a dozen beers and a few shots of Sticks's Bacardi, I said, "Fuck it. I can't spend yet another special night in a fucking shelter." I put the remaining beers into my backpack and headed downtown with Darren on the hunt for some cunt. Like that was going to happen, living in a shelter with a guy who, somewhat incredibly, was even shyer than I was with the opposite sex. After some much needed chronic, we decided to check out the main thoroughfares of Granville, Robson and Georgia Street. After talking to a few hotties, we hit the golden arches of Mickey D's and headed back to the shelter around 4 a.m.

Just as we were halfway down Robson Street, I somehow got to speaking to a couple of real hot, tight and ripe chicks who were totally hammered. I used every trick in my somewhat rusty arsenal of chat-up strategies from the bygone years, which to my amazement, actually worked half decent. God, it was so close, I could taste it. I didn't need any more head games. I just wanted what I believe all males want from time to time: one night of NSA sex with anything that had a pulse, tits and no dick.

Well, it was another case of desperately close but no pot of gold. Thanks to a combination of the fact that I had been MIA from the dating scene for years and my wingman offering next to no support (he just clammed up, leaving me to make all the moves), they disappeared into their downtown hotel, Fuck, so close but so far. That pretty much summed up my new life perfectly.

Before I really knew what was going on, it was New Year's Day, and I was helping Martha move while completely hungover. We had to go down to Vancouver Eastside, which still gives me the willies because of all the messed-up people. I could never figure out if I was like those weirdos when I was messed up on my prescription version of their street drugs. With much haste, we got what we needed there, and by around 4 p.m., I was back in the Yukon, recovering from a brutal hangover and real low, as that was the last of my friends gone from the shelter.

I guess it was similar to a bike race, where having your teammates around you gives you moral support and ultimately helps you get through all the intense ups and downs the road has to offer. I would end up doing what I always did: work harder and smarter than any of my rivals to stay ahead, and if all else fails, try to be content with my all-out effort, even if it falls short of winning. As long as I did everything in my power to win, even if I came in last—which only happened once, when I decided to hang back in a particularly challenging mountain-bike race to coach my daughter Michelle through. I knew it was exactly that course that could break her iron will, and although it ruined my chance of a decent finish, it was well worth it.

Actually, now that I think about it, I stupidly entered a fucking chess tournament back in my school days in a bet with my mates that I could get on the school team. Guess what, genius: I actually somehow got on the team. Then, in our first game, we went to Dundee High School and I managed to lose all of my five matches. I guess chess was not for me!

I had finally managed to shed my lifelong chains of being down on myself (ignoring my perfectionist crap) and was content with just finishing. Nothing encapsulates that new thought process better than Miley Cyrus's "The Climb," which actually came out during my second stay in the Yukon. The line "Sometimes I am going to lose" goes against the ultimate competitor I have always been, but in my last stint in the shelter, I realized I had nothing to prove to anyone but myself.

Everything was finally starting to take shape, and my escape was piecing itself together almost like a Rubik's cube. I had finally booked a flight out of hell and was counting the days to my departure. One of those planes that I used to watch so intently in the psych ward was actually coming for me this time.

Because I had been knocked out so many times by sucker punches I never saw coming, I left everything to the last minute. I couldn't truly believe it was going to happen, especially with my upcoming court date and another trip to the cop shop for fingerprinting sitting in my subconscious. I just knew that with my luck, the more desperately I dreamed that something positive was going to happen in my life, the more likely it would be taken away from me at the last minute, usually for the stupidest reason ever. I wasn't going to let myself get too high.

The only difference between then and now was that this time, it really had to happen, or I was fucked big-time. As Sharon said, it was truly unbelievable that I was going to leave such a godforsaken homeless shelter to travel to a wonderful summer island paradise. Even though Sharon had been a social worker for many years, even she had never seen a situation like this coming to fruition.

Thank God, after appearing at the courthouse shaking like a leaf, as everything was riding on the outcome, after about an hour of talking to this lawyer, the verdict came down that there was insufficient evidence. In reality, Roger's long history of pulling this shit on other people and my tactic of letting him hit me first had paid off, thank the Lord! Although it might sound like a huge relief and now all my dreams could actually come true, it really wasn't. I think I actually cried more over those few weeks than I ever had in the past, as it meant all those years in Canada had amounted to nothing. Like it or not, I was running like a dying dog with my tail between my legs away from everything that had truly turned this boy into a man. In the simplest form, I had failed.

Easily the hardest point was going to say goodbye to my dog and my kids when they came down to pick up Cheyenne around a week before my flight. Time to take a break; I can no longer see my keyboard, as the tears wreak havoc on my sight.

Have you ever been in a situation where no matter how hard you try, with everything you have as a person, not to cry—as I had done so many times over the preceding weeks—you lose all control over yourself and they come down regardless of your best efforts to hold them in. This was one of those times. I couldn't hold them in, as this was such a monumental and pivotal point in my life, just as moving to Canada under happier circumstances had been nearly two decades earlier. Because I had been dreading the day so much, I could not sleep no matter how many sleeping pills I popped the night before. By 3 a.m., I gave up and took my best friend Cheyenne out for a walk in the new blanket of snow. We went to the park we frequented and took a whole bunch of photos that I prayed would help me not to miss her so much.

We had been so close for so long, through all the glory years of Whistler to homeless shelters, then back to Whistler, and now right back where we were a few years earlier. Combine that with the stunning views of False Creek over the water to downtown Vancouver and over to my beloved Yaletown apartment. Sometimes moments are just so precious that you need no music or anything else to make them stand out in your head as grandiose as others, like learning to ride a bike; the day my other best canine friend, my precious golden retriever Vharie, was put down; my first girlfriend/making it to home base; graduating from university; meeting Carol and getting married; my daughters being born; leaving Scotland; making my first million; leaving my family behind; MJ's death; even getting evicted. No exaggeration or hype: this was the real deal that left me on my knees so heartbroken that there simply aren't words. My real tears would tell you all you needed to know how much this really bit hard.

I will never forget the feeling deep in my soul as Carol's Toyota Matrix rolled away with my kids and my dog, leaving me to sob like a baby for the whole world to see. I had taken all that one life can give, and I couldn't take much more. And despite my best efforts to cover it up and tell myself it was for the best, there was this massive hole in my heart that nothing anyone could do to close it.

To my amazement and embarrassment, my kids had even bought me a Christmas present, which drove another stake through my heart as I couldn't afford to get them anything. I felt like a total deadbeat Dad.

After a very long walk to get myself together—as no way in hell could I let anyone in the Yukon see my emotional breakdown—I slid off to my room for the rest of the evening. Without Cheyenne and my good mates, I was extremely fragile, but all I knew was I needed to focus on nothing except my plan to get the fuck out of homeless hopeless land and, once and for all, commence my long-awaited return to the normal life I had dreamed of for so damn long.

The final morning, I got up early to catch the early breakfast that was really only for those with jobs in the Yukon. To my amazement, my most-hated staff member there, a guy called Chuck. I liked to rhyme his name with another obvious word. He was probably hoping he'd never have to lay eyes on me ever again.

Sharon helped me like only she could, trying to get my shit together with what I was taking from my mini-storage and other odds and ends that needed tying up. Then it was off for my last Wendy's Baconator and back to the Yukon to tidy up my room. After a very tearful farewell with Sharon, my mate Chris and this Scottish mate of his Mark helped me with all my swag to the airport, where only a few short years earlier, I had tried to escape myself with nothing but a rampant mental disease.

As we left the SkyTrain station, Chris pulled out a couple of blunts, and we smoked them. It was just what I needed, as I was a nervous wreck by this point, and only chronic could calm me down. It worked like a charm.

Then it was time for final farewells before going through customs and onward to my nine-hour flight to Heathrow and its connecting flight from Gatwick to paradise found: my folks' apartments in Tenerife. All in all, it would be pretty much 24 hours of travelling. That, along with lack of funds, was the main reason I'd had only three holidays down there—another huge regret.

I realized just how fortunate I was, as unlike so many—no, most—of my friends and foes, I was the very last survivor left in the Yukon. Instead of winning my million or possibly a way bigger prize than any money or materialistic possession, I was in actuality one of the very few who could claim they had finally escaped the mire that is homelessness, mental illness and drug addiction. Was this a case of it not being the destination but rather than journey that mattered? Maybe. All I could think about was the destination and a return to a new life I had prayed about for so many years and almost tasted before it was inexcusably wrenched from my grasp on countless occasions.

I was now being given another second chance at life, and just like the title of Lance's book that I read at the start of my vicious decline to depravity, *Every Second Counts*. I was going to try to cherish this new opportunity with all my heart, as it surely had to be better than the precipice I was precariously balancing on. I was going back to the place I had come from and back to my clan. To somehow appropriately glorify my exit strategy, I watched the crazy good flick *Braveheart* on my laptop before boarding the flight.

CHAPTER 18

HOME

As is usual with my life, nothing is ever easy. After a nine-hour overnight flight with next to no sleep, as I had to be beside the bulkhead, where all the young families sit with their babies. And what do babies do? Cry—no, scream. I have to confess, as much as I genuinely love kids and am just a big kid myself, babies aren't my thing. I know I'm not the only guy out there who feels this way.

Thankfully, I had recently acquired a pair of banging Dr. Dre Beats Studio headphones from the revenue from my bike sale. They had a noise-cancelling feature but were not nearly as good as my previous Bose Quiet Comfort 15 phones. The Dr. Dre's had a much bolder bass response, and that was a total savior when it came to the seemingly non-stop crying.

It was quite the pimped-out British Airways plane, with this cool feature where you could pick your own movie. I'd never seen that before. I simply cranked up the volume on my kicking phones and watched movies all night long while fantasizing about if I was ever going to join the mile-high club—and no, I'm not talking about going to the stadium for my favourite football team, the Denver Broncos.

After a long sleepless night, I eventually made it to London Heathrow— but of course, I was departing from Gatwick. I was carrying my gigantic Dakine bike bag with my road bike and the majority of my clothes in it to give the bike some padding, as road bikes are not very strong when the forces are anything but vertical from the tires up to the seat and handlebars.

Why I really needed to take it is, quite frankly, beyond me. I needed rest and quiet solitude more than I needed grunting up the monstrous beast of a climb that is Tide, Tenerife's dormant volcano. But I had failed to climb it the last time I was there, mainly because of the weather. This highlights perfectly the highly competitive, adrenalin junkie and total perfectionist I am and have been all my life.

Dragging my roller bag and my backpack, I eventually figured out how the hell I was getting to Gatwick: via bus. I hunted down a Starbucks to get my usual java fix and then headed for the bus collection point. After I'd waited about 30 minutes, the bus arrived, and I with the help of the bus driver loaded all my gear on.

While we were loading on the bags, the driver turned to me and asked me if I was a boxer because of my screwed-up nose from all breaks due to my way too numerous fights from my younger years. Then he asked if I was Barry McGuigan, an Irish boxing legend who was one of my heroes growing up, as he always gave his all in every fight, and like me, despite his diminutive figure, kicked the ass of much bigger opponents. He proved my brain-over-brawn and "the bigger they come, the harder they fall" beliefs true.

The driver said, "No matter, just looking at you, I can tell you can put a beating on me." I was blown away, as I was nowhere near my natural weight of around 180 pounds. I always dropped a silly amount of weight at the Yukon, for obvious reasons.

Around an hour and a quick much-needed catnap later, we arrived at Gatwick. I had an overnight before catching my connecting flight at 7 a.m. the next morning. Although I was running low on actual cash, I bought myself some good old pub grub and tried to find a comfortable seat. These days, all the long seats have dividers in them so there is nowhere you can stretch out to sleep. Crazy, if you ask me. I finally found a quiet corner of the concourse and tried to close my eyes. But with my heightened complex PTSD, hyper-vigilance starts to take over in these situations, which means your brain somehow tricks you into believing everyone around you is a potential threat, so your body goes into the anxious fight, flight or freeze mode, rendering my sleeping pills practically useless. Adding to this was the fact that the security guards would wake me up seemingly just after I fell asleep to ask me what was in my bike bag.

THE HOOD

When I awoke to my alarm clock sounding, I prayed something along the lines of, "Thank you, dear God. I'm almost there to commencing a new life away from all the terrible demons and triggers that was British Columbia. Nothing can stop me now." Or so I thought.

Doing my usual routine of cutting it a bit finer than I wanted to, I found the check-in booths for my flight. I was met by a supervisor who stated that my bike bag was well overweight, and it was against UK law for them to board it as it was. All I could think of was, *Why the fuck do these things always happen to me?* Full-scale panic was the order of the day.

They pointed me to this other kiosk, and with time really running out for me to catch the flight, I was stuck with the predicament of what I was going to take to Tenerife, as a great many of my clothes in the bike bag were either bike gear or warm winter clothing for when I returned to the UK, as it was in the height of the Scottish winter. With time running out way too quickly, I repacked and then ran as fast as I could. By the skin of my teeth, I managed to catch the flight.

I don't need to tell you the dirty looks I got from other passengers on the plane, but I stayed quiet, which I have found, through way too much practice, is the best approach when I start to feel the whole world is against me. Thankfully, their disdain soon vanished, replaced by the typical and somewhat hilarious British binge-drinking epidemic with a "let's go on a bender starting now and keep it going for the entire length of the holidays" attitude.

Not long after takeoff, and after the in-flight safety blur, it was time for the stewardesses to come around with their trolleys. I decided to join in the good old British spirit and get a cup of tea, which I thought would be free. Hell no; this was one of the bargain-basement charters where you had to pay through the nose for anything you order, and my cup of tea was 3 pound something. *Dear God*, I thought, *did you go to Ceylon to collect the leaves?* But I was too tired to fight from my next-to-no sleep for back-to-back nights. I know that when I am totally drained, my somewhat dark, aggressive, bad-tempered, feisty and fiery side comes out firing. Instead I just tried not to look shocked as I searched my pockets for the cash.

Well, guess what: I didn't have enough money in any denomination to pay for my overpriced caffeine fix. So I had to grovel, something I absolutely hate doing, as it goes against my fiercely guarded, private, independent nature. This pleasant old couple who I had started some talk with about their forthcoming cruise chipped in the remaining pound so I could afford my wee cuppa tea, much to my embarrassment.

All I could think of was the disaster that had occurred in the baggage area and concern for my C$2,000-plus road bike, which I'd had to entrust (not easy for me) to a total stranger. Did I even have a pair of shorts and all the necessary items for a sunny vacation in my other wheelie bag? My logical side kicked in and told me to stop worrying about what was now in the past. I couldn't do diddly-squat about it now. *Enjoy your overpriced cup of tea and try to close your eyes, Andrew, as you are more than beat.*

Despite my usual inability to catnap, I actually managed to get an hour or so of sleep to recharge my batteries, and after some other polite words of gratitude to my saviors for my tea, before I knew it, we were coming down to land in Tenerife's South Airport. Looking out my window at the spectacular landscape, radiant sunshine, endless golden beaches, and fabulous clarity of the water, honestly, I could have been on NASA's Space Shuttle Endeavour heading for the moon, it was so far removed from the rainy, cold, godforsaken weather that Vancouver shared with my homeland this time of year. I had to pinch myself to actually believe that this wasn't just another dream that I was soon going to wake up from back in the Yukon.

No, this time it was a reality. It was so overwhelming emotionally, I had to do what I always do when life gets too much: I headed to a safe place (in this case, the plane's washroom) to cry a mixture of sad and happy tears. I guess to most people, this makes me a pussy, but please bear in mind I couldn't even remember the last time I went on holiday anywhere because of my extensive memory loss over the last drug-filled decade. I was pretty sure the last holiday I had been on was also to Tenerife in my million-dollar-man days, when I was travelling with my loving family to see my original blood family in much happier times.

I cleaned myself up and put my brave-face mask on. I was nearly on my knees with nothing left inside the tank, but I was proud that I had come this far and was at the start of a whole new life. Maybe now I could finally close the book on my past life. From here on in, I would look forward and not backwards into my rough past.

THE HOOD

Hallelujah, I never woke up in the Yukon. This time, the dream was for real. We departed the plane and went into the terminal building, where I gave my old man a big hug after another anxious moment when I couldn't initially find him in the airport. We jumped in a cab and drove the short way to their lovely resort village in beautiful Playa del Carmen, where we were met by my mum, who looked genuinely pleased to see I had made it in one piece. With her motherly intuition, she immediately saw just how shagged I was on every level.

She quickly showed me to my studio apartment, which was palatial compared to where I had just come from. All I wanted to do was sleep, but they invited me to their local haunt for lunch, and I accepted, because by now I was also starving. It felt like forever since I'd seen them last. They were living in the sun almost year-round now, and the lines on her face were somewhat magnified from the last time I saw her. But without being too biased, I'd say she'd aged with grace, elegance and beauty, which combined with her young-at-heart attitude overcame any fears I may have had that she was getting very old very quickly. My dad, on the other hand, seemed to have succumbed more to age. His worse-than-pathetic hearing was starting to wreak havoc on what I remembered as an old-school man's man with the typical logic-driven engineer's brain that draws out a flow diagram to solve any problem.

As much as I wanted to talk, I needed to sleep at all costs, so I politely excused myself from the table and headed back to my room for some much-needed shut-eye. Waking up from my afternoon nap in paradise was such a bizarre experience. I had dreamed this moment so many times before, only to have it stolen away from me when I woke up in the streets, psych ward or homeless shelter. After an initial double take, I finally started to believe I had actually escaped my life in the gutter. This was like a rebirth that I was going to take full advantage of.

My folks had finally come through and extended an olive branch to pull me out of my pit, and it would be just plain wrong not to run with it. I have been a lot of places and seen a lot of stuff for one lifetime, but I had never been in such contrasting environments. I think it must the closest anyone living has been to flying like a bat out of hell and arriving at the pearly gates. *Could it be any better?* I wondered.

We had a pleasant dinner out at the local pub, despite my being so rundown I think I could have slept for a week. I don't know whether it was my complex PTSD, the fact that I had an afternoon catnap or just pure jetlag, but I found myself staring at the ceiling that night in a vain attempt to sleep. I eventually gave up and, much like I had started to do in the Yukon, got dressed and went for a reconnaissance in the wee hours of the morning to the adjacent younger, more happening resort settlement, which is somewhat notoriously infamous in UK culture, called Playa de las Americas. They even did a reality TV program from here and another party town, Ibiza, which followed groups of girls to see how much drinking, troublemaking and sex they could fit into one vacation.

It was now 4:30 a.m., and there were still clubs open. One that I almost went into was called, somewhat appropriately, Tramps. Instead, I grabbed a favourite snack during drunken nights out—an overpriced but delicious kebab—and started to suss the place out. As I began to get my bearings and figure out how to get home, this lady of the night, as my old dear likes to call them, confronted me asking if I wanted a suck-suck, or in English, a blow job. I politely turned her down and headed home.

It took almost a fortnight for me to find myself again. In the meantime, I managed to lose my only passport: my UK one. Fuck, what else could go wrong in my dumb-ass life? The answer was not long in coming. I tried to chase up my bike bag from the FedEx affiliated company back in London, only to find out that I had to pay 250 pounds in excessive baggage fees to get it shipped to the island. I bummed that off my folks, which I hated to do, but the bag had so many of my clothes and, even more importantly, my bike. To this day, summer holidays to hot places are boring to me, as my ADHD won't let me lie in the sun for hours like some, unless I'm dying from a brutal hangover or have my head buried in a good book (I read the entire Harry Potter series in the sun).

Even though I paid that ridiculous sum of money, the bike still was a no-show, and so this very annoying saga continued. The bike was crucial for me to avoid getting bored but also to regain some physical fitness, and because exercise and the endorphins it generates were a lifelong form of therapy for me. I explain it to myself as "exercising my demons," which I obviously have more of than most.

THE HOOD

As if to prove my mum's prediction that I was an accident waiting to happen correct, while watching my beloved rugby coverage of the Six Nations championship, I was so tired I fell asleep in the sun with no shades on and burnt my eyelids beyond scorched. That night, somewhere in my mind, my imagination concocted the weirdest dreams and most frightening nightmares based on true stories loosely based on my life experiences. In the early hours of the morning, I decided to put on some moisturizer to tame the heat and found this Neutrogena sample I had scored from the Yukon. I slathered it onto my eyelids and surrounding flesh.

I eventually got back to sleep with the aid of sleeping pills or chronic, which is still the best sleep aid I have ever used as to this day, I cannot sleep without them. I awoke to a burning sensation. I checked the Neutrogena packaging and actually read the directions, only to find out it was fucking shampoo. *Doh!* For a week, I wandered about the island with swollen eyes that looked like a mixture of being Asian and being on the brink of crying. The latter, to be honest, wasn't too far from the truth.

After various fruitless trips to the local police office regarding my passport, we had to start the long, drawn-out, costly process of applying for another one. In the meantime, I was enjoying the peace of this holiday paradise. But to my amazement, my complex PTSD got no better; it just stayed the same as before. My brain still listened to every single conversation in an attempt to find out if people were talking about me. The sanctuary of my own place was a godsend, as I really was still very frail, fragile and hurting inside. Being in the very same apartment as when we visited during our happier times made the tears flow pretty much every night as soon as I turned off the lights.

As much as I loved my parents' company, they wanted to go out pretty much every night, and they didn't understand that I was still incredibly weak and simply could not. I didn't have the inner strength to oblige. An unspoken reason was because my old dear was cool until she got a drink inside her, then the "real" mum came out and attacked me with all her theories on my roller-coaster life, most of which were so untrue I simply couldn't shut my mouth and nod, as my old man begged me to do. To say we fell out large is not strong enough, but hey, she had always been that way, and I wasn't going to change her now.

There was one night that was particularly hard for me. After a huge fight, she levelled the following accusations at me:

1. I had been sucking up to and basically bought with the Fyfes' (Carol's family) money and not, as was the truth, a self-made millionaire.
2. I got Crohn's disease because of Canada and not my very driven perfectionist type-A control-freak personality.
3. They never came to see me in the psych ward because I slammed the phone down on her and they were somehow scared of me.
4. I was lucky compared to my little brother, who almost died because of a dumb-ass drunken binge and fight that his big mouth got him into, and he had to deal with all the Abigail big-sister shit that I didn't because I was too far removed from it.

Eventually, I just said, "Where were you? This is all just a big smokescreen for not being there for me when I needed you, especially in the psych ward for the hardest fucking months of my life."

At that, she stormed off. I went back to my apartment to hide my tears and went to bed, even though I knew sleep was not an option, regardless of how many sleeping pills I popped.

Eventually, after around three hours, I got a knock on my door. Everything inside me wanted to ignore it, but I knew I couldn't. Yes, it was my mum, and at the sight of her, I couldn't hold back the tears. She hugged me and kept telling me it was okay. It is for this reason that when I hear that all-too-often-said word *okay*, it triggers a PTSD flashback of that horrendous fight.

After a fruitless attempt to leave Tenerife with my dad—who had checked into it and found that all we needed was a police report about my lost passport, but I was still refused entry to the flight to Aberdeen with him, as the local police information was wrong—I had to return to Mum's apartment, where I spent the next few weeks trying to get this temporary emergency passport that was good for one trip back to Aberdeen. In truth, I was actually relieved. I was dreading a return to my old hometown. Would people accept me? Would I fit in? What happened if the rose-coloured specs I was wearing were just another one of life's tricks that can only be revealed if you actually call its bluff?

THE HOOD

After another few weeks of total pleasure, apart from the occasional drunken fight, my relationship with Mum improved. She started to get where I was coming from, both now and then. The best thing about Tenerife was not the easy lays, superb weather and bountiful beautiful beaches. No, for me, it was the delicious and great-value-for-money pub grub and the marvelous music in every bar, with a cover band to draw in the ever-shrinking number of tourists because of the ever-deepening European recession. We saw everything from a cast member of the original *Les Miserables* to covers of Billy Idol, Frank Sinatra, Meat Loaf, Freddy Mercury, Elvis, Pink Floyd and Robbie Williams, all for the price of a couple of beers.

Easily the best night was Saturday. We went to this pub/club with a great Motown cover band, and after a couple of pint-sized Red Bull and vodkas to overcome my lifelong shyness, I danced my ass off for the first time in God only knows how many years. It reinforced my belief that dancing, just like any activity you love, is in itself an amazing therapy that we all need but don't get enough of because of our whirlwind, stress-filled lives and unspoken social rules that anyone over the age of 35 has to be responsible and steadfast (that is, fucking boring). I let my walls come down for once, and although I intentionally never scored, I had a whale of a time with various honeys on the dance floor. It was like a cleanse for my brain and body. Can't these dumb males who believe dancing is a girls' sport just look at nature, where all creatures get dressed up and show off their moves in the air, ground and water? That's the best way I know of getting laid right through to maybe finally finding your lifelong partner.

The only downer was, I only had one pair of board-shorts, my Harbour Dance jogging pants and no fucking bike, as it had somehow gone to Madrid in mainland Spain and then for some stupid reason was sent back to Gatwick. It's funny, but looking back on it, maybe that was God trying to tell me I needed to accept that I was not in the right place to be trying to improve my physical fitness. I needed to focus on my emotional and mental health and attempt to repair and even eradicate all the terrifying voices and memories I had stored in my head.

After a trip up to the UK embassy in the capital, I was ready to leave the island and return to Aberdeen to start a new real life. In truth I already kind of knew what that would be like. Tenerife is almost a British colony now, with so many Brits vacationing there. I had a real good feel for my former tribe. After 18 years, I had become more Canadian than British, something I found hard to accept. If I felt like that in stunning Tenerife, I was pretty sure it would be worse when I returned to the normal work-based environment of Aberdeen.

After a short flight, I was met by my old man. He drove me back on the road I used to drive every day in my very first real job as a market research assistant with Stewart Milne Homes decades earlier. I had also used this road to see Carol in her midwifery training in Stirling, in my first car, my green Ford Cortina. It was one of those times when there are simply so many things going on in my head, all I could do was try my best to ignore them and focus on the distraction that was a sensible conversation with my dad. You know when you almost feel every thought, memory and feeling all at once, and your internal computer can no longer keep up and eventually crashes? All of a sudden, you are faced with the fight, flight or freeze impulse, and with the first two not being realistic options, I had no choice but to freeze and almost go numb as my subconscious raced uncontrollably.

Aberdeen was exactly what I remembered it to be: cold and grey, with predominantly granite buildings; a grey, dark and somewhat threatening sky; and immense amounts of green from the grass that all the cold rain feeds. Then back to the large detached house and up to the spare bedroom which again brought up so many memories of my new family's trip there over a decade earlier, before Crohn's ever existed in my life and during a very happy time with my wife and girls that was now like a stake through my heart. Believe me, I know it might sound melodramatic, but I felt devastated. I knew almost immediately that the grass was indeed greener here but only in the most literal sense.

My clansmen had deemed me a traitor and believed I had no right to come home just because I screwed up my life in a foreign country. To which all I could say, in the back of my mind, was, *I spent the best years of my life here and therefore have as much right to be here as anyone else.* With cruel vibes coming at me from seemingly everywhere and everyone, all I could do was put it down to the complicated mind tricks that are complex PTSD. Despite the huge urge to hide in my folks' house, I made a commitment that no one here was going to turn me into a recluse.

THE HOOD

Every day, without fail, I would pack up my laptop and recommence my Canadian habit of heading to the nearest Starbucks. No matter how much I tried to fit in, I was for some reason different from these people—no better or worse, just different. It was far from the first time in my life I felt like a duck out of water.

Initially, it was just me and my old man at home. That meant it was very quiet, as my dad, between being an only child and his more recent hearing loss, is now the definition of an introvert. To be honest, it was just what the doctor ordered. Tenerife had been way too much too soon for me; I desperately needed to just chill, do nothing and honour the quiet, shy and guarded side of my complicated new personality. It was kind of funny, though. Being a very logical engineer type, my old man had this amazingly strict schedule. Meals were always at the same time every day: breakfast at nine, lunch at one and tea (or dinner in North America) at 6 p.m. on the nose, just like in the shelters.

I was now stuck between a rock and a hard place. Aberdeen will always be my hometown, but it was no longer my home. It's the people who make a place, and just about all my old friends had moved somewhere else, leaving it a very cold, bleak and sad place for me. All I could do was remember the wild and crazy stuff I did when I was in my glory years. Much to the disdain of my parents, like it or not, Canada was my home—especially with my dog and kids there. My parents were the only things I really had left in my old home.

Well, that's not quite true: I also had my bike. My new specialized Tarmac SL2 road bike, which I bought with the dodgy deal of selling my old Roubiaz before leaving the Yukon, was finally back in my possession. Aberdeen was experiencing record high temperatures for February and early March, so I took full advantage and jumped on my bike most afternoons, if I could muster up the inspiration and motivation to regain my stamina. I had to start afresh, as my cardio had completely gone and a combination of alcohol and too many kebabs in Tenerife had given me a tiny beer gut. I was 20 pounds heavier than my ideal racing weight of 160. So yes, I was sucking wind bad, but it gave me something to focus on instead of feeling sorry for myself.

After the first few brutal rides, which always happens when you take the whole winter off from any stamina-based activity, I started finding my legs and lungs again. As a result, I started loving my time on my bike. Sport is like anything else: your brain comes up with every excuse to take the easy way out by simply lazing around, but when you overcome that and really go and do it, you feel a million times better and return to your pad proud you did something constructive with your time. There's also the bonus improvement of both self-esteem and confidence that it somehow awards you.

My mum followed us to Aberdeen a few weeks later. That was just perfect, as my silent time with my dad had put my feet back on the ground. My batteries were sufficiently recharged that I was ready to make human contact again.

I know it sounds somewhat strange, but like most people, I have different sides to my all-new and hopefully improved character. I once asked my good mates from the Yukon, Charles and Martha, which daughter takes after me the most. They astutely pointed out that both girls were carbon copies of me in different ways:

1. Michelle, now 22 years old, is a very athletic, thick-set and stunningly beautiful girl with a fiery, in-your-face attitude. Although she is humble at her very core, she won't take shit off anyone. As such, she relies on her physical attributes and her street smarts to the fullest.

2. Iona, now 16, looks like a female version of me, with a very curious, pure-genius yet incredibly shy and quiet demeanour until she gets to know you. Unlike her sister, she relies on intelligence rather than physical prowess and is blessed with very likable traits. She is feisty, tenacious and mischievous, yet very caring, compassionate, loving and caring. She is emotional and a pure genius of a wee soul.

Both reflect me perfectly depending on the day, mood and circumstance. If I was being really honest, Michelle is more like the old me before the shit hit the fan in my life, and Iona is much closer to the new me. Or, as the celebs like to say, they are my alter egos. But believe me they are both their own person, two beautiful girls that because of me (like my wife) were put through the wringer-guilt & grief are terrible things to deal with.

It's funny that because of my colourful past, I am now obsessed with human psychology. Through my love of some reality TV—especially shows relating to my lifelong passion for music and dance—I have confirmed that all the real people who have been damaged by terrible hardships seem to value traits like empathy, loyalty, graciousness, forgiveness and, most importantly, humility, compared to their more normal peers who are driven by cockiness, judgment, vanity, arrogance and power. It's that nature-versus-nurture thing, I guess.

I will never forget the best program I have ever seen—a superb BBC documentary whose name is now lost on me. They followed a wide spectrum of people from various class backgrounds from childhood through the rebellious teenage years, up to their adult lives. It was simply a magnificent series. Just as Celia Laval noted in her amazing letter, life can make or break you if you let it. So yes, this "leopard can't change its spots" thing is simply crap. I know deep down I have changed beyond what I could have ever believed possible—hopefully, as I truly believe, for the better.

CHAPTER 19

THIS IS IT

After about five weeks, my new UK passport arrived at my new home, and I could make real plans to return to Canada, against my folks' advice. In fairness, I also had a few real good nights out with my folks and reconnected a bit with my younger brother, Stuart, who was very respectful but a little stand-offish. This was his town now, and he didn't need an older brother to cramp his style, especially as we fell out big-time when I left for Canada. He took my folks' position on it, as, in all honestly, he usually did.

It didn't take long to find a flight, and before I could blink, I was saying goodbye to my mum, which was incredibly hard. I thought she finally understood where I was coming from and was really a shoulder to lean and cry on after we got over the initial bullshit fights back in Tenerife. After a final heartfelt goodbye hug from the old man, I was all alone in the waiting area for the Vancouver flight.

I have no idea why, but waiting there for the connecting flight back to London for the Vancouver flight, I had the worst case of complex PTSD flashbacks. It felt more like a full-blown panic attack, probably because I was really anxious about returning to Vancouver after having said my goodbyes. How were people going to accept me? I now knew what it was like to feel you don't belong anywhere—neither your old home, as you were a traitor for leaving, or your new home, as you weren't born there so could never become a naturalized Canadian.

THE HOOD

That's something I can't comprehend, as let's face it, life is short, and with air travel, the world has shrunk beyond belief. Tell me who doesn't want to explore the rest of this truly wonderful world God blessed us all with? It's like the magnificent movie I just watched called *Into the Wild*. If you want to truly understand where I'm coming from, watch that movie, as it nails everything I have a hard time accepting and portraying in my everyday life.

I had already persuaded Martha to let me crash at her new place on my return to Vancouver. She had managed to craft a very comfortable post-shelter life for herself in a rich Vancouver suburb called Kerrisdale, where she grew up. The thing was, her previous Yukon tenants had moved out after clashes of personality, especially Karen. It turned out—and I always had my suspicions that I tried to alert Martha of back in the Yukon—she was a common criminal who wasn't going to change her stripes anytime soon. After sorting out the dog situation with Cheyenne, Martha got back to me with the great news that we could crash with her until something else turned up, as it was practically impossible for me to find anything while still in Scotland.

After another drawn-out trek to London and then across the pond, I arrived totally bagged from a nine-hour transatlantic flight. Despite trying to get to sleep, I met a really cool mum and her middle-aged daughter who I had a real chill chat with. I was already dead anxious about how my return would go down. After arriving, I was immediately diverted to Canadian customs with the dregs of humanity, as I had a brand-new UK passport on a one-way flight into Canada. All the illegal-alien red flags flew. I had never gotten around to the stupid lengthy process of getting a Canadian passport, as you have to get a citizenship card first, and both were stolen from me by my street attackers.

Thank God, after four very scary hours lining up and eventually getting to speak to someone, I assured them I was not like all the other scammers there but a full-fledged Canadian citizen. Jumping back on the same SkyTrain that only 10 weeks ago I had used to escape Canada, I was more determined than ever to make this return stick. Instead of running away from my fears and memories, I was back for one more try to prove all my doubters wrong. I remember slogging all my gear up the Davie Street hill to Martha's office and then going for a coffee until she finished her workday. We jumped in a cab back to her pad, which I'd helped her move into back in January. It was way better than all my recent more-than-humble abodes.

It took me a few months to find my way around my new hood. It almost seems wrong to call it a *hood*, as in reality, it is one of Vancouver's richest suburbs—such a contrast from the downtown Eastside and my shared accommodation in Whistler. For once, I had found a place that didn't hold as many of the terrible triggers for my worsening complex PTSD, and there were plenty of parks for Cheyenne to roam.

To this day, I still feel guilty for putting my family and my adorable collie through all the trials and tribulations for which I could blame no one but myself. No dog deserves what I have put her through. I say again, more than any person or thing, Cheyenne has saved my life. Every time I felt, and still feel, like giving up and giving in to all the lies and promises suicide offers, I look at her lovely smile. How could I do that to her after her astonishing love and loyalty?

Finally, here was a home where both of us could start over. This time, it had to happen. Problem was, I really didn't know whether I was coming or going. I decided to use my time as practically as possible. First thing was to try to gain my persons with disability (PWD) designation. In truth, I should have been granted that over a decade earlier, but as with most government handouts, they make you jump through every fucking hoop. There aren't too many ex-millionaires attempting to get an extra C$300-plus per month, so I think I was kind of setting a precedent, which is always the hardest slog.

Next up was getting my taxes up to date. Unlike before, when I always had my taxes in on time, I hadn't filed them for over four years. Staying alive was more important than any material wealth.

Trying to find a job in Vancouver was, like everywhere in this global recession that had already cost me everything, nearly impossible, despite my at-minimum two hours a day of trying. What I really needed was time to get my head straightened out. Thankfully, my new hood was very quiet and very conservative. Apart from a few Inuit homeless people, the scourge of poverty was next to non-existent here. Instead, there were suburban roads lined with million-dollar mansions and silver-spoon teenagers driving exotic automobiles, with a predominance of European marks like

Ferrari, Lamborghini and Aston among the more run-of-the-mill Mercs, Beemers and Audis. For some strange reason, anything European in North America is cool, classy and stylish. It's just the opposite in Europe—a strange and costly twist of fate us humans seem to have bought into. The grass is always greener.

Less than a decade ago, I was buying fancy toys myself, but I always stopped before wasting that kind of green on a depreciating asset and put a limit of 100 grand on my favourite status symbol. God only knows how many people could be saved from the street with the MSRP of these insane toys. In fairness, or maybe as a lame excuse, my lifelong love of cars was more as a pure art form in itself, but yes, the additional street cred they gave their owners had not completely left me either.

To be honest, it's actually way worse seeing the cars I used to own, which were more than a few, as I changed my rides almost every two years. What a fucking waste. I cried the day the collection company came to take my pimped-out red Audi TT S-edition and my cool red Toyota TRD Tacoma away forever. To this very day, I still haven't had the disposable income for a car for as far back as I can remember—probably over six years. I could handle it okay until my oldest daughter, Michelle, got one. It was a very bitter pill to swallow, along with my pride.

Living without a car makes picking up a chick almost impossible in this town, day and age. Sad but true. It is just like this sad sandwich board I saw the other day proclaiming, "Men are like coffee—the richer the better!" We all strive to be like those celebrities from the silver screen, rock stars of music and superstars of sport. They get paid a ludicrous amount for what entertainment and escapism they provide us worker ants.

After a few months, I started to realize that the reason Martha let me stay was more than just a strong friendship. She wanted to be friends with benefits, which was simply never going to happen. Everyone who knows me is aware that I am probably the fussiest guy ever when it comes to women, as unlike most men, to me, no sex is better than bad sex. Call me shallow if you want, but with my inherent shyness and complete hatred of rejection, I have to be physically attracted to a girl before I am going to attempt to chat her up.

To highlight this, I had been seduced by Britney from the Yukon shelter when she invited me around to her new pad and fed me beer and blunts, then jumped me. As gross as it was, I simply needed it bad, as I had self-inflicted my celibacy for way too long now (close to six years) because of the AA and NA warnings of the inherent dangers of dating during recovery, and yes, more than anything, a man has his needs. Unfortunately, she was both fat and far removed from being a virgin. Between fear of my penis falling off due to the high risk of picking up a STD and the fact that I couldn't even get a boner because of her figure, I never even penetrated her. I just gave her my best oral until she could come no more. Only problem was, I forgot my sleeping pills. After she climaxed for the last time around 6 a.m.—I literally did go all night—I left around 8 a.m. while she was still sleeping.

One great thing about my new hood was that it was just around the corner from the University of British Columbia, one of Vancouver's main universities. There were more than a few hot twenty-and thirtysomethings, and yes, many yummy mummies. If I did require companionship, I had plenty to choose from.

Unfortunately, it wasn't long before I realized my Martha was also a closet alcoholic, something she never was in the shelter. Every time she got drunk—which was pretty much every night after work, as she would buy a half bottle of Ballentine's whisky or Polar Ice vodka depending on her available cash flow—she would hit on me. Fuck, why does everyone have an ulterior motive? Why can't people just help their fellow human out to be nice without wanting or needing something in return?

It all came to a head when I came home from smoking a blunt with my mate Chris at his place to find Martha hammered. She welcomed me into our shared bedroom, where we had two single beds. On her bed, she had laid out a teddy, lube and a vibrator. After a little polite conversation, she started to hit on me. WTF was I supposed to do? Fuck her to keep the roof over my head? It simply wasn't happening.

We had an unreal conversation in which she laid it on the line: I should stop looking at all the young pussy and give more mature women a try. She had, metaphorically speaking, a dog collar around my neck. I was living there for free, and in this day and age, you don't get something for nothing.

I spoke to the landlord agents, who confirmed my darkest fears: she had proclaimed that I was her Gaelic boyfriend. She soon developed new back problems that gave me no choice but to apply Deep Heat for her every night, which in truth made me cringe. It also reinforced the fact that I had to move on. When the bachelor suite across the hall became available, although it was a stretch to afford the monthly rent, I really had no choice but to claim it for myself. I moved in the early fall.

By then, I had managed to secure my PWD payment finally, and also a ski and snowboard coaching job at the local Cypress Mountain. Only problem was the pure logistics of getting the 15 clicks to the ski hill, as I had no car and no driver's license (the previous driving-without-insurance ticket being still on my record), and I had absolutely no snowboard equipment. I had only applied for a ski instructor's position, but all of a sudden, they wanted me to step up and become their snowboard evaluator as well, teaching their instructors how to instruct and ride better. It was similar to the position I had held in Whistler.

They also wanted me to take on this specialist Australian travel company, whereby I taught their riders not only how to ride better but also how to teach so they could ultimately gain their Canadian Association of Snowboard Instructors (CASI) certification. It was very similar to the job I had done with YES tours and as a leader of CASI Level 1 courses back in Whistler.

Looking back, I should have never accepted that role, as although I knew I was a better rider than skier before my major tib/fib crash, I hadn't been on a board for I couldn't even remember how long. I also had no equipment and no money to buy any. It was my stupid pride and "I can do anything, especially if it helps someone out" attitude that put me in this position. There was no way I could give them a glimpse into my past to try to explain my predicament.

I had also scored a small part-time job with the landlord's agent delivering thousands of those flyers most people just throw away. Why isn't there a law outlawing that spam shit that goes into everyone's email inboxes and slow-mail postal boxes? It was a very physical job, but by then, I had built up some cardio from riding mainly my road bike all summer, and I had started my usual gym routine in preparation for a new snow season. After a few days with a sore back because I didn't focus on proper lifting technique, I got it dialed in. The extra work, however hard with its manual labour wreaking havoc on all my injuries (especially my messed-up shoulder and back) and below minimum wage, gave me some cash and a bit of a buffer after my rent and hydro was paid. Even so, I was living off fumes—around C\$200 a month with the cash from my casual delivery job, even with my new PWD C\$927/month, as my rent was C\$850, a situation I couldn't deal with on a long-term basis.

Those few very, very lean months with almost total starvation rations provided the ideal stepping stone. With some very reluctant help and really nasty correspondence from my folks, I just had to survive until my Snow School job kicked in around the middle of November. Martha offered me her SUV to get to work, and Cypress very grudgingly let me use their worse-than-crap rental equipment until I could get my order from my Burton Pro-form in. This really was just a facade, as I knew I couldn't afford it until I started earning serious green from Cypress.

As always, it didn't take very long for life to come back and bite me in the ass. In my first day on snow, I managed to break two ribs from a combination of being rusty and the worse-than-useless rental gear. I bailed hard three turns into my first day on snow since my time in Whistler, Fuck. But like always, I never ever quit. I persevered and did everything I could to ride at a decent level with their shit equipment, because I needed the money, and I had a real good in with a couple of cute Australian girls up there, especially this Suzie chick who unfortunately was in the skiing group. We definitely had a strong crush thing going on. If you're still out there and ever read this, please, sweetheart give me a shout, as I really, really liked you.

On my day off, I decided to head back up there to get a ski day in to improve my two-plank technique and to hit up Suzie, but just like always, when I do anything wrong, I always get caught. This time was no different. On my way home, the inevitable happened: I got pulled over by North Vancouver's finest for driving without insurance and with an expired license. In fairness, the cop was actually really cool. After hearing my humble yet honest plea that I had got out of a homeless shelter and was trying desperately to make something of my life, he let me off with the lowest fines possible. But it put to an end my snow job and possible fling with my Aussie hottie.

After another couple of months of sending my résumé anywhere and everywhere and very real starvation rations, I managed to score a job at the hearing company where Martha worked. In the meantime, Martha was in a bad way financially, so she decided to take in this Latin loser from the homeless shelter. He seemed harmless, but I still knew it was an idiotic idea.

In no time, he had done what all the crooks do: found her Achilles heel, namely her lifelong alcohol addiction, and used it to manipulate her. Very cunningly, he used whatever little green he had to buy her a 40-ounce bottle of Ballantine's whisky, which was like handing a kid the biggest bag of candy. Before I could blink, she was hammered 24/7, had pawned her laptop for the whisky kitty, and eventually got an eviction notice for nonpayment of rent because all her spare cash was going to booze.

Luckily, she found a new residence in Vancouver's prestigious English Bay apartments, but I knew the writing was on the wall there too. The rent was the same as it was in Kerrisdale, which was beyond her disposable income after the C$600-plus booze and cigarette habit was taken off. As with all addicts, these were now her number-one priority.

It was hard for me to watch a friend go down the road I had traveled a few years earlier, albeit with a different addiction: pills rather than booze. The results are just the same. Another totally non-functioning addict was precariously balancing on the precipice of losing everything because of an addiction. It was very sad.

Things came to a crisis point when she started turning up for work drunk and blaming it entirely on her recent change of prescription antidepressants, then taking a long weekend without even a phone call. I knew exactly what was going on. Although it was incredibly hard for me, I waited until she started talking about ending it all to get the professionals involved. I couldn't understand it, but everyone from the office was putting me forward as her knight in shining armour while doing next to nothing themselves.

After a few weeks, I could take it no longer. I contacted Sharon, who reinforced my belief that I was not strong enough to deal with this myself. I might dive in and save the drowning damsel in distress and whilst saving her, sacrifice my own life. That's something I could not allow to happen. I was finally getting my life back to almost normality.

Don't get me wrong: my current job was still very far from my ideal. Being a totally dull, no-challenge data-entry clerk earning just above minimum wage was not my dream job. But hey, as much as I hate the saying, beggars can't be choosers. I hoped this would be a stepping stone to something befitting my obvious management and entrepreneurial skill.

Then Alan, the main audiologist and shareholder in the company, took me aside and threw a sucker punch I never saw coming: I was to be laid off. He tried to justify my firing with the lamest excuse ever, that because of Martha's problems and another integral person taking maternity leave, the data-mining project was no longer needed, as they couldn't handle the extra business my work was providing. Like I was born yesterday, fuckwit! My mother didn't raise no fool! I knew it was because Martha had talked them into to giving me a job, and with the impending financial crunch they were experiencing, without her having my back, I was the first to get the chop. In reflection, Martha both got and lost me the job.

After 40-plus years of working my ass off in whatever job I did and never being fired, I now had back-to-back firings, neither truly my fault. All I could think of was Sharon's warning before I left the Yukon the second time to move to the North Shore shelter: my comeback was not going to be smooth and easy. It was a minefield littered with speed bumps, curveballs and sucker punches. All I could do was keep trying.

After a couple of months trying to pick myself off the ground, dust myself off and make sense of all of the shit—and even a quick 15-day visit from Martha before she headed into a rehab clinic—I had four walls that I couldn't afford the rent on, no job or purpose in life, two harsh and totally incurable diseases in Crohn's and complex PTSD, and the very real threat of ending up back in the streets. I was trying everything in my power not to relapse, as the temptation to numb it all with drugs is powerful when you see no way out.

CHAPTER 20

MAN IN THE MIRROR

Like most songs whose lyrics I used to sing with happy abandon, without a clue what they were about, probably the hardest of all to listen to is the one in the title of this chapter. It's not only so true, it also really hits a nerve: "If you want to make the world a better place, take a look at yourself and make the change." I can't tell you how many times I have sung that song, along with his other amazing ballads.

Whichever way I sliced it and diced it, there was no way I could regain the life I had back when the biggest decision was what car I would buy next or which hill or bike trails I would hit next rather than how the hell am I going to pay my rent or how am I going to eat this month. Talk about a shift in your priorities! Trust me, I do not exaggerate. It often comes down to whether Chi or I is going to eat. My best friend in the world always takes precedence, of course. Only problem is, when I don't eat, my Crohn's/IBS pays me back with very real pain.

Every morning, I wake up and open my eyes. I close them again and open them in the hope that I am simply waking from the worst nightmare ever. But no: same thing every time. Like a sledgehammer smashing into my skull, the reality of my present situation coupled with how I used to live invariably draws tears from my eyes, and I curl up in a ball and try to figure out how I am going to face another day of my new life.

It gets so tiring to put on a brave face every day, hiding all my fears of the past and present and hoping for a future with a fake smile and BS polite conversation with everyone who wants to pet my dog. On the good days, you get up, tell yourself it's all going to be okay and work out for the best, and pray you don't have to talk to anyone, as conversation could open the door to the things you can't tell anyone. You know they will judge you and most likely tag you with the bad/evil stereotype of a drug addict, homeless person and psycho. And they'd have plenty of reason to. Consider these events of my past:

1. used to be a multi-millionaire, but fueled by prescription meds and just like a common gambler, got greedy and rolled the real estate dice one too many times, losing everything and then some
2. was happily married with the ideal life in Whistler and could now be classified as a common criminal and wife-beater
3. was evicted, beaten up badly and lost all ID while sleeping on the streets
4. was a prescription drug addict for well over a decade
5. spent over a year in homeless shelters with some of the worst criminals out there
6. was confined to a psych ward with severe psychosis/schizophrenia for close to the maximum stay of six months

And the present didn't look much better:

1. bankrupt, at last count with negative C$54,000
2. all RRSPs, life insurance, fund portfolio spent when tripping on prescription painkillers
3. creditors calling from 7 a.m. to 10 p.m. every day of the week
4. "between jobs," aka unemployed bum
5. missing the things most people take for granted: a house, kids, fancy car, flat-screen TV, iPhone/iPad
6. suffering from a mental illness called complex post-traumatic stress disorder that brings with it hypervigilance, trust issues, anger issues, anxiety, insomnia, negative voices; jumps even when a car door closes; finds terrible triggers at every turn
7. has another real nasty incurable disease called Crohn's which works together with the complex PTSD, especially the stress component

And as for my future, who knows? I'm just trying to get through each and every day with its challenges the best I can and avoid the spectre of relapse, violence, homelessness, worsening mental health, psych wards and ultimately suicide to make all the voices in my messed-up head finally fucking stop.

Let's face facts: would you want to speak to me if you knew the above about me? As much as your empathetic side might tell you yes, your logical side would override it and tell you to run as fast as you can in the opposite direction. And to be honest, not so long ago, I would have been right there running with you.

You can only truly understand something if you experience it for yourself. On the bad days, you curl up in a ball and cry until you have no tears left. Then you search everywhere to find the motivation to drag your sorry ass out of bed, because really, what's the point? Your life has no purpose. I think the medical term for it is depression, something I never understood before. Even as I write this, the war begins in my head between the angel who tries to convince me to be positive and the devil who tries to do me in. The angel begins by saying something along these lines:

> You have got through the worst of it. Just look how far you have come in four years! On Christmas Day four years ago, you were in a locked psych ward, incapable of remembering your daughter's name! Or more recently, you were all alone in the Yukon homeless shelter dreading every waking second, looking for a coffee shop that was open, and once you found one, crying your eyes out in front of the few customers while emailing your kids in Mexico and folks in Tenerife.

But then the devil fights back:

> Don't believe that bullshit. Here's another Christmas Day and you are still all by yourself, no real family with you, no girlfriend or any real friends, no tree or decorations, no presents, a desperate loser with no job

and next to nothing, who can hardly even afford to buy a coffee or more importantly a real meal tonight.

The devil has a point. Instead of a fancy turkey or chicken platter like the rest of the world, I am sitting down to my two-day-old C$2 McDonald's Junior McChicken and rice meal with my baby Cheyenne. Yes, pretty sad! The devil continues:

> Any minute, you could return to that homeless shelter, and that could put you right back into relapse, and who knows—maybe another trip to the loonie bin. Why are you putting yourself through this? Just go through to bathroom, chuck all those pills down your throat and put paid to this misery you call life. You have already tried everything to make this comeback stick, but you are too tired, low, beat and broken to play the game of life and love anymore.

I know my family will hate me for saying this, but I know that without my adorable canine friend Cheyenne, the devil would have won that war a very long time ago. Lassie really did save Timmy down the well and my world this time.

I still don't really understand fully how the love of an animal can make your life worth living. It's a kind of magic. As I said before, it would be lame and very unfair to leave her in the world alone. I know my ex-wife would probably give her away, as she has no time for Cheyenne, who somehow represents me. Chi was always my dog. In truth, without Cheyenne, I probably would have never survived my time in the homeless shelters, as she was the only normal in a fucked-up world that even after reading this, you still can't begin to imagine.

I thought I was a really tough and strong person before I ended up in there. As an accomplished athlete and businessperson, I had beaten almost every rival, conquered all of life's challenges and overcome every insecurity I had ever faced. I thought I had a good handle on life. What's crazy is not so much being literally crazy in the psych ward, when I didn't even know my own name, but back in my glory years as a real estate tycoon when I thought I really understood this life. Only now do I realize that like so many others, I was clueless.

There is something that is very hard to describe, quantify and rationalize, as you run the risk of misperception when you proclaim that because of your past you somehow have a greater exposure to and therefore understanding of the circle of life than most people. You are probably right now, just as I would have back then, calling bullshit to any such claim, or as my old dear likes to say, "We all have our stories and have been through our own battles." I honestly believe that to be true. But genuinely, there is something I have gained from such a magic to tragic history. It's like going from a black-and-white old tube-style television when you're a teenager to a full-colour flat screen when you're an adult. My trials and tribulations have somehow given life a whole new dimension, like the new 3D sets you can get with an awe-inspiring surround-sound AV system.

Again, I'm not saying this makes me any better or worse than anyone else; rather, it gives me a whole new perspective on life, because apart from going to prison (something I have flirted with because of my never-back-down philosophy) or war and/or killing someone, there aren't many scenarios I haven't been through. Therefore, I think I comprehend, but I cannot say for sure.

If you still don't understand what I am trying to say, watch the following movies:

1. *Patch Adams*
2. *Into the Wild*
3. *Angel Eyes*
4. *American Sniper*
5. *Avatar*
6. *A Beautiful Mind*
7. *The Pursuit of Happiness*

Add to that A&E's *Dogs of War* TV series. Try to not only understand but feel these characters' journey and the underlying warnings and inspiration through pain they contain. If you still don't get it, track down a remarkable documentary which, by an uncanny irony, just came on PBS called *Happy*. It gives credence to and provides empirical evidence for everything I have been trying to explain in this true story and everything it has taught me, which no book, song, lecture or course could ever teach.

What is hardest to explain is that for some reason, I am honestly not jealous of the multi-millionaires in my new hood of Kerrisdale, a rich Vancouver suburb with million-dollar mansions complete with all the mod cons that only money can buy, like top-of-the-range German M/S version cars and dream vacations around the world. Actually, the hardest thing to cope with is not their material wealth but seeing happy families. As much I really do love kids, on my bad days, I have to ignore them. My heart breaks for the lost decade with mine, and even now, I see them for less than four hours every six months.

Praise be, Carol was not taking them to Mexico this Christmas, so I thought I might see them on that special day for the first time since we separated almost seven years ago. But because I got a last-minute cashier and shelf-filling position in the local liquor store, which feels like I am right back doing the first job I ever had way back in my Fine Fare combined with the Wine Lodge teenage years, I still ended up all alone. Damn, here come the tears again. There is something about being all alone on Christmas Day that compounds my already bleak loneliness.

Again, that is why I love music so much. There is always a song that describes my feelings so much better than I can. I think that's why, as much as I used to despise all the hate, anger, swearing, attitude and everything about hip hop and rap music, I now have such a special affinity with it— not because it's way cool but rather because I have been there, done that and truly understand what they are saying in their songs.

In fairness, their journey is different from mine. I went from middle class to stupid riches to pitiful poorness, and most of the musicians and movie stars did it the opposite way around. I never really thought about it until Sharon, whose experience is second to none, pointed out that it is much easier to be born poor and stay there, as you don't know any difference, than my voyage, which had me start as middle class/almost nouveau rich, become a self-made millionaire and reach the richest 1 percent of Canadians in net worth, then lose it all and land in the proverbial gutter. Regardless, I still share their frustrations, as I have seen most sides of this messed up world we now live in and wondered at the following:

THE HOOD

1. No one speaks to anyone anymore, and the word *respect* has been long forgotten, replaced by cutthroat competitiveness and judgmental people hating each other for no real reason apart from sheer jealously and/or misinterpretation.

2. There's an ever-growing divide between the sexes, to the point that we have now embraced being gay as the new normal and being straight means you're an old-school square, instead of embracing our differences as sexes. If we only learnt to compromise and communicate, we could actually make a pretty good team, as very often one sex's weakness is the other's strength and vice versa.

3. Your success is based on material wealth rather than the type of person you are at your core.

4. The divide between the rich and poor and the resultant slow destruction of the middle classes is ever-increasing. How on earth did we get to a place where in the states, for example, 0.1% of the top wealthy people now own 90% of all wealth (and power, because unlike any time I have ever seen on my half century on this planet, money equals power. Just look at how Donald Trump won, no *bought*, his way into the most "powerful' position in the world.) I say again, if the whole pie chart is 1,000 people, and one person owns as much if not more than 900, it's crazy. How did we let this happen? As in the George Orwell classic *Animal Farm*, although the Western "democracy" bags on communism, based on pure facts, maybe capitalism has its own animals (greedy power-hungry humans) growing legs, which represents the massive corruption everywhere, even in Canada, Europe and the worst offender of them all, the USA. It is always our goal to make more (income) and produce more. Why does the GDP always have to be positive? That just means we are going to exhaust all of our God-given blessings like unsustainable raw materials that our newly man-made universe has put in a place that are almost too powerful, as they are like keystones in a bridge. That's what they'll tell you.

5. Massive injustices like homelessness, drug addiction and mental illness aren't seen as the diseases they rightfully are. Most still

believe they are something you choose or a natural weakness, lack of willpower or failure of self-discipline.

6. We let corrupt politicians, who we look up to, get away with running our world and literally lying as badly as used-car salesmen to get into and stay in power, when invariably, they go back on their election promises because of high-powered lobbies and the promises of election funding for campaigns that brainwash us to vote for them.

7. If you're an environmentalist, you are somehow thought to be less of a real man. It's hinted that you are some gay, green, metro half-man or a hippy dude stoner rather than someone with a genuine concern not for yourself but for the world your kids and their kids are going to inherit.

8. We have become so judgmental, and so many issues have arisen from that. We all claim the higher ground and look down on "sinners"—and then intentionally forget everything that the Bible states over and over again, like forgiveness, empathy, compassion, and second chances. These are now dirty words, replaced by biases against so many of life's temptations and turmoil that, unbeknownst to any one of us, we could all fall into in a heartbeat.

9. The demise of religion—more critically, the degradation of the core values and rules that religions promote on how best to live your life—is gathering speed. For example, Bibles in hotels, airlines, and other public places have been replaced by nothing more than verbal pornography like *Fifty Shades of Grey*, because it's supposedly way cooler and somehow more relevant than the Bible will ever be. Tell me, what is more important than the Ten Commandments!

I could go on and on and on, but I won't, because you either get it or you don't. You either think I am old school and need to update my core values very quickly, as this is the world we live in today and fuck, was it really all roses way back when we allowed child molestation, corporal punishment, and discrimination against women, certain races and sexual preferences, and diseases? Or on the other side, you think I am some naive, idealistic daydreamer who has suffered too much brain damage from all the drugs I did. To be honest, that's actually true; my long-standing psychiatrist stated it is very similar to post-concussion syndrome and most likely will decrease my life expectancy.

There's no denying that our twenty-first-century lifestyle has more to do with electronic gadgetry than real, genuine, social face-to-face, hand-on-hand interaction, which I'm convinced we need now more than ever. Instead, we hide behind our fancy cars, houses, hedges, email, cellphones, texting, and Facebook to express all our hatred and hurt.

Believe me, I get it. Had I read any of this book a decade ago, I would have stopped reading by now and justified my cessation with similar arguments. We accept the status quo, as it is so much easier to bear than trying to solve the gigantic injustices, issues and problems we now face as a race. Really, that is what life is: a race to get richer, more powerful, more confident, more beautiful, and more accepted than our fellow human beings. It's a race to an early grave.

I wish I had all the answers to these problems, as I like to always give constructive criticism, pointing out a problem but also providing a solution. This time, I don't have all the answers, even with so much time to analyze the world. I do, however, believe that like MJ, if we gained a greater understanding of young children and animals, as they are closer to Mother Nature's value system, we would be in closer harmony to what God intended us to be like. I also do not believe all the crap, similar to Hitler's chosen ones/superior race, that humans are the greatest supreme species on Earth. Instead, just like the dinosaurs and so many other species that were once great, we could become extinct if we don't change our ways. Nature, including the magical animal kingdom, the deepest oceans, and the world's other untamed/uninhabited paradises, offer so many clues to the answers we seek.

If you ever get to see the remarkable story of Nim, the chimp raised by humans in the CBC special *Project Nim*, you will know where I am going with this. Unlike most, I believe humans are not superior beings. Instead, we are just another species on this planet. It's not us and the environment; we, along with all of God's creatures, *are* the environment. Who can explain how, for example, my beloved dog knows I am coming home before I get anywhere near the door, or as soon as I walk through the door can read my non-verbal cues and know what mood I am in and respond in an appropriate way? If we all began working together rather than in competition, then just like the messages contained in *The Lion King*, *Avatar*, and ultimately the Bible, we would align ourselves with the forces of nature as opposed to constantly butting heads with her. I strongly believe that's a fight we are bound to lose.

All this macro, big-picture, change-the-world stuff is cool to think about, but at some point, I need to look at my own life and figure out how on earth I am going to make this comeback stick, even when everything and everyone seems to be against me and everything I was as a human being has gone up in flames. The temptation to numb my immense issues and problems with chemicals is simply overpowering when things are not going my way. Recovery from addiction is the hardest, rockiest, most speed-bump-ridden dead-end road I have ever been down. Only now can I fully understand how so few (4 percent) make it back from drug addiction and homelessness. That figure is one of the things that makes me absolutely determined to be one of the few. It's the reverse-psychology trick that I used to amazing effect in so many other challenges in my crazy life.

How the hell am I going to put a wrap on my true story? I wish I could do the Disney happily-ever-after, frog-to-a-prince, every-cloud-has-a-silver-lining deal, but I can't quite yet. I don't even know if I ever will be able to again.

Today, after having a job and financial security for five months working with Martha in her hearing company, earning minimum wage doing the most boring data-mining to find sales opportunities by methodically going through and cleaning up their customer database with the aim to create sales leads, I got laid off as soon as Martha relapsed on the booze, costing both her and me our jobs. As such, I am hanging on for dear life in my 400-foot studio rental apartment in Kerrisdale—actually the only address I have lived in for more than a year in God knows how long. I applied to BC Liquor Store and, after a couple of interviews, scored a casual cashier and graveyard shelf-filler position. It was only guaranteed for the special Christmas month, and I was laid off all over again. I'm left with all the financial stress and lack of direction, purpose, and worthiness that being unemployed brings. Sometimes, it is easier to not have a taste of real life and money than to have it for six weeks only to lose it again.

THE HOOD

Without a job or source of income, trying to survive in the world's second-most expensive city with a monthly balance sheet that reads C$927 government disability payment minus rent of C$850 a month, yes, I am living a lie big time. The numbers simply do not add up. My only possible escape from yet another trip to the streets is to find another job in a hurry. And despite the world and their dog telling me I have a very impressive résumé, I still cannot get the business middle-management position I believe my qualifications and experience deserves.

So I need to swallow another very big and bitter pride pill and get a job stocking shelves, working as a cashier or being a sales representative in a retail store. God, that's what I did 30 years ago in my first-ever job at Fine Fare. Have I really wasted the majority of my life? No, I didn't, but yes, I did end up in the same place.

I try to find solace in the fact that it's not the destination but the journey and what that journey has taught me. I just wish I could have missed out on the intense, dark, painful times on my bad trip from heaven to hell and back again. I still find some peace in my mum's words: "I respect you more for trying and failing than not having tried at all." I wish I could have avoided the failed part because it is brutal, especially when you consider what floored me was a man-made recession by some crooks in banking and international stock exchanges. Unlike Trump and General Motors, I was not "too big to fail," which rules out any of us small-to medium-sized entrepreneurs. Should it not be the other way around?

Do I have regrets? Hell yes! In all honesty, if I knew then what I know now, I would have never left Carol—but in a weird way, I know I did the right thing for everyone, as our love was gone. I can't be like the rest of the world, living in a relationship that is built on nothing more than a comfortable friendship. I need the old-school lovers-for-life, if that even exists anymore.

Ever seen *Shrek Forever After*? Shrek gets bored of his seemingly dull and boring family life. He is tempted to change everything up by signing with the sketchy Rumpelstiltskin, who messes up his life. Only then does he realize, too late, the old but oh-so-true saying: "You don't know what you've got until its gone."

How can I sum up my life any better? I did the same, with prescription drugs being my downfall. My biggest worry is based on my history. The last two Winter Olympics have been dire for me: I destroyed my leg so bad it almost needed amputation during the Nagano games and during our very own Vancouver Olympics, I was certified and committed to a locked insane asylum for five months. God only knows what the Russian one has in store for me, especially considering my weird and wonderful relationship with the number three. Please don't let it be another stay on the streets or in a homeless shelter or worse still, a locked psych ward. I simply cannot handle returning to any of those nightmares ever again.

All I seek is a normal life. I want to have everything that seemingly everyone else takes for granted. I'm so tired of being broke and not knowing where my next rent cheque or meal will come from. Sure, I would love a prestigious career complete with a fancy streak-of-lightning car, pimped-out media system, and a million-dollar mansion in the most sought-after hood in the city I truly love and call home: Vancouver. God, if I could only turn back time to correct the devastating mistakes I made along the way, I would. But I can't, so I try to find solace in the miracle that is me still being alive on this planet. Some days, that's enough. On others, I just want the world not to judge me and, yes, leave me the fuck alone to just be.

Believe it or not, I am not always lonely when I am alone. I truly appreciate my freedom, independence, and the blessed company and unconditional love of my real-life angel and canine friend, Cheyenne. She is simply the best friend I have had and will ever have.

The biggest Catch-22 with complex PTSD is that you never know whether people are indeed talking about you behind your back or are just having their own conversation and a trick of the mind somehow twists it to apply to you. That's what the hyper-vigilance does. You are on your guard every single waking hour.

With my tragic yet magic journey has come so many deep and painful scars that my brain still has a hard time finding any kind of peace, especially with my never-ending struggle to keep my head above water. I know people look at me differently, as a polarizing figure if you like, just like my icon MJ without the fame. People either like, love or loath me because of my burdens, demons and somewhat unique past. Very few are willing to grant me a second or third chance and take me for what I am now instead of judging me throughout the many transformations that make me the man I am. What I simply cannot comprehend is that people don't understand the nature and nurture that molds us into who we are. Of course I am a bit off the wall, as my path resembles so few others that I feel different from the other guys, as indeed I am.

It's just like the two very shy collies I met down on Spanish Banks beach on my bike rides. They were mistreated for the first year of their lives by a bastard master who locked them in his garage (why we don't have more appropriate punishment for animal cruelty is beyond me). Their trauma altered their personality, potentially for life. I know more than you will ever know. People who don't and can't comprehend me and know nothing of my traumatic past put my shyness down to a lack of confidence rather a very real disease (complex PTSD) which, at its core, means a complete mistrust of people based on previous experiences. Let's face it: how else do you learn?

As I refer to music to try to find words for my thoughts, I think of the lyrics of the incomparable Scandinavian supergroup Abba's timeless classic "The Winner Takes It All." A truer song has never been written. Music has been my lifelong therapy for dealing with all my emotions, but especially the darkest pain, when everyone left me for dead on the scary city streets and in the locked psych ward.

Sport has also been a port from all the perfect storms in my life. It represents a blow-off valve for my dark side: the pure angry, fiery, feisty heart on the sleeve when my bad temper just wants to lash out but can't because of our new human rules. The rest of the animal kingdom still uses fighting to sort out disputes, and without that outlet, we all turn into twisted bitches.

Answer me this: why the fuck is it okay to kick the living shit out of people in the name of sport but it's not okay when the ice rink, football field, UFC cage or boxing ring is replaced by asphalt on the street. Go figure! I am not saying mindless violence is the best solution to differences, as it's not, but just think of what am trying to convey. We no longer discipline our kids with some sort of physical discipline. Is that not the reason why you see so many out-of-control kids? I believe that in this case, there must be an elevated punishment for gross misconduct or real hatred between people, just as in most animals' social hierarchy.

In the words of my still-favourite band U2, I feel like I am "running to stand still" and "still haven't found what I'm looking for." So much so that I think I have given up the quest for Utopia. Hopefully, I'll find that in heaven. I've replaced it with a simple search to find inner peace, serenity and tranquility. Please, Lord, give me the strength to not give in to the easy solutions of drug relapse and/or suicide. Help me ignore the attacks of ignorant, judgmental people who see me as something I am not: an inherently bad man.

As much as I would love to change the world, I am only one simple man, and as much as I try to be the absolute best person I can be, I am an imperfect human and can only be what I am and continue to strive to be: the very best man I can be given my challenging health problems. Living constantly with the knowledge that Crohn's pain can hit at any moment bites hard. But more especially now, my greatest adversary is my complex PTSD, which contaminates my every single thought, action and situation, from my head to my very heart and soul.

Don't get me wrong: I do not seek sympathy. All I ask for is that instead of misjudging me, you will take my true story at book value as an inspirational message and/or honest warning of what can happen to anyone, anywhere, at any time. From these harrowing experiences, a somewhat original and unique perspective on life is born.

Truth be told, that somewhat shy and naive little boy dancing to MJ at the pool in paradise, trying to heal the world, is still alive and kicking inside me. But this boy has grown up, and unfortunately my experiences have replaced the innocence and naivety of my youth with reality, as in the words of Green Day: "the innocents can never last" in today's urban jungles. So yes, there is also a man trying everything to survive, grow, and who knows, maybe even someday return to a place of normality.

I do have a really good grip on my own SWOT analysis, and with it, my own very personal dreams and aspirations, which all seem to centre around gathering information and turning it into knowledge of the priceless yet oh so precious love of what we call our home, planet Earth. In particular, and unlike the majority material-wealth mafia, my growth is based on learning new things each and every day. Maybe someday I will explore the rest of the world and the things that travel can give us all, like the miracles of language, culture, heritage, history, topography, geography, faith and love.

It's tempting to write out all the lessons I have learnt, but as I have said repeatedly in this book, you can only truly learn them by experiencing them for yourself. So instead, I will leave you with this one simple thought: life is like a board game, whether it be Monopoly, Risk or, possibly most appropriately, Snakes and Ladders. I genuinely believe we are in almost total control of our destiny with the decisions we make each and every day. These decisions vary in magnitude, but regardless, I believe there is a cumulative effect. The key is to find the ideal balance between risk and return.

Believe me, I know better than most how fine a line we walk trying to balance all the external and internal forces, especially when we let our evil side motivate us, namely vanity, ego, power, revenge, and greed. There is a very thin line between success and failure (and for that matter, genius and crazy), and risk has a pivotal role. Love it or hate it, Lady Luck still plays her cards. I truly believe God came through in my darkest hours, when, for example, I nearly lost my newborn baby but didn't; I avoided my left-leg amputation; I could have had a permanent colostomy bag after my bowel resection; and I survived many suicide attempts.

I genuinely hope you enjoyed reading this book as much as I did writing it down on a blank sheet of paper night and day for the last three years. I urge everyone to do the same and write your own life story, as quite honestly, it is one of the most fruitful, cleansing, and inspiring things I have ever done. When you do it, you will find out most of the answers you seek to so many of life's questions we all are bound by and struggle with.

There is so much more to my story, like all the real troubling tapes I haven't even listened to or touched on from when I walked the streets of Vancouver with a voice recorder in my pocket to leave behind memories of my struggle with money, eviction, mental illness, drug addiction and ultimately homelessness. I was hell-bent on killing myself and wanted to leave a warning from beyond the grave to everyone not to make the mistakes I paid so dearly for. I genuinely believe I have more than paid my dues, as they say.

Possibly even more shocking—if I could find a way to access my old email addresses, as I can't remember the passwords—would be the messages I wrote to my folks and my kids almost every day chronicling my exploits, when I knew deep down inside my brain had gone to a place that most of you will thankfully never see and feel. Believe me, from the very little grey matter left that lets me remember, these emails are extremely intense. My parents have advised me that I wouldn't want to see them. And yet, I have to ask them: why did not only they but everyone leave me for dead?

At the end of the day, when all is said and done, I am only human. If you ask me what is the greatest lesson I have learnt, I will leave you with this saying that somehow summarizes my journey to riches and my plight thereafter: Don't aspire; instead inspire. Put as simply as possible, through all of life's roads, the good, the bad, and the ugly, love is truly life's greatest prize, as it alone can give you everything you need to survive this life and give you the armour you need to deflect all the haters' attacks and life's curveballs and speed bumps.

Love is beyond anything you can buy with money. It is the truest form of happiness we all so desperately seek. Always remember this lesson it has taken me my entire life to fully understand: your life should not be about proving your haters wrong but rather proving yourself right.

Only love lives forever.

THE HOOD

CHAPTER 21

INSPIRED IDEAS

I only decided at the last minute to include some of my crazy thoughts and dreams for the planet just in case I am not the only one that is concerned with her health. And yes like some of my favorite artists, you probably guessed by now I am a bit of tree huger, greenie not because it's gay, but exactly the opposite, it is only right we stop coming up with these lame excuses for ruining our oh so precious Earth with our need for greed. In no particular order:

- **Nurture:** thoroughly examine the School Curriculum and refine the subjects bearing in mind the new World of electronic data that offers most of us every answer to pretty much any question within reach. As such make it much more practical for life now, for example: sign language as a second language, money and domesticated sense, ambidextrous, supreme balance, etc.
- **Work:** why do the majority of us still work 9-5, 5 days 40 hour week or close to that in a workplace when some of the work could be done better in our own homes and/or more in-line with our own body clock? If we were current, the world economy is now 24hour so make more work like that, i.e. stretch out the heavy traffic times (usually before and after work times) and end gridlock and the need to build more roads, bridges etc. In North America grant workers a fair 5 week vacation per year as it is in most of

QUIETSTRENGTH

Europe not including public holidays. Instead of the predicted 60% of us working being made unemployed with the unbelievable rate of improvements in IT (including robots) why not turn that scary statistic on its head to substantially reduce all our working lives to enjoy life. Why we start work right after school all the way through to our old age is forever a mystery to me.

- **Drugs:** I believe like a growing number of us that drugs are undermining our performance levels, health and ultimately death rates. Gang power is based on the money. As such I would legalize everything, yes everything. Whether we use Government dispensaries like in BC the government liquor stores or drug stores this way we can regulate; quality, quantity, addiction and relevant recovery and rehabilitation. But possibly most importantly we can use the crazy revenue this would bring we could invest in anti-drug strategies, tax breaks etc.

- **Radically change corrections and prisons:** there must be a better way based on prevention before detention, reduction and rehabilitations and make them work like in the old chain gangs. Too big a topic that thankfully I don't know enough about but something needs changing bigtime, especially Police training, an independent Police complaints Committee and officers trained in relevant psychology, gangs, social injustices etc.

- **Motion Control:** of everything especially street lights and like the watches that never need a battery, can we not use this dynamo type of energy in other applications like cell phones, tablets etc. Combine motion control with proper use of solar power, motion control & reflective paint (on street signs & on the tarmac) we could make every road as energy efficient as possible.

- **Green power:** why do we not utilize solar panels on buildings, especially the towering skyscrapers that utilize glass as their exterior finish? What about harnessing tidal power as it has awesome power to mould our planets landscapes & harnessing the power of thermo power from the Earths centre, wind power and all the other natural sources of energy. Copy France whereby all new builds over a certain size have to be fitted with solar panels and where needed, new builds incorporate a predetermined allotment of low income housing. Build Solar panel farms in high sun areas like all over Africa – Canada alone could get 70% from its entire energy need just from the sun!

- **Green cities:** Copy green cities like Singapore by planning and planting more greener to combat pollution, increase more traffic free zones, replace concrete/ tarmac sidewalks with AstroTurf (less impact=less hip, knees surgeries) etc.

- **Magnets:** Can we not research using the polarity of magnets to also create free and completely clean power? If we replaced the explosion in combustion engine and use magnets to push and pull the pistons. Or can we somehow utilize static electricity in some form – yes I am no engineer to evaluate their empirical opportunity potential. Follow that with Newton's Cradle for maximum efficiency and you might get the best engine we have ever invented if any of this is possible.

- **Catalytic converters:** why do we not use a similar product to that used by modern cars on every factory and household chimney, especially as most of the heat just goes straight into the air, there must be a better design.

- **Outlaw all SPAM:** We all have limited time on this planet so why waste it on being forced to have advertising coming out of everywhere.

- **Salt converters:** can we not use the most tried and tested way of cleaning the oceans in our everyday lives of cleaning water and a better way of extracting the salt out of oceanic waters to solve our upcoming water shortages (check out The last call at the Oasis documentary if you still erroneously believe that there is plenty water to go around)

- **Road versus rail:** can we not make rail transportation a more efficient, practical option for not only people transportation, but even more importantly the main mode of transferring all our heavy goods. For people transfer to get cars off the road, why Canada especially with it being the second largest country landmass wise does not have a high speed bullet train network like its French & Japanese competitors? That way we will also be able to minimize the heavy freight on our highways & city streets &

therefore reduce the many millions budget of taxation dollars for infrastructure including road building & maintenance, & reduce the brutal levels of road rage and accidents on our city streets and rural highways.

- **Rapid Transit stations**: could we not build more comprehensive master plans that not only include further expansion of them, but make them even more practical and cost effective option for commuters with bike rental/ secure storage and an integrated **electric or hydrogen powered** bus schedule. I truly believe we should be able to use water (H2O) in our cars if we investigated it further. And hey maybe even make the closed transit stations along with empty buildings temporary night shelters for the homeless

- **Homeless, mental health and addictions task force**: there must be a better way in dealing with this ever growing population, bi-product of our modern day excesses or as I like to call it, what comes out of the muffler/ tailpipe of Capitalism. A completely comprehensive and integrated initiative that includes all the crucial agencies that deal with this eternal problem – social workers, homeless centres, medical institutions, doctors, crisis agencies, emergency services, and politicians must develop a coherent strategy based on the sharing of resources & communication between all that come into contact with these people who are not aliens, just normal people like you and me that just fucked up sometime – again we don't realize how close we all are to becoming part of this ever growing problem. Last but certainly not least, can we come up with a way that we can have a mental health sufferer can be recognized & hopefully treated like everyone else that has a disability, a Livestrong like band but a bit more creative (still working on that one)

- **Music:** Could we not put on an anual international/ Worldwide concert similar to Live Aid, U2 Superbowl after 911 with a bit of Woodstock thrown in. & yes like U2 we could all the names of people we lost to these diseases, not just as we do at present at Award shows we drool over the celebrities, why? because in my mind they have more than enough media exposure, rather the ordinary man & women throughout the World that lost their life by: Drugs (both prescription & street) Mental disease & Homelessness & do it every year

- **Universal:** a/c cables & possible charging through WIFI?
- **Solar powered AI Tourist maps powered:** with Tourism being the world's largest industry, can we not partner with a google maps type of provider to make them as interactive as in your cell capability.
- **Cars:** why are they not made out of aluminium &/ or carbon fibres as like road bicycles, isn't it all about power to weight ratios when it comes to not only improved fuel economy, but also torque, acceleration and top speed – a more obvious win win scenario there isn't. Why is there is no cars not just minivans designed like the old VW camper to maximum indoor capacity where the driver sits above the engine like a scaled down mini-bus instead of losing all that space with a large hood? And finally is it not possible to have air suspension, a pull out ramp for easy loading especially for trucks, SUV's and any hatchback, multi-link steering with both axles aiding in steering so we truly turn on a dime, even somehow incorporate the advantages of camber in bike tyres into the automobiles.
- **Customization:** imagine going online and you can not only build up your dream car but include hood scoops, flared wheel arches but also your unique paint schemes that the customer can draw from their own computer. Hell why can't do that with any and every product, bikes, homes, clothing, electronics etc. Especially in regard to cars, why can't we have 1 Ford dealership for a city like Vancouver that you can test drive any car you ever dreamed of and then you just order it on-line or just drive off the lot or at home delivery Like how many millions of cars liter show-rooms & warehousing all around the World.
- **Reflective paint:** for signs on the tarmac & at the road side to utilize the lights from headlights instead of some form of wasteful lighting. In the same vein, could we not design all new Chameleon style camouflage for our military, a moving fluid mirror that reflects everything around it except the sun?
- **Biodegradable plastic**

- **Programmable and mobile traffic lights:** for construction work like used all over Europe. Men at work sign persons all over Canada are paid well above the minimum wage, think of the cost savings to us the taxpayers.

- **Cleaning:** Steam & enriched oxygenated water to clean everything without using chemicals that end up making our clean water toxic and God knows how many water born modern diseases that are caused by our overuse of these incredibly dangerous chemicals.

- **Olympics:** start to recycle the already built monuments to sports and tap into the billions that have already gone into staging such a celebration of sport by going back to previous host cities. Plan it better so the Special, then the Disabled and only then the main Olympic festivities so our challenged athletes get the exposure they need for so many reasons.

- **Flip to toilets:** yes simply retrofit by adding the oh so simple mechanism utilized in flip top bins into a toilet so no-one has to lift and lower the seat with their hands to improve sanitation

- **Baths:** why do we still use the centuries old design of baths, is there not some kind of form fitting foam, gel etc. a la foot beds in shoes for a bath that will customize its moulding to the owners body shape to make them more comfortable. And also can we not encourage some of the athletic footwear brands to start an executive business suite appropriate line to make all our feet & resultant physical issues by providing foam, gel, whatever foot beds & have custom fit yet replaceable souls.

- **Waterproof and bombproof:** more electronic devices like the Sony Expedia cell phone, Walkman mp3 phones & some of the new cameras. Especially something you can use when you're having a bath or a shower to record your thoughts, ideas, jobs etc. as it is well known most of us come up with our best concepts in the safest place in our existence because I believe it brings us back to the womb?

- **Internet Shopping:** expand the current tip of the iceberg shopping with internet grocery stores, clothing, everything. I believe this will be the future that WILL revolutionize our main streets, shopping malls more than we can ever imagine, just as the internet and mobile/ cell phones already have. And just I case I never mentioned it before buy shares in Amazon!

- **Improve ourselves by studying nature more**: especially in the fields of biomechanics of, for example a cheetah that can accelerate faster than pretty much every man made toy and/ or a study the psychology of babies, kids, dogs, cats, in fact all wildlife to solve our problems like insomnia, stress management, learning techniques. And utilize this knowledge in improving our educational systems with incorporating modern electronic devices with well-designed games for both our brains and bodies (like why do all these cool computer games come out without utilising the boundless possibilities of the X-box Kinect/ WII type sensors or where it is going VR)

- **Electronic voice, handwriting & Scanners:** why don't more electronic devices with a camera do not have a program that scans either the hand written and typed into word processing programs, like take a picture of it like bank cheques just now? Yes the technology now exists in a basic form to be able talk, write to text programs that would leave a laptop's keyboard useless. So why not invent the new laptops to be dual screen with the option of putting them together to make a small television for the increased usage of computers and the Internet as the only household TV provider and finally drive a nail into the coffin of all these over-priced television service providers. Having two systems, an old school paper world and the all new and improved electronic world need to be combined in a more effective & efficient one system deal to improve work inefficiencies and in turn reduce our massive ecological wastage.

- **Emergency personnel & Doctors:** in their training both initial and Continued Professional Development (CPD) by experiencing what they provide, namely: Doctors taking some of the chemicals they give us and Emergency personal (Police, Fire, Paramedics) and politicians spend a predetermined time period living on the streets in the dark and cold side of the tracks.

- **Hospitals:** Maybe they do this where you live, but as far as my time in pretty much all the major hospitals in the city of

Vancouver is concerned by implementing additional offerings that you could pay for like: Massage, Reflexology, Acupuncture, Yoga, Dog emotional support, an A La Carte menu, even play some music to escape the Hell that is hospitals. And somewhere we need to reduce the profits these Pharmaceutical Giants are raping our people and in the end torching us and the environment. To me these are inseparable, we are the environment stupid and we need to fix what we have already broken like the overuse of so many prescription "medications" cleaning chemicals and…..part of our environment causing crazy malformations of all kinds of cells, not only in our bodies but EVERYTHING!

- **Social power:** Call me a bad loser but it really is it not about time we used our voices to initiate change so many topics like those noted above (but certainly not limited to) The power of the people must always be greater than the people in power. Our power is our work ethic which is used and abused by the rich to justify their social standing in our human hierarchy model that never seems to change. Just like the newly stoked environmentalist movement, the only way we can facilitate this is again copy the French "yellow jackets" whereby the World stops working at a predetermined time to affect pure, just and right equality for all of us, not just the all genders, races, loves etc. but for a much fairer distribution of wealth which I don't think Capitalism has an answer for.

Yes I hear you already with all the usual derogatory comments from all the small, insular and shallow minds like the "easier said than done" or "it's all been done before". But maybe when you have time all by yourself, maybe you will see they are not as lame or crazy as they first might seem. Please remember it has been five years since the writing of the Hood and as such some might have already been done

Fini

ABOUT THE BOOK

The Hood chronicles the true life of its author, from his troubled childhood in Scotland through his glorious golden years to his traumatic fall from grace in Vancouver, Canada. It is a true, real-life story that highlights and challenges pretty much everything we all take for granted in our modern lifestyles. Throughout his journey, the author gives not only a blow-by-blow narrative but a whole different perspective on this thing we all call life.

It is an astonishing story that the very few who have heard it compelled him to write, as it could not only offer inspirational self-help for those experiencing similar struggles in their own life but also a drastic warning of what can happen in a heartbeat to anyone, anywhere, anytime on this planet we call home.

Put simply, this is a must-read story that no matter whom you are—male or female, black or white, gay or straight, rich or poor, sick or healthy, CEO or garbage collector—*everyone* should read. From his genuinely sensational life story, Andrew explores the very core of our civilization and presents a remarkably different perspective on what we all now use as measures of success, like power, wealth and must-have toys. Through his trials and tribulations offers an alternative course for humanity to gain what we all privately seek deep down inside: acceptance, friendship, confidence, faith, hope, true happiness and pure love, which fly in the face of today's more materialistic goals.

Rather than being some naive, idealistic, ivory-tower novel, the book is based on the real world. It is a tale that even Hollywood scriptwriters would have a hard time dreaming up. Even if it doesn't change the world, it might just change your world.

ABOUT THE AUTHOR

Born and raised in Aberdeen, Scotland, Andrew is the second son of three in the middle-class Hunter family and attended Robert Gordon's College, a private all-boys school. After a troubled childhood, he became the only son to graduate with a business-studies upper-second-class honours degree and Chartered Institute of Marketing diploma specialization from the university of the same name.

After marrying the love of his life and opening his own cutting-edge sports retail store, Andrew accepted the position of manager of snowboard operations for Whistler Mountain and emigrated with his wife, and their newborn daughter, to British Columbia, Canada, in 1995. It was here that his amazing and completely unpredictable life really unfolded and laid the foundations of this truly remarkable novel.

All Andrew seeks now is forgiveness for his many demons and relief from their horrendously deep scars. Maybe, just maybe, by telling his story through appropriate media, he can give back to the community that both condemned and saved him. His to-hell-and-back story might be the inspiration needed by anyone who is struggling in a very dark place, as it proves you can never, ever give up. Nothing is impossible.

Printed in the United States
By Bookmasters